The Mysteries of Mary

The Mysteries of Mary

Growing in Faith, Hope, and Love
with the Mother of God

Father Marie-Dominique Philippe, O.P.

Saint Benedict Press
Charlotte, North Carolina

Translated from the French by André Faure-Beaulieu.
Revised by Marcia Potempa and the Brothers and Sisters of Saint John.

Original Title: *Mystère de Marie. Croissance de la vie chrétienne.*

© Librairie Arthème Fayard, 1999

1958 La Colombe, Editions de la Colombe, Paris. English.

All Scripture quotations (unless specified otherwise) have been taken from the Revised Standard Version Bible, Catholic Edition; New Testament © 1965, Old Testament © 1966, Division of Christian Education of the National Council of Churches of Christ in the United States of America.

All quotations with the original French references have been translated directly from the French by the translators.

Nihil Obstat: Fr. A. Doolan, O.P., *Maître en Théologie.*
               Fr. R. Omez, O.P., *Maître en Théologie.*
Imprimi Potest: Fr. J. Kopf, O.P.
               Provincial Prior.
Imprimatur: Paris, June 18, 1958.
               Pierre Girard, s.s.v.g.

The Nihil Obstat *and* Imprimatur *are a declaration that a book or pamphlet is considered to be free from doctrinal or moral error. It is not implied that those who have granted the* Nihil Obstat *and* Imprimatur *agree with the contents, opinions, or statements expressed.*

Cover design by Milo Persic.

Cover image: *The Annunciation*, c. 1627 (oil on canvas), Charles Mellin (c. 1600–49) (attr. to). Musee Conde, Chantilly, France, The Bridgeman Art Library International.

ISBN: 978-1-935302-38-4

Printed and bound in the United States of America.

Saint Benedict Press
Charlotte, North Carolina
2011

CONTENTS

He found him in a desert land,
and in the howling waste of the wilderness;
he encircled him, and cared for him,
he kept him as the apple of his eye.
Like an eagle that stirs up its nest,
that flutters over its young,
spreading out its wings, catching them,
bearing them on its pinions,
The LORD alone did lead him,
and there was no foreign god with him.

Deut. 32:1-12.

But the path of the righteous
is like the light of dawn
which shines brighter and brighter
until full day.

Prov. 4:18.

PREFACE

A THEOLOGIAN can present in various ways the mystery of Mary, Mother of God. By following and using St. Thomas he can develop a treatise of *scientific theology* on the mystery of Mary. The order that St. Thomas gives us in the *Summa Theologica* can then be kept and supplemented since, thanks to the mystery of the Immaculate Conception, all theological studies of the mystery of Mary spread a new light, enabling us to enter more deeply into the mysteries of her personal sanctification, her divine motherhood and her cooperation in the mystery of Redemption. We can also see how one may complete, in the treatise on Christ, what St. Thomas already elaborated so brilliantly. Such theological research is animated by the increasingly pure and penetrating "understanding" of the mystery of Mary as the Father's beloved daughter, the Word Incarnate's beloved Mother, and the beloved Mother of all mankind.

What we are seeking to do above all in scientific theology is to discover the order God has established among the various mysteries of Mary's life: the order He has established between the mystery of Mary and the mysteries of the Incarnation and Redemption; the order between the mystery of Mary and the mystery of the Church. Indeed, the theologian considers whatever he studies in the light of the wisdom of God. His greatest desire is to participate as much as possible in this light to the extent that faith allows. His most spontaneous impulse is thus to ask himself constantly how God in His wisdom sees the mystery of Mary, the mystery of her Immaculate Conception and the mystery of her Motherhood. Such a question obliges him to come back with ever increasing eagerness to the very sources of Revelation, since through Revelation God Himself teaches both the believer and the theologian. His desire to enter ever more deeply into the understanding of the mystery urges him to draw parallels between the mysteries in order to compare them. In order to enter more deeply into the mystery of the Immaculate Conception, the theologian compares and contrasts this mystery to that of original sin. He compares the fullness of grace implied in this mystery of the Immaculate Conception to Adam and Eve's fullness of grace in original justice, as well as to the fullness of the grace of Christ.

Finally, to penetrate further and shed more light on the richness of the mystery, the theologian puts his philosophical knowledge at the service of his faith. He can then use the various analogies suggested by the mystery itself. To develop the mystery of Mary's divine motherhood, he uses the analogies of human motherhood and of contemplation. Divine motherhood is a mystery of contemplation. Mary is Mother in the fullness of her faith. In her divine motherhood, she is blessed in her faith. Divine motherhood is also a mystery of real motherhood. These two analogies enable us to bring to light all that sets apart the mystery of Mary's divine motherhood; we could say that these analogies shed a certain "negative" light on the mystery itself which generally gives the theologian an even stronger desire to return once more to the source of Revelation in order to adhere more fully and purely to the mystery as it was revealed to us by the Holy Spirit. The richness of such research and such theological contemplation is plainly seen.

One could also try to develop a treatise of *biblical theology* concerning the mystery of Mary. Then one would try to specify the special place that the revelation of this mystery holds in the Old Testament as a prefiguration, and the place this mystery holds in the New Testament: in St. Paul's Epistles, the Synoptic Gospels, the Book of Revelation and St. John's Gospel. One would bring into light the way in which this revelation was carried out progressively and the predominant aspects and secondary aspects by which this mystery is revealed to us in Holy Scripture. Lastly one would try to specify the meaning of this mystery in relation to other revealed mysteries: those of God, of Christ and of the Church.

One could also try to develop a treatise of *positive theology* (or maybe it could be called: a theology of Tradition, of the life of the Church) about the mystery of Mary. One would then need to show how, little by little, the mystery of Mary was developed and clarified in the Church, leading to the two great proclamations of the dogmas of the Immaculate Conception and the Assumption. How did this clarification come about? What were its predominant orientations? The

parallel between Mary and Eve comes to mind, as well as
Mary's different relationships with Jesus and the three
Divine Persons. It would also be necessary to ponder why—
at least as far as a theologian can know!—there is this development and why this order in the development. Indeed,
nothing is left to chance, particularly when it concerns the
proclamation of dogmas. Thus there is a temporal order in
God's guidance of the Church, an order which is a reflection
of God's wisdom. The theologian must be very attentive to
this. He must try to discern the meaning of this order in
God's guidance. Why these most recent dogmas regarding the
mystery of Mary? Why the dogmas of the Immaculate Conception and the Assumption? Why does the Holy Spirit, who
guides the Church, orient our faith in such an imperative way
toward the "Woman" of the vision in the Book of Revelation?
Is there not a mysterious connection between these incredi-
bly luminous, glorious revelations about Mary, our Mother—
the sign in the sky—and the intense and overpowering rise of
contemporary forms of atheism? It was at the Cross that she
was given to us; it is when the Church is crucified that she is
given to us, so that the faithful disciples may not be alone.

Finally, the theologian could develop a treatise of *spiritual theology* (mystical theology) about the mystery of Mary.
In this particular perspective, one would primarily try to
show how Mary, who has been given to us as a Mother, can
and must help us fully live our Christian life. One would try
to see how this Mother educates us, and educates us as a
mother, showing us through her example and her life, how we
must live the mysteries of faith, hope and the growth of charity. In the domain of faith, hope and growth of charity, Mary

comes first. Only she can really be a model. Not only does
Mary show us the path we must follow by being the perfect
model of the growth of charity, but as a Mother she also has
a certain influence on us, through her presence, her intercession and her maternal action. Mary is truly for us like a
maternal *milieu* which helps and comforts us. Lastly, and
above all, she is given to us at the Cross as a Mother, to be the
one we receive from Christ Crucified as an intimate and
secret pledge of His love. She is given to us so that we may be
divinely disposed to receive Christ's Spirit, the Paraclete.

Spiritual theology thus considers three great aspects in
the mystery of Mary: Mary, model of the life of faith, hope
and growth of charity; Mary, maternal *milieu*, prototype of
the Church; Mary, gift of Jesus Crucified, the one who disposes us to live by the Holy Spirit. In this essay of spiritual
theology, we shall consider only the first of these aspects. The
other two aspects must be considered in connection with the
mystery of the Church and the mystery of the Gifts.

It is quite obvious that these various ways of presenting
the mystery of Mary, far from opposing one another, actually
complement each other. Scientific theology of the mystery of
Mary, far from excluding spiritual theology, calls for it; since
this mystery of Mary, Mother of Jesus and of mankind, needs
to be developed in an immediately practical way. We must
specify how, in fact, Mary concretely carries out this role as
Mother; we must specify how she educates us and teaches us
through her silent life.

We must understand clearly the order that exists among
these various ways of theologically considering the mystery of
Mary. Each of these theological considerations, according to

a certain aspect of the mystery, takes priority over the others, which means that these considerations are absolutely original and irreducible. We can say, for instance, that the perspective of biblical theology is fundamental and, in this aspect, is first in the order of discovery (*l'ordre génétique*). The perspective of scientific theology is the most perfect in the sense that it alone looks at the mystery for itself, trying to grasp its proper meaning and its proper nature. In this respect, it takes priority according to the order of nature. The perspective of spiritual theology is the ultimate and most practical one in the sense that it alone considers how we can live this mystery. In this respect, it takes priority (a priority according to the order of finality).

In these various theological considerations, we find something analogous to the various branches of philosophy: metaphysics, philosophy of nature, human philosophy. Each of these branches enjoys a certain priority in relation to the others. The philosophy of nature is first in the order of discovery (*l'ordre génétique*); metaphysics in the order of perfection; human philosophy is first in the order of finality. However, there is a very great difference between the branches of theology and the branches of philosophy. The latter are more profoundly distinct from each other than the various theological considerations, for the branches of philosophy have distinct formal objects and material objects, whereas the various theological considerations have the same formal and material object, but make the various modalities of the same mystery more explicit. Hence the unity of theology is much more profound than that of philosophy. Thus it is better not to speak of *branches* of theology, but rather of various perspectives of *Doctrina Sacra*.

If even in philosophy, the philosophy of nature and human philosophy cannot be fully developed without the actual influence of metaphysics, it is the same, and much more rigorously so, when it comes to the influence of scientific theology over the development of biblical and spiritual theologies. Not only can spiritual theology be perfectly developed only when presupposing scientific theology, but spiritual theology must remain under its actual influence. Of course, this does not mean that spiritual theology applies the conclusions of scientific theology to determine what we have to do, for the conclusions of scientific theology are not really "usable" and cannot be directly applied to the concrete reality of our Christian life. Spiritual theology develops and clarifies a proper aspect of the revealed mysteries (the aspects of exemplarity and gift), but to bring out this aspect of the revealed mystery according to an order of wisdom, presupposes the most perfect and precise knowledge of the mystery in and of itself; thus spiritual theology implies scientific theology. That is why this theological treatise on *Mary, Model of the Growth of the Christian Life* implies the scientific theology of the mystery of Mary and that of our life of grace, faith and hope. However, we have intentionally chosen to clarify and consider only the precise aspect proper to spiritual theology, an aspect which the other theological perspectives cannot show us. We emphasize this point to avoid any misunderstanding.

INTRODUCTION

FROM the immediately practical viewpoint of mystical theology, it is not enough to consider the nature of charity, to grasp its properties or even to consider its wonderful fulfillment in the heart of Jesus Crucified and Glorified. It is not enough to see how this divine friendship binds the heart of Jesus to His Father and to His members in the Holy Spirit and how it takes possession of all the strengths, qualities and virtues of Jesus so as to make Him fully live the evangelical beatitudes. It is also necessary to understand how this mystery of love that is communicated to our souls must in actual practice grow by gradually taking possession of all our human strengths, qualities and virtues.

As long as we are still on earth, can we not compare charity to the leaven that must make all of the dough rise, or to the mustard seed that must become a large tree so that the birds can come and rest in its branches (cf. Mt. 13:31-33)? St. Augustine states that "divine love in us has a beginning—*sua initia*—a growth—*sua augmenta*—a perfection—*suam*

xviii   The Mysteries of Mary

perfectionem."[1] That is why we must consider the various stages of Mary's Christian life as a model and as an "exemplar" of the growth of charity.[2] We shall first recall a few theological points.

How Can There Be a Real Growth in the Mystery of Divine Love?

Only an imperfect being is capable of progress, of growth. A perfect being is beyond progress because of its very perfection, whereas a being that has not yet attained its full stature, which has not yet developed all its capacities, which has not yet made the most of all its resources, is still capable of growth and of greater perfection. With respect to divine life and charity, progress will thus only be possible for one who possesses charity only "partially"—in a participated manner—and who has not yet reached the measure that God, in His wisdom, has fixed for him. We know indeed that "grace was given to each of us according to the measure of Christ's gift"—"*secundum mensuram donationis Christi*" (Eph. 4:7).

The growth of charity thus presupposes a certain imperfection in the one who lives it; it is the imperfection of one who has not yet attained his end. This imperfection comes in fact from the state of a believer—as one who does not see—and from the state of hope—as one who does not

---

1. *Sermons,* 5th Series, 368, Ch. 4.

2. The mystery of Christ as model and "exemplar" of charity will be considered in another book.

possess. The mystery of faith and the mystery of hope enable one who loves to progress from light to light, from love to love, from holiness to holiness. Since he does not see and does not possess, he is really in an imperfect state which makes him capable of growing in love, of "being renewed everyday" in his divine life.[3] Hence the Book of Proverbs affirms: "But the path of the righteous is like the light of dawn, which shines brighter and brighter until full day" (Prov. 4:18).

From a practical point of view, we must never forget that the growth of charity cannot be understood without the mysteries of faith and hope. Charity in itself, in its proper nature, cannot explain this growth, since in itself it is nothing other than affective and intimate union with God. "He who abides in love abides in God, and God abides in him" (1 Jn. 4:16). Any act of charity directly reaches God in His personal mystery of love, and, for this very reason, its proper object is the ultimate end of every creature. Now, the moment man is united to his ultimate end, the only thing necessary, he must rest in it. Considered in itself, charity is perfect and implies no imperfection. It demands rest in God and achieves unity with Him.

When it is possessed by a man living in faith and hope, charity only achieves this divine rest and this unity of life in an imperfect way. Because of the imperfection of the state of

---

3. "So we do not lose heart. Though our outer nature is wasting away, our inner nature is being renewed every day" (2 Cor. 4:16). Cf. Rev. 22:11: "Let the evildoer still do evil, and the filthy still be filthy, and the righteous still do right, and the holy still be holy."

the one who possesses it, charity is in a situation which is almost abnormal, almost "violent" we might say, since by its very nature it is meant to blossom into a perfect friendship implying the beatific vision. Because of faith, the exercise of charity always remains imperfect here below, as it is never completely free from certain necessities pertaining to the subject. This imperfect situation gives charity the possibility to grow and gradually reach its state of perfection, of perfect union with God.

Thus from the viewpoint of mystical theology, the mysteries of faith and hope must be considered as essential parts of the mystery of the growth of charity. The mystery of the purification of faith and the mystery of hope are practically inseparable from the mystery of the growth of charity and are ordered to it. Charity gives faith and hope their finality.[4] It is in order to allow divine love to grow that those who believe and hope must go through terrible purifications. Hence from a practical point of view, we must not consider these mysteries separately. On the contrary, we must show their profound connections, their multiple interactions, and their reciprocal causalities. While speculative theology, in its scientific analysis, must study each of the theological virtues for itself and consider its proper characteristics, mystical theology, while taking into account the analysis of scientific theology and making use of it, must try to grasp in a concrete way the mystery of the growth of Christian charity in all its complexity and richness.

---

4. Cf. 1 Cor. 13:1-3.

Nature and Properties of This Growth

The growth of charity is the growth of participated divine life in our soul. This growth is mysterious by nature, as is divine life itself. However, by resorting to certain analogies, we can draw closer to the mystery without intending to explain it.

The divine life in which we share through Christ and in the Holy Spirit is the most perfect life we can lead. Nothing is more vital, in the strongest sense of the word, than charity. Thus the growth of other kinds of life which we may experience and analyze within us and around us are only very imperfect vestiges and images of this deeply hidden mystery of growth. These vestiges and images nevertheless remain very valuable in helping us to probe this mystery.

The growth of living beings having a vegetative life appears to us as an imperative internal impetus toward a perfect blossoming. Living beings take food not only for self-preservation but also in order to actualize all their vital capacities, initially possessed according to an implicit and imperfect modality, withdrawn into themselves, as it were. Think of all the vital capacities contained in a seed or even in a tiny animal that has just been born. The growth of living beings is thus spontaneous in the sense that it is ordered by the demands inherent and proper to imperfect living beings as such. But this spontaneity is determined; it is orientated and has its own particular rhythm. Each living species has its orientation and its specific rhythm of vital growth. The growth of a grain of wheat obviously does not develop in the same way as that of a dog. Each individual also possesses certain special characteristics modifying the rhythm and the direction of its vital growth. The vital evolutions of two brothers from the same family can be very different. This diversity will arise from internal and external factors; in any case, the vital *milieu* will have a great influence. We shall return to this question of vital *milieu,* of its role, and of its efficiency in the development of the living being.[5]

This rhythm of life covers more or less diversified periods. But one thing is certain: any living being having vegetative life experiences a beginning to its upward movement of growth, reaches certain plateaus, then a summit, a certain state of fulness and perfection; after which comes the reverse movement toward progressive degeneration.

The mystery of the growth of charity is analogically the same. Charity also possesses its imperative and spontaneous vital impetus. Grace, from its source, is a divine "seed" which needs to blossom and take possession of all that it can get hold of, not only to live and survive, but also to grow and radiate. The growth of charity also possesses an orientation and a rhythm. There is a certain law governing the vital growth of divine love, a law proper to divine love, and this law is more imperative, more demanding and stronger than any other law of growth. If it is terrible enough to prevent or stop a budding human love from blossoming normally—people nowadays talk constantly about "repressions," pointing out all the damage and complications caused by these violent restraints or psychological shocks that deny free rein to deep vital

---

5. The study of the vital *milieu* would fall within the context of a study on "The Church, Vital *Milieu* of the Growth of Charity."

impulses—one can guess how much more terrible and full of unfortunate consequences are those more or less admitted, more or less violent, refusals that block the deep, strong, and vehement aspirations of divine love. Just because we do not hear as much about divine "repressions," this does not mean that they do not exist or that their importance is minimal! But they are more mysterious and elusive to our psychology.

We should not forget, however, the diversity of these growths. They are very different, and it is important for us to take note of it.

The rhythm of growth for creatures with vegetative life can be represented by a kind of curve with an apex and a decline. The rhythm of the growth of charity, considered according to its nature, must be represented by an ever-ascending line, having undoubtedly a few plateaus, but without any apex followed by degeneration. Since charity has a divine vitality, it can always grow as long as the subject remains in the fidelity of faith.[6] This growth has no measure other than the one God appointed for it, and this measure can only be attained at the end of earthly life. With this mystery of the growth of charity we are in the presence of a continual *sursum corda* [lifting up of the heart]. While there may be deaths, radical falls through mortal sin, there can be no decrease nor slow, gradual descents.

---

6. St. Thomas, *Summa Theologica*, II-II, Q. 24, Art. 7: "*Ipsa charitas secundum rationem propriae speciei terminum augmenti non habet; est enim participatio quaedam infinitae charitatis, quae est Spiritus Sanctus.*" ["For charity itself considered as such has no limit to its increase, since it is a participation of the infinite charity which is the Holy Ghost."]

Since the growth of beings with vegetative life takes place in sensible beings, this growth necessarily implies a certain exteriority of the diverse parts, due to the aspect of quantity. The starting point of a growing being is necessarily exterior to its end. The growth of charity, belonging as it does to the divine order, no longer implies this exteriority. That is why one can say that each starting point in this growth is at the same time a summit, and each summit is like another starting point. Each act of charity both reaches God in Himself and disposes one for a new impetus, for a new, more perfect act.

Finally, while the growth of beings with vegetative life does depend on certain equivocal causalities proper to the *milieu* in which it occurs, it depends first and foremost on an immanent vital principle which is the proper and formal cause of this growth. While the growth of charity does indeed depend on our efforts and good will, it depends primarily on the grace of God and the Holy Spirit. St. Paul states quite clearly: "I planted, Apollos watered, but God gave the growth. So neither he who plants nor he who waters is anything, but only God who gives the growth" (1 Cor. 3:6-7).

To express these profound diversities when speaking of the growth of charity, Scripture not only uses comparisons taken from beings with vegetative life (the mustard seed for instance), but also uses images evoking the artistic construction of a finished work: "Every one who comes to me and hears my words and does them, I will show you what he is like: he is like a man building a house, who dug deep, and laid the foundation upon rock" (Lk. 6:47-48). St. Paul says something similar: "For we are God's fellow workers; you are

God's field, God's building. According to the commission of God given to me, like a skilled master builder I laid a foundation, and another man is building upon it" (1 Cor. 3:9-10). In the Old Testament, the construction of Yahweh's tent carried out by Moses is also extremely significant.[7] These comparisons, in contrast to the first ones, show that the growth of charity is God's principal work, that the Holy Spirit is its divine architect, so to speak. He acts as "God's finger" and He also uses instruments. As for works of art that have no decline, no degeneration, it is God's wisdom itself that has fixed the limits to this growth.

One last point is that these two types of comparisons show us that there are two very characteristic orientations of the growth of charity: first the implantation or the foundation-laying, the foundation-digging; then the ascent, the expansion or the building, the upward construction which corresponds well to the growth in intensity and extension; a phase of hidden inner growth, and a phase of blooming and radiance manifested by flowers and fruit. These two orientations are interrelated as the two movements proper to life: that of assimilation, of accumulation—life which tries to preserve itself—and that of communication, of gift—life blossoming out and diffusing itself.

Mary Is Model in the Order of the Growth of Charity

Because of the very mystery of the hypostatic union, from the first instant of His earthly life, Christ possesses a

---

7. Cf. Exodus 25 to 40.

fullness of love that is infinitely perfect. It is beyond the mystery of the growth of charity. As Only Son of the Father, Jesus cannot grow, for He is infinitely perfect. Hence He cannot be the model of the mystery of the growth of charity. Moreover, from the first instant of His life, Christ lived by the beatific vision in the heights of His human soul, further heightened by grace. It would be repugnant for the divine life in Jesus' soul to be in an imperfect state, susceptible to progress.[8] His divine life is immediately stabilized; its dimension is that of the Beloved Son with whom the Father is well pleased.

The pure creature who lived most by Christian grace, who exploited all its riches while still being immersed in the realm of faith and hope here on earth, is the Most Holy Virgin. Through Gabriel's salutation and the *fiat,* Scripture testifies to the exceptional fullness of grace and charity which the Holy Virgin possessed at the Annunciation in her state as a believer. Tradition presents her to us as the creature who experienced the closest intimacy with God and Christ, the one who received the greatest love from the Father and Christ. The dogmas of the Immaculate Conception, of the divine Motherhood and of the Assumption present her to us as being looked upon by God and Christ in a unique manner, as having received from Them the greatest graces and

---

8. We know how St. Thomas interprets this passage from St. Luke's Gospel: "Jesus increased in wisdom and stature, and in favor with God and man" (Lk. 2:52). To him it is not a question of progress according to the "habits of wisdom and grace" but only "as regards the effects" in the sense that He performed works manifesting an ever greater wisdom (*Summa Theologica,* III, Q. 7, Art. 12, ad. 3).

mercies that a pure creature can receive. Some theologians further specify that the fullness of her initial grace is more perfect than the grace present at the end of the earthly lives of the greatest saints. The fullness of her grace in the final act of her earthly life is of course incomparably more perfect still. And since she never committed any sin or refused the divine will anything, we can then conclude that she is indeed first in the order of the growth of charity; she is the one who took advantage of her time of trial in the most perfect and divine manner. If she is first among those who are to grow in the order of divine life, she is therefore the model of the growth of our Christian charity, since the first in a given genus is the model and exemplary cause of all those who are in that genus.[9]

Speaking of true devotion to Mary, St. Pius X notes that perfect devotion to Mary must imitate her example:

> It is a divine law that those only attain ever-lasting happiness who have by such faithful following reproduced in themselves the form of the patience and sanctity of Jesus Christ: "for whom He foreknew, He also predestined to be made conformable to the image of His Son; that He might be the first-born amongst many brethren" (Romans viii., 29). But such generally is our infirmity that we are easily

---

9. St. Ambrose, *De Virginibus in Nicene and Post-Nicene Fathers,* First Series, Vol. 10 (Peabody, Massachusetts: Hendrickson Publishers, 1995), Bk. II, Ch. II, §6, p. 374. Cf. *Les plus beaux texts sur la Vierge Marie,* presented by P. R. Regamey, La Colombe, Paris, 1946, p. 56.

discouraged by the greatness of such an example: by the providence of God; however, another example is proposed to us, which is both as near to Christ as human nature allows, and more nearly accords with the weakness of our nature. And this is no other than the Mother of God. "Such was Mary," very pertinently points out St. Ambrose, "that her life is an example for all." And, therefore, he rightly concludes: "Have then before your eyes, as an image, the virginity and life of Mary from whom as from a mirror shines forth the brightness of chastity and the form of virtue" (*De Virginib.* L. ii., c. ii.).[10]

Should we not say, as some people do, that she is too perfect to be our model? Such an objection shows a misunderstanding of the proper nature of a model. The more perfect, ideal and pure the latter, the more it can play its role as model by fully exerting its attraction as exemplary cause. The model is, by nature, an ideal but a concrete ideal, already realized in a more perfect being which goes before us. Because a model is an "ideal," it can attract and fascinate us. The more perfect the model, and in a certain way the more transcendent, the more immanent and intimate it can be.

The growth of charity in Mary is truly for us a pure, incomparably beautiful ideal. But this ideal of growth is at

---

10. Encyclical *Ad diem illum*, §20, February 2, 1904. Acts of Pius X.

the same time as close to us as it is possible to be. Is it not the growth of our divine Mother's heart? The growth of a virginal and immaculate heart is that of a maternal, merciful and welcoming heart.

The Mysteries of Mary

PART 1

THE MYSTERIES OF
MARY'S GROWTH IN CHARITY

CHAPTER 1

THE IMMACULATE CONCEPTION: THE INITIAL CONDITION OF MARY'S CHARITY

S INCE the growth of Christian charity is a movement, an
ascension, we must determine its starting point and its
terminal point in order to try to grasp its specific character.
Any movement is first characterized by its starting point, the
terminus a quo, which it leaves behind, and by its goal, the
terminus ad quem. If it is a vital movement, this *terminus a
quo* is not only what is left behind, it is also the initial quality of the living being; and the *terminus ad quem* also implies
the ultimate manner in which this terminal point is possessed. Then, in terms of these two extremes, we can consider
the various stages of this movement. That is why, when considering the mystery of the growth of charity in Mary, we
must first consider its starting point and its terminal point.
Then we must point out the various stages of this divine
ascension: the joyful, sorrowful and glorious stages.

The starting point of the mystery of the growth of charity in Mary's soul must be understood in the light of the

mystery of the Immaculate Conception, for this mystery reveals to us God's unique mercy toward Mary and the way in which He manifested all His predilection for her from the beginning. In this mystery, we are presented with the foundation laid by God for the great work he wants to do in Mary. This mystery shows us the extent to which God wanted Christian grace to be rooted in this tiny human being totally bound to God from the first moment of her conception, and how radically He wanted to separate her from all complicity with sin.

The Apostolic Constitution *Ineffabilis Deus*,[11] in proclaiming the dogma of the Immaculate Conception, states very clearly that:

- Mary is preserved from the stain of original sin from the first moment of her conception;

- This exemption from original sin is a very special act of mercy granted by God in view of the merits of Christ;

- This doctrine is revealed and at least implicitly present in Scripture and Tradition.

---

11. The dogmatic definition of the Immaculate Conception (Pius IX, December 8, 1854. Boston, Massachusetts: St. Paul Books and Media, p. 21) states: "We declare, pronounce and define that the doctrine which holds that the Most Blessed Virgin Mary, in the first instant of her conception, by the singular grace and privilege granted by Almighty God, in view of the merits of Christ Jesus, the Savior of the human race, was preserved free from all stain of original sin, is a doctrine revealed by God and therefore to be believed firmly and constantly by all the faithful."

This is what is properly defined by the Church.

Even though Mary is a descendant of Eve and fully belongs to the human race, she is nevertheless exempt from the hereditary flaw to which we are all subjected. Not only has she never known sin (*culpa*), but, in addition to this, she was not touched by the "*fomes*" of concupiscence. The privilege of the Immaculate Conception completely separates her from what we call the "old man," the man of sin.

The Practical Consequences of Original Sin in Us

Indeed, we know that the direct consequence of Adam and Eve's first sin of personal pride was to place all their descendants, the entire human race, in a fallen state, in comparison with the initial state of the Garden of Eden. The grace that made them God's intimate friends is lost. The preternatural gifts of integrity and immortality, which, in this state of original justice, perfectly harmonized the deepest demands of grace with those of nature, are lost. This nobility as son of God and king of the universe suddenly disappears through this sin of pride, and man remains in a state of enmity toward divine love and of painful and austere servitude with respect to nature. Through original sin all mankind is condemned to be in a terrible situation, invaded by sin and as though submerged by the flood. After inner harmony comes division, struggle. Concupiscence leads our passions toward sensible goods and proudly excites our intelligence against God's loving and merciful will. What was normally supposed to be subordinated and subdued—the lower part of human nature—keeps trying to dominate and rebel against the upper part. The latter, having lost its subordination with respect to the ultimate end, in other words, being deprived of love, no longer has any firmness and stability. It is easily carried away by the attraction of sensible earthly goods.

The first sin thus caused a break, a terrible opposition between the human race and God. This human race is in fact handed over to Satan, so to speak. God allows him to take temporary possession of the human race.

All of Adam's descendants are born in sin (except Christ and Mary, though in very different ways). Satan thus has a certain hold over them from the moment of their conception and from the time of their birth. He knows them. Having for a time possessed the stronghold of our soul, the devil knows its most vulnerable points. He knows human nature with all its capacities, its noble and great tendencies, as well as the cowardly and base ones, far better than the best psychologists and psychoanalysts! He knows all the multiple interactions that can exist among various instinctive tendencies and all that is hidden in them. With his claws, with his own imprints as it were, he has marked Adam's descendants in their sensitive nature to such an extent that even after baptism, although the sin is erased, the trace of this first condition remains nonetheless present. Our three concupiscences attest to this. New birth to divine life—in Jesus' blood—does not take the members of Christ back to the earthly paradise. The cherubim, placed at the gate of this paradise, gives a clear indication of God's express will not to allow Adam and Eve's descendants to return to this initial beatitude, despite the burning nostalgia that can sometimes seize them. Baptism reinstates humanity in the Father's house like true prodigal sons, giving them grace, the wedding garment, but it does not do away with the concupiscences, the bad instincts. That is why an inner struggle remains. Satan has been thrown out of the "citadel." He does not rule over it any longer—the victory of the Cross keeps him away—but here on earth, during the entire period of trial, he still has his "fifth column."

God's Prevenient Mercy Toward Mary

In the midst of this human race, Mary was preserved like "a lily among brambles" (Song 2:2). From the beginning there was never any complicity with evil, with sin, with Satan in her. In a unique gesture of predilection, divine mercy preserved her from this. Divine mercy arose, so to speak, to confront this hereditary contagion of sin, to set aside this predestined creature, or more precisely, to place her, as it were, beyond this sin of nature that invades the human race and respects none of its members. We can see the Old Testament prefiguration of this prevenient mercy in God's gesture toward the newborn infant Moses. This son of the Hebrews was supposed to have been thrown into the waters of the Nile. But this child is "so beautiful" that he cannot be put to death. After hiding him for three months, they put him in a basket among the reeds near the riverbank.[12] Wrapped in this mercy of preservation as in a "divine ark," Mary remains the only pure creature who is not touched by sin. God holds her in His jealous love in such a way that He does not allow any-

---

12. Cf. Ex. 2:1-10.

one except Himself to touch her. She came from God's hands totally pure; she will, in fact, return to Him totally pure.

Separation Between Satan and Mary

The devil never had any direct hold on Mary, neither in her soul nor her body. Among all Adam's descendants, she is the only pure creature that totally escapes the devil. He knows nothing whatsoever about this little child of men. She is a "closed garden," divinely closed. To him she is a mysterious enigma that puzzles and irritates him. Filled with dread, he guessed that she was his rival. The revelation of her divine motherhood was probably the very cause of his revolt. In his pride, he did not accept the fact that a pure creature could be the Mother of his God and thereby know an intimacy with God that he, Lucifer, would never know. Seeing this descendant of Eve escape his grasp, he sensed that she was the one whom God had chosen as Queen of heaven and earth, of men and angels. Confronted with her he is forced to admit that he is alien, vanquished and powerless.

We must clearly understand the practical attitude of Satan with respect to the mystery of the Immaculate Conception in order to understand better the following words of Scripture: *Inimicitias ponam inter te et mulierem;* "I will put enmity between you and the woman, between your seed and her seed" (Gen. 3:15). In His wisdom God allowed the devil, through original sin, to have a certain hold on Adam's descendants. In his pride, Satan considers this divine permission as a right. One of the practical consequences of pride in creatures is immediately to establish any permission granted on a temporary basis as a permanent right. Does

Satan not introduce himself to Jesus in the desert as the "prince of this world," as the one who has the right to rule over the universe and tyrannize men? Faced with the mystery of a descendant of Eve untouched by the hereditary stain, instead of keeping quiet and admiring a special gesture of God's totally gratuitous mercy, he considers himself defrauded of his rights. This mysterious little child appears to him as a failure in his power as the "prince of this world." Refusing out of pride to admit that it is normal for God's mercy to act with complete freedom, and that His mercy is accountable to no one, he is angry inside and tries as much as possible to ignore the existence of this extraordinary creature, claiming that she is nothing. For this proud intellectual, the only real things that exist and have the right to exist among the realities that he respects and which are within his particular competence, are those that he knows! But since he cannot absolutely deny the fact of this existence, he tries in every possible way to minimize this creature enveloped in God's prevenient mercy and hold her up to ridicule. He always tries to make caricatures of her! This mystery is intolerable for his pride. It is all too clearly the "sign," of a mercy that he cannot accept and that he loathes; a mercy that shows him God's absolute right over all creatures, even over this fallen human race. He himself, however intelligent he may be, has no rights but those received from God or those which depend on God's permission. His days of domination over the earth are numbered; he is not the one who has fixed their duration.

Thus Mary is Satan's proper and personal enemy from the beginning, his indomitable enemy who totally escapes his grasp just when he considered himself to be master of the situation, master of the world. Thanks to this privilege, Mary is indeed completely separated from sin and from any complicity with evil or with the prince of this world.

This radical separation from evil and this absence of the "the tinder for sin" (*fomes peccati*) enables us to grasp how distinct is the starting point of the growth of love in Mary. In the *terminus a quo,* everything that is irreconcilable with divine love is completely rejected, left aside, whereas it is never completely so in us. A certain measure of selfishness and pride still remains in a latent state in our most divine aspirations of love. We shall be completely free from this only in glory.

Inner Harmony, Fullness of Love

To understand the original character of the starting point of the mystery of the growth of charity in Mary, we must not only consider how distinct is the separation of the Virgin's soul from sin; we must also consider the unique quality of this vital seed that God communicated to her at the beginning, for what we are looking at is the growth of a living being.

The absence of the *fomes peccati* enables us to affirm that, although Satan is there as an exterior enemy, as a tempter in the strongest sense of the term, furious and irritated in his pride, Mary's soul is nonetheless preserved from inner struggles and divisions. For that very reason there WILL not exist in her the squandering, wasting of time, hesitations, delays, soul-searching and selfish pauses that inevitably exist in all inner struggles in which the enemy has complicities in the soul. Her soul is totally oriented toward God, her sole Good, her Creator and her Father. She is attracted and polarized solely by Him. *Dominus possedit me in initio viarum suarum.*[13] There is no selfishness in her. She loves herself as God loves her; that is why everything in her being is in perfect balance and harmony. All her faculties, all her vital forces are organized with a view to divine service. All that she possesses—intelligence, will, sensibility, passion—is perfectly ordered to serving God. In her we find the perfections of the state of pure nature, the normal attitude of the creature, which consists in being God's docile and loving servant.

This inner harmony and orientation toward God give her soul a marvelous simplicity and purity, which God had communicated to His image in the Garden of Eden and which were like the living echo of His own simplicity. God made man simple; sin made him complex and multiple. Is not Mary, as Scripture says, a perfect reflection of the Creator who "glorifies her noble birth"? (Wis. 8:3). She is an even more perfect image of her Creator and of her Father than was Eve in the state of innocence, for she is closer to the adorable unity of the Triune God. Her soul is utterly luminous and clear: pure crystal that mirrors the light of God, that lets the radiance of the Sun shine through without retaining or darkening it. Is not Mary the morning star? This harmony and light clearly show us all the splendor and beauty of her soul. But the beauty of Mary's soul, unlike Eve's, remains hidden. It is an inner beauty; all the glory of the King's daughter is

---

13. Prov. 8:22: "The Lord created me at the beginning of his work."

inside. It is a veiled beauty: "Your eyes are doves behind your veil" (Song 4:1b). Eve's beauty, on the other hand, is a beauty that disposes her to be Adam's spouse. The inner beauty of Eve's soul blossoms forth and radiates over her whole body and sensibility, through the preternatural gifts. Mary's beauty disposes her to be God's confidante, the virgin *par excellence.* It is not a beauty for men, but a beauty entirely reserved for God. "It is the glory of God to conceal things" (Prov. 25:2). This harmony, clarity, purity and simplicity actually come from Christian grace. Mary does not return to the Garden of Eden by virtue of her privilege! Her grace is not a grace of original justice; it is really a Christian grace that implies deeper and more exclusive divine demands and that uses a body capable of undergoing suffering and a soul susceptible to sorrow, capable of bearing the pains due to sin.

The starting point of this growth of love is thus very simple and pure, without any internal duality or division, but it is also very hidden. Can we not see a sign of this in the very fact that the Holy Spirit did not reveal this great mystery to us immediately, since the way in which God reveals His secrets to us is not extraneous to the very nature of the revealed secrets? The Holy Spirit wanted Tradition to keep this mystery for a long time as a "secret" of love from which one lives, but about which not much is said.

We must specify that this Christian grace is given to her in its entirety from the very beginning. This fullness of grace and charity is not strictly defined in the dogma of the Immaculate Conception, but we can say that it is implied. The bull *Ineffabilis* speaks about this clearly and explicitly. We must now consider this fullness of love in order to understand more perfectly the power and the divine virtue of this initial seed.

> From the very beginning, and before time began, the eternal Father chose and prepared for His only-begotten Son a Mother in whom the Son of God would become incarnate and from whom, in the blessed fullness of time, He would be born into this world. Above all creatures (*prae creaturis universis*) did God so love her that truly in her was the Father well pleased with singular delight. Therefore, far above all the angels and all the saints so wondrously did God endow her with the abundance of all heavenly gifts poured from the treasury of his divinity that this mother, ever absolutely free of all stain of sin, all fair and perfect, would possess that fullness of holy innocence and sanctity than which, under God, one cannot even imagine anything greater, and which, outside of God, no mind can succeed in comprehending fully.[14]

This is the magnificent royal dowry that God gave to the one He chose for Himself to become one day His beloved Son's Mother. This fullness of grace brings us, in a new and even more intimate way, into the mystery of God's

---

14. Bull *Ineffabilis Deus,* December 8, 1854 (Boston, MA: St. Paul Books and Media), p. 3-4.

very special mercy toward Mary, since grace is the proper effect of God's merciful and paternal love for His creature.

Mary was loved by God more than "all other creatures" from the very first instant. All God's favor rested on her. He wonderfully lavished all His graces upon her.

St. Thomas gives us a theological explanation of this fullness of grace: "In every genus, the nearer a thing is to the principle, the greater the part which it has in the effect of that principle. . . . Now Christ is the principle of grace, authoritatively as to His Godhead, instrumentally as to His humanity."[15]

The Blessed Mother, because she was going to be closer to Christ than any other creature since she was to be His Mother, received from Him a fullness of grace which surpasses that of other creatures. This fullness of grace is a very perfect echo of Jesus' fullness of grace and depends upon it. It surpasses by far that of all the other saints. For she was given this fullness of grace so that she might be capable of being the worthy Mother of Jesus.

Thus from the moment of her conception, Mary possesses this fullness of Christian grace, which implies a fullness of faith, hope and love. Like an incomparable divine seed, this grace essentially needs to grow and take root in this totally pure "good soil," to take hold of what is most intimate in this being, to expand, to blossom, to become "the greatest of all shrubs . . . so that the birds of the air can make nests in its shade" (Mk. 4:32).

---

15. *Summa Theologica* III, Q. 27, Art. 5.

The Proper Foundation of This Temple of God

We specified the starting point of the mystery of the growth of charity in Mary by showing, on the one hand, the total separation of her soul from evil and, on the other, the unique quality of the divine seed initially placed in her soul. Finally we must consider the proper foundation of this divine edifice, this temple of God, that the Holy Spirit wants to construct in this pure creature. Not only must every movement be built on something fixed—and the more this support is firm and immovable, the more rapid the movement can be—but any edifice must also be built on rock if it is to withstand the tribulations of time.

Mary is given this privilege of exemption from sin and fullness of grace and charity in anticipation of the mystery of the Cross. It is a Christian grace that comes directly from the Father's mercy in anticipation of the merits of Christ Crucified. Considered in this light, the mystery of the Immaculate Conception shows us the great victory of the Cross over sin and over the devil. This mystery is the purest, most profound and most intimate triumph of Redemption. The efficacy of Redemption is radical and complete in Mary's heart. It takes possession of her whole soul, in which there was no flaw. In this mystery, Mary is indeed the living herald of Him who is to come and who is to be crucified, since she is already completely snatched away from the devil's clutches.

Through this mystery, we penetrate the infinite efficacy of Christ's blood, capable not only of purifying the sinner, of restoring him to favor by giving him "new clothes," a "wedding garment," but also of radically redeeming him by protecting him from all blemish, from all harmful contact. Christ's blood redeemed Mary in the most complete and radical manner possible. Through this mystery, she is the first to be redeemed in the very strict sense of primacy in the order of redemption. In Mary, everything that could be redeemed was redeemed immediately and from the beginning, in order to be handed over to the love of God. Jesus spared nothing for this wonderful redemption. It was for her that He suffered the most. He could not have given her more or suffered more for her. She is really the Good Shepherd's first fruit and first conquest. The proper foundation of this mystery of growth is hence the Father's mercy communicated through and in the heart of Jesus Crucified. It is on "stone," on "rock," that the Holy Spirit lays the foundation of His edifice, His masterpiece. This was necessary since it was to rise to such heights!

In the mystery of the Immaculate Conception, Mary is indeed the model given by the Holy Spirit at the starting point of the growth of our Christian charity. She shows us what our birth into the life of glory will be. In heaven we shall all be immaculate as she is. Christ's blood will then take complete possession of our soul in order to give it this total purity in divine love. In this mystery, Mary is clearly the prototype of the birth of our divine life. Our Christian grace draws us directly and efficaciously toward this mystery, which is not foreign to us; it is an essential part of our divine life. But the birth of our divine life has already begun. Every movement of love makes us live by everlasting life. All our charitable impulses will be fully efficacious only to the extent that their starting point is intimately united to this mystery of Mary. All our efforts and resolutions to grow in divine love, if made outside the Immaculate Heart of Mary, are always tainted with pride, vanity or selfishness. As previously noted, because of the consequences of original sin, these resolutions still imply a certain compromise with evil, a compromise that is perhaps unacknowledged, very subtle and very hidden, yet real. Hence the break with sin is not complete; we still have some mud on us! The initial impulse is thus somewhat contaminated, and often for this very reason, it will not last. It will come to nothing. On the surface everything appeared splendid, very pure and beautiful, but there was a very hidden "crack," something binding us to ourselves and to our pride. The bird was still tethered by a string! After a first flight full of generosity, it fell down again. If our resolutions to grow in love (all our different Christian resolutions ultimately come down to this one resolution to grow in love) are made voluntarily with Mary, by relying on her Immaculate Heart and by entrusting them to her, they will then have an absolutely divine purity; they will be truly efficacious. Mary, in her mystery of the Immaculate Conception, is thus the proper place for every authentic starting point in the growth of love.

CHAPTER 2

THE DORMITION AND ASSUMPTION: THE END OF MARY'S GROWTH IN CHARITY

THE same liturgical feast ties together the death, the resurrection and the assumption of Mary. For Jesus, the liturgy distinguished between these various mysteries. We must try to understand why this is so in order to grasp the teaching that lies herein.

In her death, Mary is the model of the finishing point of the growth of charity. Her death must show us the ultimate demand of this mystery, the ultimate demand of charity, its finishing point. In her resurrection and assumption, Mary is the model of the glorious life of the adopted sons of the Father.

Through this mystery of death and assumption, she shows us the intimate bonds that unite life on earth and life in heaven, by showing us as well all that separates the *nigra sum* of the earth from the dazzling *formosa*[16] of glory, all that

---

16. Song 1:5: *Nigra sum sed formosa:* "I am very dark, but comely."

separates the final stage in the desert from entry into the
promised land.

Mystery of the Dormition

The glorification of Mary's body is asserted as an article
of faith in the Apostolic Constitution *Munificentissimus Deus*
of November 1, 1950. It is not specified whether this glorification occurs from the separation of her body from her soul
or whether it occurs while her body is still living according to
earthly conditions. That is why we must clearly specify from
a theological point of view that the mystery of Mary's dormition is handed down to us by Tradition, whereas the mystery
of her glorification is a dogma defined as an article of faith.

Without at this point going into the various theological
disputes regarding the death of Mary, we can, from a practical
standpoint, consider that the oldest and most constant Tradition in the Church affirms her dormition as a real death.[17]
Although Tradition gives us the fact of Mary's death, it does
not give us any details that we might consider as being certain.[18]

---

17. Cf. M. Jugie, *La mort et l'assomption de la Sainte Vierge, Bibliotèque
    vaticane,* Rome, 1945.—Cf. A. Hoffman O.P. *Expleto terrestris vitae
    cursu* (*Divus Thomas, N.R. Th.*, 1953, t. 2).

18. Cf. J. Duhr, S.J., *La Dormition de Marie dans l'art chrétien* (N.R. Th. 82,
    1950, p. 135 sq.). Duhr notes that around the middle of the VIth cen-
    tury, Byzantine art shows Mary as already dead, and Western art depicts
    her in agony, dying. Cf. Gen. 23:1: Sarah's death and the length of her
    life (127 years) are mentioned. She is the only woman in the Bible whose
    age is mentioned at the time of death. Is Sarah not the prefiguration of
    the Mother of believers? She is the first one for whom her burial is men-
    tioned. Let us also take a note of Genesis 25:7-12: "Abraham breathed
    his last and died in a good old age, an old man and full of years."

The lack of details is a particularly striking fact, which must instruct us. For everything is guided by the wisdom of God, especially in matters regarding Scripture and Tradition, and above all when it comes to such an important fact. "Precious in the sight of the Lord is the death of his saints" (Ps. 116:15), since this death is the entrance into God's glory[19] and since this entrance is the ultimate work of mercy and human freedom. What is true of the death of all the saints is ever more so of Mary's death.[20]

To enter more deeply into the mystery of Mary's death and to grasp the teaching which the Holy Spirit wants to give us, we must compare her death to Jesus' death. There never were two deaths more different and yet more similar: more different from a social, exterior, visible point of view; yet more similar in God's sight from an interior point of view.

Our Lord dies on the Cross, on a mountain top, opposite the holy city but outside of it. He dies in front of the whole universe, and at His death the universe trembles, darkness

---

19. St. Thomas Aquinas, *Commentary on the Gospel of St. John,* 21, Lect. 4, §2633 (Petersham, Massachusetts: St. Bede's Publications): "the death of the saints gives glory to Christ."

20. Just as God's gesture of prevenient mercy that saved the little new-born Moses from Pharaoh's wrath is an image of God's wonderful prevenient mercy toward Mary in her mystery of Immaculate Conception, so the few words given to us by Scripture concerning Moses' death can also be considered as a prefiguration of Mary's death: "So Moses the servant of the Lord died there in the land of Moab, according to the word of the Lord, and he buried him in the valley in the land of Moab opposite Beth-peor; but no man knows the place of his burial to this day. Moses was one hundred and twenty years old when he died; his eye was not dim, nor his natural force abated" (Deut. 34:5-7).

covers the earth, and the veil of the temple is torn in two.
Our Lord dies condemned as a criminal and a slave, mocked
and ridiculed in the eyes of all His people. He dies betrayed
and abandoned by His friends. He dies as a bloody victim,
handed over into the hands of His executioners. It is amidst
struggle and discordant voices that He communicates His last
wishes, His ultimate words, His testament of love.

Mary does not die with Him. Mary must agree to
remain on earth and to die when God wills it, with a bloodless death, an infinitely simple death. The human tragedy of
the Cross no longer exists. The reason why Tradition has kept
only the fact of her death is surely so that everything would
remain hidden and buried in silence.

We might be tempted to lament the silence of Tradition
and consider ourselves as orphans who do not even have the
consolation of keeping in their hearts the last words and gestures of their mother. When unable to be present at the death
of a loved one, we know how eagerly we try to find out at
least what his last words and actions were from those who
were there. Just think of the reaction of all the mothers and
wives who learned of the death of their sons or husbands on
the battlefield, far from their country, far from their family.
How they would have liked to know how they died! How
they would have liked to question those who witnessed their
death!

John tells us nothing about Mary's death. John was certainly a witness, since Jesus had entrusted Mary to Him and
had given her to him as Mother, and John had taken her
"into his home"; but he tells us nothing. He, who spoke so
strongly and clearly in his Gospel about Jesus' death, tells us

nothing about the death of she whom he had loved as a mother. He, who had understood so well all the treasures of her heart, keeps quiet.

We need to understand this fact correctly. In reality, Mary is hereby leaving us a maternal, unwritten testament, left buried in John's heart, and sealed by the Holy Spirit in his heart as son and priest. Is John's voluntary silence here not the most perfect sign of the mysterious silence of the heart of Mary dying for her God? The most divine, the most efficacious and most forceful way of telling us the secret of this maternal heart which accepts a death totally absorbed in love and completely silent through love, was indeed this profound silence of the witness who bears witness to silence through silence.

Mary's entire life was silent and hidden, for as Scripture tells us: "It is the glory of God to conceal things" (Prov. 25:2). It is therefore normal that her death, which concludes such a life, should remain hidden, inaccessible to human eyes, to the gaze of the curious. Her death evades human history so that it may be reserved exclusively for God. She dies without any human glory so that she may be entirely for the glory of God and for the life of her children. Mary's testament could not be anything other than the silence of love. She who keeps God's Word[21] could only impart to us Jesus' testament in the silence of her faith.

---

21. The French expressions *"Parole"* or *"parole de Dieu"* (i.e., Sacred Scripture and Tradition) is consistently translated as "God's Word," whereas the French word *"Verbe"* is translated as "Word of God" or simply as "Word" [Trans.].

Interiorly and in the sight of God, no two deaths are more similar than those of Mary and Jesus. Jesus consents to die out of pure love to accomplish the Father's will: "Not my will, but thine be done" (Lk. 22:42.). Mary consents to die out of pure love to accomplish the Father's will, to be more like Jesus, to follow Him to the end.

All other descendants of Adam and Eve, including Adam and Eve themselves, cannot accept death out of pure love; it is a penalty, which is imposed upon them and which they have to accept. Of course, they can accept this punishment with love, as sons who acknowledge that they have really deserved it and who know why their Father imposes it upon them. Nevertheless, the penal characteristic of death still remains. Since Mary was not affected by original sin, she is exempt from this penalty; therefore, if she dies, she freely accepts her death out of pure love. She can thus have the same purity of intention regarding death as Jesus had, although the reasons that explain their respective exemptions are clearly different. Just as the first action of her life was one of surrender, her last action is also one of surrender. However, one is made in joy, while the other is made in an absolutely pure love that takes in all the suffering and sadness of her earthly life.

Indeed, the love of Mary's heart reached a wonderful fullness in the final stage of her life: the fullness of love willed for her by Jesus. Jesus finds His greatest delight in her and communicates to her all that He can give her of the love of His heart. Hence in this final act, the intensity of love in Mary's heart meets the intensity of love in Jesus' heart. She is totally similar to Him, as similar as it is possible for a totally pure creature to be united to the love of Jesus' heart and in His heart to the Father's will.

Certain theologians have rightly claimed that the fullness of love in Mary's heart in this final act of her life was similar to that of Jesus' heart but with a different modality: Jesus being the source and Mary receiving everything from this source. To enter more deeply into this mystery, we must always consider it in the light of the Most Holy Trinity without losing sight of the difference. In the Most Holy Trinity, the Son receives from the Father. In the Mystical Body, Mary receives all the fullness of charity from Jesus. There is a similar fullness of love in Jesus and Mary yet in two different modes: one being "principle," the other "derived." And it is precisely in this ultimate communication of love, which so closely unites Mary's soul to Jesus, that her soul can no longer remain joined to her body: Mary must die. It is truly a death of love, a death provoked and realized by Love.

In a very fine passage from his *Treatise on the Love of God,* Saint Francis de Sales, echoing an entire tradition, speaks of the dormition of Mary, saying that she dies of an ecstasy of love.[22] The word "ecstasy" needs to be interpreted correctly. It is not a charismatic ecstasy, which always implies a certain violence, a certain visible, extraordinary, almost miraculous element. (All charismatic grace, as we know, is ordered to the

---

22. Cf. *Treatise of the Love of God,* VII, Ch. 13 and 14. Cf. Pseudo-Modeste: Mary died "gazing on him and deeply moved, as always, by the holy yearning of her divinely maternal heart" (*An Encomium on the Dormition of Our Most Holy Lady, Mary, Mother of God and Ever-Virgin* in *On the Dormition of Mary: Early Patristic Homilies,* translated by Brian Daley, S.J., Crestwood, N.Y.: St. Vladimir's Seminary Press, 1998), p. 98.

sanctification of others.) This aspect seems to have no *raison d'être* in the death of Mary since everything is hidden, everything remains reserved for God. John, who was probably the only witness, must bury everything in his heart as child and as priest.

Thus we have here an ecstasy that is wholly divine and interior, wholly reserved for God. Outwardly, it must have been a sweet sleep. As St. Germanus of Constantinople says, "[you] had to experience death simply as a falling-asleep; you had to undergo your passage from this world as an awakening."[23] And St. Andrew of Crete affirms: "Mary's death was, we might say, a parallel to that first [ecstatic] sleep [of Adam], which fell upon the first human being when his rib was removed to complete the creation of our race."[24] It is the dormition of the "old servant" whose work is accomplished, who no longer has any ties to the earth, and who completely surrenders herself to the love of her God. It is also the dormition of the Virgin who, very gently and in peaceful joy, leaves this earth to go and meet the Bridegroom who is calling her. This is truly the death of God's handmaid and the death of the Bride who dies solely for her God and for her Spouse and wants to die only out of love for Him; who dies while keeping in her heart the words of the Bridegroom and wants to add nothing to these words in order to show just how much they are truth.

---

23. *On the Most Venerable Dormition of the Holy Mother of God: Homily I,* in *op. cit.*, pp. 158-159.

24. *On the Dormition of Our Most Holy Lady, the Mother of God: Homily II,* in *op. cit.*, p. 121.

It is also the death of a Mother who dies for her children. Her death is a motherly teaching. Mary wants to teach us how to live Christ's death through the example of her life. She wants to reveal to us what is essential in the death of the Crucified Christ so that we might not stop at the external details, at the grandiose, tragic, spectacular, even aesthetic, aspects of this mystery of Calvary. She wants us to enter right away into the wound of Jesus' heart and there understand that His death is a death of love and of obedience to the Father's will. She wants us to understand that this is what counts the most and that the external, bloody aspect has meaning only to the extent that it manifests this intimate, divine love. As our Mother, Mary wants us to consent to die in the same manner, imitating the Crucified Christ not outwardly, but intimately, in the very depths of His will and heart.

She wants to teach us to accept all deaths, big and small, in silence and out of pure love. She knows how difficult it is for our human nature; we have such a need to tell ourselves and others that we are suffering, that we are not understood by those close to us, that we are martyrs. In our suffering we always need some spectators; and if others turn their backs on us, we become our own spectators. This explains moreover why our daily deaths are not divine enough, not sufficiently His in love. We are depriving Him of something. As Mother of our divine life, Mary does not want this. She wants for us a death of total love, a holocaust in which everything is consumed out of love for Him and to acknowledge His sovereign rights of love.

According to Tradition, this mystery of the death of the Virgin Mary is intimately united to the mysteries of her resurrection and Assumption. In fact, the Church has brought everything together in one and the same feast. Here again is a teaching that must not be forgotten. Through her death that complements Jesus', Mary reveals to us not only what is essential in the death of Jesus but also the necessary link that exists between His Death, His Resurrection and His Ascension. She wants to help us understand that every death accepted out of love in a totally divine manner, completely hidden from the eyes of the world, immediately implies a resurrection, an ascension: "Today you will be with me in Paradise" (Lk. 23:43). This is true for all those who accept to die with Him. This is very important for our daily lives. Every divine death implies an immediate resurrection, which may be very hidden but which is real.

The Final Act of
Her Earthly Contemplation

The final act of love that Mary's heart accomplished on earth brings her long exile to a close and enables her to enter into the beatific vision, into her contemplative life in its fullness, which is wholly blossomed and totally divine. The contemplative life in the beatific vision is the first blossoming of this divine life, and it takes place in a certain continuity with our Christian life on earth. Indeed it should be understood that there is both a certain continuity and a certain discontinuity between the divine life that the Virgin Mary led here on earth and her life in heaven. There is a substantial and objective continuity in the essential structure of her divine love. There is a discontinuity from the viewpoint of the subject—that is when focusing on the *exercise* of her love—

a discontinuity which springs from the transformation of faith into the light of glory.

It is important to clearly understand this in order to grasp both the similarity and the difference between the structure of Mary's contemplative life on earth and the structure of her contemplative life in heaven. Otherwise one may fail to grasp what is uniquely specific to the contemplative life of the *viator* [the wayfarer], and one always runs the risk of lapsing into errors (condemned by the Church) that try too hard to transform the earth into an anticipated heaven.

Actually, the final act of divine life accomplished by Mary on this earth was indeed an act of contemplation totally directed toward the Father, in and through the mystery of Jesus, under the divine motion of the Holy Spirit. This act of contemplation occurs in the ecstasy of love we mentioned previously, an ecstasy that tears her away from herself to hide her in God. This ecstasy of love, however intense and perfect it may be, necessarily remains totally enveloped in the darkness of faith and the poverty of hope. It is not yet the ecstasy of her intelligence, but in fact an "ecstasy of love" that does not imply full possession. There is still a tension, an aspiration, an ultimate desire, which tears Mary's soul away as it were to hurl it into the love of God.

Since this "ecstasy of love" necessarily begins with the final act of faith of Mary's life, this act, in what is most characteristic to it, then comes to an ultimate perfection. It is exercised in a totally divine manner, under the motion of the gift of intelligence. Here we are presented with an incomparable and unique adhesion of faith that necessarily implies a maximum of certitude, stability and permanence. It is the ultimate foundation of the contemplative rest of Mary's soul, since this full adhesion of faith puts her in direct contact with the Word. There is no longer any fluctuation of her intelligence, no longer any extrinsic agitation that might disturb this adhesion. This adhesion really exhausts all the potentialities of her intelligence. But at the same time everything occurs in the utmost darkness: the non *visum* [the not seeing] has never been so acute, for the mystery of "the gift of the Son" has never been so deeply lived. We are presented with the ultimate demand of the mystery of the subsisting first truth that wants to take full possession of the creature's intelligence.

The darkness of the joyful and sorrowful mysteries and of the first glorious mysteries is transcended. They remain but according to a special and unique modality; for, in this final act of love, Mary is very close to the great revelation of heaven. This ultimate disposition and this proximity thicken in a certain way the veil of her faith, while at the same time making it more luminous. Above all, this proximity makes the veil more difficult to bear. We need to grasp this ultimate captivity of the human intelligence by faith because of this mystery of darkness. Mary's excessive love can remain completely hidden from others and from herself; it can be totally reserved for Jesus and for God. Mary can die without glory, not only without human and social glory, but also without any personal glory. She can be exclusively for Him, totally surrendered in the complete captivity of faith, living her last *nescivi* [I did not know], no longer doing anything but loving.

This act is really the final trial for her, the one that sums up everything and leads to the final *sursum corda*, in a love that sees nothing but is sure of the Beloved's infinite love.

This final act of love of her earthly life also contains her final act of hope. Mary's hope, like her faith, then reaches its full perfection, to such an extent that nothing is left for her but to disappear. She has fulfilled her role.

The final act of hope of Mary's earthly life, exercised under the motion of the gift of fear, has an intense, burning desire, an extraordinary desire to see God, to possess Him fully and to be totally possessed by Him. This burning desire is also very poor. It is entirely surrendered to God, to the Father's gracious will. Mary knows then more than ever how useless a servant she is and how much everything is given to her out of sheer mercy. In this final act of hope, which ends her earthly life, she abandons herself completely to God as the poorest of all creatures, totally dependent on God's mercy, incapable of standing on her own in His loving presence. But at the same time her heart leaps for joy, for it is thirsty for Him who is everything in her life and who has always been for her the "one thing necessary," the sole reality.

In this final act of love, faith and hope, where Mary is so close to her Father, to her Son, where she is consumed by the Holy Spirit, a wonderful patience and ardor blossoms in her heart. The *in manus tuas commendo spiritum meum*[25] is fully lived. She is ready to remain in the desert if such is God's good pleasure, yet she longs to see Him, to be entirely possessed by Him and to give all to Him, with an intensity she had not yet experienced. Mary fully lives on all the ardent love that Jesus lived in His final earthly act on the Cross, at Calvary. Her charity is in unison with Jesus' charity.

---

25. Lk. 23:46 (Ps. 30:6 Vulgate).

Glorious Life of Heaven in Mary: Her Birth into Heaven, the Light of Glory

In this ecstasy of love, God interiorly imparts the light of glory to her. This light of glory has the same fullness of intensity as the final act of love, since it is the degree of charity that measures the special intensity of each beatific vision, and not the intellectual capacities of the soul. This light of glory enables her to see God from within, in His mystery, to see Him as He sees Himself, "face to face," to know Him as she is known. It is the Word of God Himself—He who is the primary source of her intelligence, He who is the Father of all light—who, from within, takes hold of all of her intelligence and reveals Himself in full light. Mary contemplates the Word who is present in the inmost depths of her being, her spirit, her heart. Seeing the Word, she sees the Father and the Holy Spirit. The beatific vision, allowing her to participate directly in the life of God in full light, is necessarily a Trinitarian contemplation since God's life is a Trinitarian contemplative life: a contemplative generation of love and a luminous spiration. Mary is associated with this Trinitarian life through the Son and, in the Son she is the Father's daughter. She loves in the very light of the Word.

Because Trinitarian life is in fact inseparable from Christ's glorious life, Mary contemplates in her beatific vision her Son's glorious human nature hypostatically united to the Word. Her Trinitarian contemplation is at the same time, and indissolubly, a contemplation of the glorious Word Incarnate. She sees all the love of the Father for His beloved Son, and she lives on this love, with the Father and the Holy Spirit. She sees all the splendor of this love in Christ's soul and risen body and especially the splendor of the wound of His heart, which is the burning source and center of all the light and warmth of the heavenly Jerusalem. In this contemplation of the Word Incarnate, she sees all the divine ties that the Holy Spirit has fastened between her and her Son. She contemplates God's gesture of prevenient mercy toward her, understanding the unique privilege of her Immaculate Conception. She contemplates the sheer gratuitousness of the mercy of her God, He who "has regarded the low estate of his handmaiden" (Lk. 1:48), making her Mother of His only Son and associating her so intimately with all His work of Redemption. In the vision of her Son, and in the vision of her divine motherhood, she contemplates the entire Mystical Body, the entire mystery of the "new Jerusalem, prepared as a bride adorned for her husband" (Rev. 21:2), and in this "holy city" she enters into the mystery of each of our souls. She sees us in her beatific vision as God sees us, from within, in full, divine transparency.

The theologian Father Bernard states the following concerning Mary's glorious life and her motherhood in the beatific vision, in his work *Le Mystère de Marie:*

> Her noblest activity is evidently to see God and to love Him. Now the Blessed Virgin is so essentially a Mother that she cannot help seeing all her children in God and loving them in Him. This is her spiritual maternity in its highest aspect, for here we see a creature who has the privilege of seeing those whom she

brings forth the way God sees them, and of carrying them constantly in her eternal heart the way God Himself carries them. It would be impossible to conceive anything greater in her activity or more profitable for us than this tender gaze in which she enfolds us and with which she penetrates us.[26]

Mystery of Ecstasy and of Silence

Mary's beatific vision implies both an intellectual ecstasy and an ecstasy of love. It is the Word of God Himself who takes hold of what is most intimate and profound in her intelligence to illuminate it and actualize it in a divine way. By manifesting Himself as He is, the Word becomes the proper good of her contemplation. Mary's intelligence, uplifted by the light of glory and as it were assumed by the Word, directly contemplates the Word of God as the Latter sees Himself. Then the Word becomes the living form of her contemplation, according to the striking analogy expressed by St. Thomas in *Contra Gentiles* that just as in the mystery of the Incarnation Christ's human nature subsists through the Word of God, so in the beatific vision the beatified intelligence lives in and through the Word of God.[27]

What is realized in the ontological order in the mystery of the Incarnation is realized in the vital order in the mystery

---

26. Père Rogatien Bernard, O.P., *The Mystery of Mary*, trans. M. A. Bouchard (St. Louis: Herder, 1960), Ch. 46, p. 243.

27. Cf. *Contra Gentiles*, IV, 54.

of the beatific vision. This vision is both an intellectual intuition, the purest that can exist (that is why it is said to be a vision and a judgment of existence, the most realistic possible, since this vision is a penetration of the subsisting Truth) and a direct contact with the reality *par excellence.* We can understand how infinitely this divine mode of the beatific vision transcends the connatural mode of the human intelligence. In this act of the beatific vision, Mary's intelligence is truly enraptured by the Word. It is enraptured in the proper sense of the word: the intelligence leaves its own modality, so to speak, to live in unison with the Word, to fully adopt His manner of knowing. That is why it is only this contemplation that really has an ecstatic mode. But since the Word, while transcending the proper object of Mary's intelligence, is at the same time immanent, He is more intimate to her intelligence than her intelligence is to itself. This contemplation also possesses a mode of absolute interiority and recollection, since it unites Mary's soul to Him who is present in the inmost depths of her being, who is the very source of her entire being and of her whole life.

It should be clearly understood that this mode of recollection and interiority of the beatific vision is not at all a reflexive attitude, as though there were a new act of knowledge that considered the subject in a state of contemplation and analyzed the very behavior of the knowing subject. No, it is one and the same act of a contemplative and objective gaze that possesses all the perfections of intellectual rapture and recollection. Thus we are in the presence of an objective and divine recollection that surpasses and transcends all reflexive and subjective recollection.

This intense recollection occurs in silence. In her blessed contemplation, Mary's intelligence utters no "word" of its own. She remains eternally fixed in the Word of God, totally absorbed in Him, completely secluded in His divine solitude and His Trinitarian life. The beatific vision, in what is entirely proper to it, cannot be communicated since it is the Word of God Himself that specifies or informs the intelligence uplifted by the light of glory; and likewise it is the Word of God Himself who is the end of its proper act of contemplation.

Mode of ecstasy, mode of recollection, mode of intimacy and of silence; all these characteristics clearly indicate that this beatific vision, which is formally a contemplation of the intelligence, bringing all its capacities to bloom, also implies a full blossoming of love. The beatific vision necessarily implies an ecstasy of love since divine life is Light and Love. Contemplation of the three Persons is both "pure gaze" and "pure gift." The primary characteristic of this ecstasy of blessed love is the fact that it is eternal. For eternity, Mary is surrendered in a perfect and unchanging gift to the Father, in the Word and through the Holy Spirit. Nothing can stand in the way of this gift any longer. And although this gift is in fact substantially the same as the gift of the final act in her earthly life, it nevertheless knows a new dimension. It is no longer hidden; it is radiant and in full bloom. It is realized in splendor and beauty. It bursts forth like a flower that, until then, could not blossom and had to remain a bud. Think of the beautiful comparison made by St. Francis de Sales: charity here below remains like a cocoon; it is only in heaven that it can appear as a wonderful butterfly that spreads out its multicolored wings in the sun's rays.

If we wanted to analyze more profoundly the act of gift of Mary in the beatific vision, we would see that, like the act of the intelligence, this act also implies all the perfections of the mode of ecstasy and of the mode of recollection. In this act of gift of perfect love, Mary is one with God and with her Son. She lives Their very life. She is totally Theirs and being totally Theirs, she leaves herself totally. She no longer belongs to herself at all, yet at the same time, she is more than ever intimately present to herself. We might say that to the extent that she had forgotten herself for God during her exile, that she had died to herself as it were, like the grain of wheat buried in the earth, to this same extent, in glory, she finds herself again for God. In the vision of glory she lives the life of the Trinity; the life of God is the life of her soul. We know that we can perfectly find ourselves only by being totally in God. Christ's words are still true: "He who loses his life . . . will find it."[28] Here on earth we live mostly by this "loss"; whereas in heaven, it is this "gain" that shines forth in splendor. Substantially, in divine love, loss and gift are always simultaneous and coextensive; yet the experience of this is totally different during the time of tribulation than once in heaven, where the gift of love occurs in full light and in a perfect divine mode, free from all earthly constraints and all the conditions of the subject who still lives in faith.

Mystery of Presence

This contemplation of pure gaze and pure gift enables Mary to live in the presence of the three divine Persons and

---

28. See Mt. 10:39; Jn. 12:25.

of her Son, a presence similar to the one that exists among the three divine Persons. The Father is present to the Son and the Son to the Father in the Holy Spirit, in such a way that the Son is in the Father, *apud Patrem,*[29] that He dwells in Him and that the Holy Spirit dwells with both of Them. In the same way Mary is present to each divine Person and dwells with each of Them. She is *apud Patrem, apud Verbum et Spiritum Sanctum.* This presence of penetration is realized in and through her Son, in His light and in His love.

The solitude and silence of the beatific vision are a divine solitude and silence that are not incompatible with the Trinitarian communal life, the eternal generation of the Word and the eternal spiration of Love. Mary is fully associated into this communal life according to the measure willed by God. While remaining a creature infinitely far from God's transcendence, she is as though integrated into God's personal mystery in and through the mystery of her Son. She is for eternity the Father's beloved little daughter, heiress to His entire family treasure. She is eternally called by Him to live His secrets: the generation of the Son—who is also her own Son—and the spiration of Love.

Comparison Between the Two Modes of Divine Life: Their Diversity and Continuity

We can see immediately the very great differences that exist between Mary's final act of contemplation on earth in her ecstasy of love and this unique, eternal act of heavenly contemplation. The captivity of the intelligence on earth through faith and its complete exaltation in heaven through the light of

---

29. "Toward the Father": Jn. 1:1-2.

glory immediately lead us to understand the psychological abyss that separates the two stages of divine life in Mary. On the one hand, the intelligence living in faith always remains in a state of expectancy and imperfection; thus it can only blossom into a certain contemplative life if charity takes possession of it. On the other hand, the intelligence uplifted by the light of glory is fully alive, and its act of vision constitutes the essential and substantial element of the contemplative life in heaven. The act of faith, considered in itself as distinct from charity, truly constitutes the foundation, the principal element, of contemplative life; but it does not formally constitute its substance. The act of faith, considered in itself, is an adhesion to divine revealed truth; it is not yet a contemplative gaze. This adhesion will become a *contemplative gaze* only thanks to charity and in charity, since here on earth charity alone reaches God directly as He is, from within and in an intimate way. Thus this contemplative knowledge will be all-imbued with love; it will be a penetrating and experiential knowledge thanks to love; and hence, in a certain sense, it will be far more characterized by "touch" and "taste" than "gaze" and "vision." In heavenly contemplation, the intelligence uplifted by the light of glory recovers its rights and its primacy, but it had to accept losing them here below in order to give absolute priority to love.

However strong the discontinuity between heavenly and earthly contemplative life may be, we must not forget their continuity which, although admittedly very hidden from our human perspective, is nonetheless real and profound. This continuity comes from the object and from the essential structure of charity. On earth, as in heaven, it is the same mystery of God in Himself that is attained and contemplated.

Anything that is extrinsic to this mystery is not part of divine contemplation. For this very reason, every reflexive and subjective attitude is contrary to divine contemplation. Substantially, it is the same charity that imposes its own demand of silence, interiority and gift of self; regardless of the *manner* in which the demand is made. What is certain is that charity always makes these demands, for it is part of the very nature of divine love, an absolute and jealous love that cannot stand being compared to any other love, that cannot stand discussions, arguments, and empty chatter. It demands that our entire "self" be totally surrendered to the love of God—a God who eagerly tries to reveal Himself or at least to give a sense of His presence in the inmost depths of our being: "The Kingdom of God is within us" (Lk. 17:21), "He who abides in love abides in God, and God abides in him"(1 Jn. 4:16).

Glorification of Mary's Body, 'Extra Verbum' Life

Mary's life in heaven does not only consist of the beatific vision. The latter is of course its essential and principal element, but it is not the only one. There is a radiance, as it were, of the glorious vision into all the other faculties of the Most Holy Virgin. The glorification of her body is to be understood in relation to this radiance. The beatific vision in itself is absolutely independent of the resurrection of the body. In itself, it is in no way altered by this resurrection since it is unchanging and eternal like the very beatitude of God.

The dogma of the Assumption affirms that Mary's body was raised and taken up into heaven.[30] It matters little here

---

30. Apostolic Constitution *Munificentissimus Deus,* November 1, 1950.

to know whether there was an interval of three days as for Jesus or whether, on the contrary, this glorious assumption took place without an interval, straight after her death. That which is formally the object of our faith is the mystery itself of the glorification and assumption of Mary's body, since her body did not undergo any corruption.

This resurrection occurs according to the model of the resurrection of the glorious body of Jesus. Mary's glorious body resembles the glorious body of Jesus in an especially unique way. Her body resembles His more than any other elect's body will ever resemble it. Regarding the resurrection, as regarding the beatific vision, Mary is first among creatures; she is the closest to Jesus. She is the new Eve alike to the new Adam. It is normal that, even in this physical order concerning the reality of the human body, Jesus should return to Mary a hundredfold what she gave Him. It was in her that Jesus' body was formed; it is according to the model of Jesus' glorious body that her body is glorified.

There is therefore a wonderful proximity between Mary's glorious humanity and the glorious humanity of Jesus. She is Jesus' glory. Jesus is glorified in her as the Father is glorified in Jesus. All the beauty of Jesus' glorious body can be found in her.

St. John Damascene states: "It was fitting that the Mother of God should receive the blessings of her son."[31] Is she not portrayed by John in his heavenly vision as the

---

31. *On the Holy and Glorious Dormition and Transformation of Our Lady, Mary, Mother of God and Ever Virgin: Homily II* in *op. cit.*, p. 218.

"woman clothed with the sun" (Rev. 12:1), *pulchra ut luna,*[32] since her beauty and radiance come from the sun?

Communal Life with Jesus

If we want to specify more clearly the fullness of Mary's blessed life in heaven, we must first of all examine her communal life with Jesus, then her maternal rule over the whole militant and glorious Mystical Body and her queenship over the angels. Finally, we must understand how this communal and merciful life divinely coincides with her liturgical life.

Between the glorious humanity of Jesus and that of Mary there is a communal life in which Jesus and Mary's divine charity blossom in a totally new way with wonderful freedom and fullness, penetration and comprehension. The life in Nazareth, the life of the Holy Family, is extended and transfigured in heaven. Jesus' glorious humanity is the center, the hearth, of this new family life. We must even say that it is the wound of His heart that is the burning source of this family life, illuminating this communal life and giving it its proper tonality. Everything comes from the wound of Jesus' heart, and everything must return to it. Jesus eternally exerts upon Mary His authority as king, priest and prophet. He continues to communicate His secrets to her, since every gaze and every word that Jesus directs toward Mary is really an illumination which comforts the Most Holy Virgin's heart and intelligence. Jesus continues to exert upon her heart His influence as a Beloved Son, as a Good Shepherd who knows her by her name, who loves her more than all the other sheep,

---

32. "Beautiful as the moon": Song 6:9 (Vulgate).

with an infinitely sweet and intense love of predilection. The attraction of the wound of Jesus' glorious heart on his Mother's heart is inexhaustible; it flows from an infinite fullness of love. In glorious poverty, Mary receives everything with thirst and gives herself with love. She is totally relative to Jesus. Everything in her glorious maternal heart lives solely for Him.

Work of Mercy

It is thanks to this profound and intimate unity that Mary accomplishes with Jesus this joint work of mercy and fraternal love toward the whole Mystical Body. She is eternally the Mother of the members of Christ: Mother of their divine life, a mother who never ceases to beget them to this divine life; a mother who never ceases to watch over them, carry them, feed them, sustain them, educate them and direct them toward the heart of Jesus and toward the Father while teaching them to be completely docile to the inspiration of the Holy Spirit.

With a perfect knowledge of our souls—a knowledge she has received from Christ, since all the secrets of our hearts are revealed to her—she gives and communicates to us this divine life as adopted sons of the Father (adopted yet real) and as members of Jesus. She knows us and calls us by our name; she has received this knowledge from the Good Shepherd Himself.

This knowledge is a practical, loving and efficacious knowledge. It is a mother's knowledge concerning her children, one which binds the mother's heart and intelligence to her children's heart and intelligence. We have here as it were a very intimate communication of life, within a loving knowledge. Mary as mother, is completely given to our souls, through Christ and the Father. And it is in this very gift that she is Mother and that she begets us. This gift has a maternal modality that cannot be separated from the gift we are given by Christ and the entire Holy Trinity. She can give herself as Mother to our souls, giving birth to divine life in us, only through the will of the Son and of the Father, under the shadow of the Holy Spirit.

In His wisdom, God willed to fully establish Mary as Mother of His Son so that she might fully be Mother of His members, in order that she might eternally play this role as Mother of our divine life. That is why the gift of this divine life which she gives to her children is realized in this particular modality of maternity. She is the vital *milieu* where their divine life can blossom. She is the one who carries and envelops their Christian life, who disposes their souls to the action of the Holy Spirit and who, in a very intimate and delicate way, completes in them this action of the Holy Spirit so that God's graces may be completely efficacious.

This helps us to understand the manner in which she is present to each of her children in the intimacy of their divine life, their Christian life. It helps us to understand how there is a kind of special mode to our grace that connaturalizes us with Mary's grace and spontaneously inclines us toward her and enables us to live in unison with her divine life. It is in this sense that we must clearly understand that her motherhood for those still on earth is on another level, beyond, as it were, the instrumental action of the sacraments.

We should point out that for those who are still living on earth, Mary's presence in the intimacy of their divine life is a supernatural presence that remains hidden and veiled and is the source of our highest aspirations and our most ardent desires. Although hidden, this presence is efficacious and real; it is the presence of someone who maternally acts in us, who gives us God's life and who never ceases to prepare us and make us docile to the motion of the Holy Spirit.

Of course, the Holy Spirit can give us the divine experience of Mary's motherhood of choice and preference with respect to our souls. He can make us consciously live from this invisible and maternal presence of Mary in the intimacy of our divine life. He can teach us to say "Mother" while looking at Mary, just as He teaches us to say "Father" while looking at our Creator. He can unveil for us and help us experience the unfathomable depths of this motherhood; He can lead us to understand the divine quality of her love. At the Cross, Mary accepted separation from Jesus in order to become the Mother of John's divine life. Jesus asked her for this sacrifice so that she might become our Mother, and Mary accepted it with love. Thus she preferred the divine life of her son John to the joy of her Son's physical presence, to her Son's earthly life. This choice is eternal. It is with this "quality" of love that we are loved.

The Holy Spirit can bury us and experimentally hide us in the depths of the maternal mercy of Mary's heart and ask that we remain there, as though in seclusion, like a little child *in sinu Mariae*. The Holy Spirit can ask us to choose her as a Mother in a very special way, with a choice that seeks to match the divine quality of her own choice. He can require from us an attitude similar to John's: to choose her as a Mother in order to obey an imperative order from Christ, in order to obey His last will and take her "into our home," intimately into our life, as he did, to live exclusively with and by her. It is a divine dwelling that is very hidden, very solitary, and very silent in which the Holy Spirit can establish us. We have here a very special covenant of love between our hearts and Mary's heart. Each one of us lives in this covenant, but we are not all divinely aware of it.

Moreover, Mary cooperates in Christ's governance upon us, a governance that consists in directing us toward the Father, in leading us through love toward the paternal home. This governance, which comes from God's wisdom, is both forceful and gentle, *fortiter et suaviter.* Mary's maternal rule over us primarily concerns the blossoming of our Christian life, the perfection of our life of faith, hope and love. Mary always hastens the Hour of Christ, as at Cana, and she always wants us to go faster. She cannot stand certain delays, certain moments of nonchalance. She acts "forcefully," demanding a great deal from us, like a loving mother who has great ambitions for her sons whom she loves so much. But she acts gently, with infinite delicacy, from within so to speak, as though we were acting on our own. She steps aside to leave room for our own initiatives. She is present in our life of silent prayer to help us live more divinely in Him. St. Thomas tells us that if we consider the wedding at Cana in a mystical way, it concerns the marriage of our soul with Christ. Mary is always invited to this wedding, and she plays the part of *conciliatrix nuptiarum,*[33] introducing our soul to Christ. Thus she acts maternally in our entire life of silent prayer to render it more divine and to

---

33. See St. Thomas, *Commentary on the Gospel of St. John,* II, §343.

remove the human, intellectual, aesthetic or imaginative modes and to give it a divine mode of simplicity and love: "Be as innocent as doves" (Mt. 10:16), "Whoever does not receive the kingdom of God like a child shall not enter it" (Lk. 18:17).

This governance especially intervenes in the realm of our human imagination, our memories, our "psychological selves." This is in fact where most of the battles and struggles are fought, where the majority of temptations occur. Mary pacifies, calms, simplifies, gets rid of our psychological complexes; she unties them with her maternal and delicate love. She also acts in our sensibilities and our physical strength, enveloping everything in her maternal grace.

Thanks to this action of maternal mercy, her presence, which is realized first of all in the depths of our divine life at its very source, can take hold of our entire human, imaginative, intellectual, affective and sensitive life, according to God's gracious will. This maternal action can take hold of everything. Since Mary possesses her glorious body in heaven, her maternal action can even include more extraordinary modalities: with more sensible or imaginative forms; as also happens for the presence of Christ's glorious body with respect to His members who are still here on earth. Mary can visibly appear to her children exiled on earth to comfort them, encourage them and to remind them of the demands of their Christian life. Obviously, such apparitions are always of a charismatic and transient order. They are like "divine signs" to reawaken our faith or reduce our incredulity, and they are also like "foreshadowings" of life in heaven.

In heaven, for the elect, Mary's presence is lived in full light, and all its potentials are made perfectly explicit. Mary still performs this merciful yet forceful maternal role with respect to the elect. She illuminates each of the elect and gives herself to each one in particular.

With respect to the angels, she exercises a "queenship" and not an intimate "motherhood." She enlightens and illuminates them, but does not give herself to them as a mother. Thus her children enjoy an intimacy with her that the angels cannot enjoy.

Liturgical Life

Her communal life with Jesus and her maternal life with the elect and her children on earth will also blossom into a magnificent liturgical life of prayer, devotion, adoration, thanksgiving, praise and petition. This celestial liturgical life is distinct from contemplative life, yet it is in perfect harmony with it. Though this celestial liturgical life remains distinct from the contemplative life, it is nevertheless in perfect harmony with it. It is, as it were, the radiance of this contemplative life in our human moral life and the place where the contemplative life takes hold of our moral life.

This life of adoration actually blossoms in her mystery of compassion lived according to a glorious modality. It is the intimate and eternal holocaust of her heart united to the heart of Jesus. It is the glorious holocaust of the spouse and Mother. The "seven swords" that pierce her heart correspond to the single lance thrust that pierces Jesus' heart.

This glorious adoration is also a song of praise. While Mary in heaven is indeed a "host"[34] of holocaust, she is also

---

34. "Host" comes from the Latin *hostio* meaning "sacrificial victim" [Trans.].

a "host of praise." Everything in her praises God; everything that is in relation to her praises God through her. It is a praise of filial love that is steeped in intimacy and joy. This praise implies true thanksgiving: thanking God for all that He has abundantly and lovingly communicated.

Finally, she is our "advocate" before the Father and before Jesus. She never ceases interceding on our behalf, requesting graces of love for us. She never ceases pleading our cause with Him whom the Father established as Judge of mankind. She never ceases repeating to Him the words He Himself addressed to the Father on our behalf: "Forgive them, for they know not what they do" (Lk. 23:34). The burning source of this liturgical life is the heart of Jesus and the heart of Mary, which are in fact inseparable. The victim and the Priest are inseparable for eternity.

This liturgical life in heaven, which ends and measures our liturgical life on earth, participates in eternity; it is directly under its influence and dependence. This liturgical life eminently contains all that the Most Holy Virgin lived during the various stages of her life, which we commemorate during the liturgical year: the liturgy of Advent, Christmas and the Purification; a maternal and joyful liturgy; the liturgy of the Agony and the Cross; the liturgy of the Resurrection and of Pentecost. Everything is united in a glorious mode and is realized beautifully in the splendor and radiance of love. In this glorious liturgical life there is not the slightest stain, the slightest obscurity. Everything in it is divinely luminous and ordered.

There we see all the richness of this blessed life; all the divine blossoming of the life of charity: this life that considers God and blossoms in the immutability of the glorious vision is an ecstatic and solitary contemplative life, divinely communal, in the heart of the Trinitarian life; this life that considers one's neighbor and blossoms into bonds of mutual and luminous friendship, in a glorious life that divinely radiates the solitude of contemplation.

In Mary, these bonds of fraternal charity are in fact bonds of filial dependence on Jesus and bonds of maternal mercy toward the members of His Mystical Body. Through the gift of piety, her charity takes possession primarily of the exercise of the virtues of mercy and religion and, through the virtues of mercy and religion, this charity takes hold of all the other virtues. In heaven, Mary lives all the beatitudes in unison with her Son's heart. Indeed the beatitudes constitute the particular "human-divine" climate of the glorious communal life and they manifest to us all its riches and various ramifications.

PART 2

THE MYSTERIES OF JOY:
BUDDING OF MARY'S CHARITY

CHAPTER 3

THE VIRGINAL CONSECRATION: MARY'S SURRENDER TO GOD

AFTER having shown the point of departure and the terminal point of the mystery of the growth of charity in the Most Holy Virgin, we must now examine closely the various stages of this growth.

First Consecration

The first act of charity of Mary's heart that is revealed to us is the consecration of her entire being to God. In the mystery of the Annunciation, when the angel Gabriel tells her that she will be the Mother of God, Mary responds by asking: "How can this be, since I have no knowledge of man?"[35] This question clearly indicates the intimate intentions of Mary's heart. This virgin, "betrothed to Joseph" has given herself entirely to God and belongs exclusively to Him. Her betrothal to Joseph marvelously conceals her total gift to God.

---

35. Lk. 1:34 (New Jerusalem Bible).

This total consecration of her being is Mary's first response to the prevenient mercy of the Father. It is her heart's first fervent movement toward the love of God. In this response, Mary divinely makes use of all the privileges of the grace of being immaculate. This act is the fruit of a heroic love that strives toward God as perfectly and as quickly as possible. Like all donations, it implies a separation, a sacrifice. Out of love for God, Mary sacrifices her human motherhood, if such is the will of God, and this sacrifice is made in the darkness of faith. She cannot know what God has in store for her. It is the act of faith and hope that God requires of Abraham when He asks him to leave the land of his ancestors to journey toward the promised land. "The Lord said to Abram, 'Go from your country and your kindred and your father's house to the land that I will show you.' "[36]

---

36. Gen. 12:1. We could here quote the words of St. Gregory of Nyssa about the departure of Abraham from his country to respond to God's call: "[Abraham] went out by Divine command from his own country and kindred on a journey worthy of a prophet eager for the knowledge of God. For no local migration seems to me to satisfy the idea of the blessings which it is signified that he found. For going out from himself and from his country, by which I understand his earthly and carnal mind, and raising his thoughts as far as possible above the common boundaries of nature, and forsaking the soul's kinship with the senses,—so that untroubled by any of the objects of sense his eyes might be open to the things which are invisible, there being neither sight nor sound to distract the mind in its work,—'walking,' as saith the Apostle, 'by faith, not by sight,' he was raised so high by the sublimity of his knowledge that he came to be regarded as the acme of human perfection, knowing as much of God as it was possible for finite human capacity at its full stretch to attain" (*Answer to Eunomius' Second Book* in *Nicene and Post-Nicene Fathers,* Second Series, Vol. 5, p. 259).

By totally consecrating herself to God, body and soul, Mary must leave all that is connatural to her: *egredere de cognatione tua* (Gen. 12:1). She must forget her Father's house, *obliviscere domum patris tuae,*[37] to direct her steps toward a promised land, as yet invisible, which God will give her.[38]

This act really presents to us the dawn of the evangelical law. The spirit of this law, in its most demanding and purest aspect, imposes itself upon Mary's heart and takes possession of her whole being.

Mary's question to the angel Gabriel at the Annunciation thus indirectly reveals the intimate and hidden love of her heart for God. She chose Him in preference to all other realities.

The Holy Spirit did not directly reveal to us the first *ecce venio*[39] that she pronounced in the secret of her heart, for He reserved it for Himself, as it were. We can nonetheless guess that this was her attitude through her objection, which is so simple, so clear, and uttered so spontaneously to Gabriel, as if it were the most normal question in the world. This question also reveals a very particular demand of her love from a social and communal point of view: she is betrothed to Joseph while belonging totally to God. Thus her love brings about a new community within the old

---

37. Ps. 44:11 (Vulgate).

38. Cf. Gen. 24:16 and 43. Rebecca, a prefiguration of Mary, is presented to us as a very beautiful young maiden, a virgin (*betulah*). No man had approached her, and she also has a virginal innocence (*almah*). Cf. Ex. 2:8; Is. 7:14; Song 1:3, 6:8; Ps. 68:25; Prov. 30:19. This expression recurs seven times in Scripture.

39. Cf. Heb. 10:7 (Ps. 39:8 Vulgate).

Israelite community: a family community of persons vowed to God who unite first of all to love Him in a more divine manner, and to love each other for Him. This is the dawn of the Christian community; all other Christian communities are rooted in this community and cannot be separated from it.

Mary's consecration, which the Holy Spirit reveals to us in such a veiled manner, is the model of every first stage, of every first orientation in the mystery of the growth of Christian life. Actually, the first gesture of the Christian soul is to present itself to its God, its Creator and its Father. One can only present oneself to one's Creator and Father through total surrender, of body and soul; surrendering oneself into His hands, promising Him fidelity and expecting everything from Him. This is the perfect act of consecration, which is the fruit of a total trust in the Father-Creator's all-powerful mercy. The first act of cooperation of the Christian soul responding to God's merciful action can only be such an action of surrender. Through this consecration, the soul freely and divinely makes the most of the grace that God has granted it. It acknowledges the fact that it can cooperate with God only by giving itself completely to Him, letting Him act with perfect freedom. We can present ourselves to God only by allowing Him to draw us toward Him. We can progress in divine love only by allowing God's love to take possession of us. A creature's first *sursum corda* can only be a total consecration, leaving the soul absolutely free for God. Then God will communicate what He wills, thus determining the creature's will. But God can communicate His will only if there is first this intimate presentation, this profound consecration, in the creature's soul. God always respects human freedom. He acts directly and imposes Himself only to the extent that we allow Him to act. St. John of the Cross speaks of a "freedom of the heart for God." He clarifies that "With this the soul is disposed for all the favors God will grant it. Without it, he does not bestow them."[40] The consecration is really meant to allow for this interior freedom of the heart, orienting it totally toward God.

We should specify that certain modalities of this first act of charity of Mary's heart are revealed to us by Tradition and Scripture. It is very useful to consider these attentively.

Modalities of This Consecration

Once it has been cleared of all the apocryphal legends that give us superfluous details which the Holy Spirit did not see fit to sanction, Tradition gives us the sole fact of Mary's consecration to God: Mary's Presentation in the temple, for a consecration to the service of God. Scripture tells us nothing explicit about it. Mary's first official action, like her last—Mary's Presentation in the temple and her death—were to be as though buried in Tradition, according to the good pleasure of divine Wisdom.

It is important to realize that the mystery of the Presentation is the starting point of the whole of Christian Tradition. Christian Tradition begins with this mystery, this first personal act in Mary's life. Thus the mystery of Christian Tradition is in fact inseparable from the mystery of Mary's life.

---

40. St. John of the Cross, *The Ascent of Mount Carmel,* Bk. III, Ch. 20, §4 (Washington, D.C.: ICS Publications, 1991), p. 303.

If we refuse to accept Tradition, we inevitably mutilate the mystery of Mary, and we will no longer be able to understand it in the manner willed by the Holy Spirit. We can no longer grasp it from within. This is normal, for a mother's mystery is always a mystery of affective intimacy, which is averse to being put down in writing. It is a mystery that can be lived and communicated only in and through love.

Through the mystery of the Presentation, Tradition leads us to understand that Mary gave herself totally to God, that she separated herself from her family, Joachim and Anne, even though they were very holy, in order to enter God's house and dedicate herself to His service.[41] She wants to be God's servant, and nothing else. Mary performs this first gesture of love in the secret of her heart. St. Albert the Great tells us that it is under the sole inspiration of the Holy Spirit, without any human advice, that Mary gives herself to God to be His possession: *solo inspirante Spiritus sanctus absque omni humano prompto consilio et exemplo*. We must understand clearly God's absolute rights over her who wants to become His exclusive property. Despite the obligation for all young girls of David's house to marry in order to perpetuate the

---

41. St. John Damascene affirms: "[She was born in Joachim's house] and was brought up to the temple. Then planted in the House of God and increased by the Spirit, like a fruitful olive tree, she became the home of every virtue, turning her mind away from every secular and carnal desire, and thus keeping her soul as well as her body virginal, as was meet for her who was receive God into her bosom: for as He is holy, He finds rest among the holy. Thus, therefore, she strove after holiness, and was declared a holy and wonderful temple fit for the most high God" (*Exposition of the Orthodox Faith* in *Nicene and Post-Nicene Fathers,* Second Series, Vol. 9, Bk. IV, Ch. 14, p. 85).

royal lineage from which the Messiah was to be born, Mary, without disregarding this obligation, nonetheless accepts the Holy Spirit's imperative call. She separates herself from her family; she sacrifices her motherhood; she deprives herself of the right to love someone of her own choice and to be loved by him, in order to be loved only by God and to love Him alone.

Cajetan points out that this gift of herself to God can be carried out only under the condition that "such is God's good pleasure." Indeed, in making this act, Mary cannot ask anyone's advice. She must keep it as a divine secret since she is the first to perform a like act with such purity. She has no model before her. She is the "leader." Hence she must act with all the more dependence upon God, entirely surrendering to His will for her.

This condition in no way diminishes the absoluteness of the gift, which is total; yet it manifests to us the modality of this act. This gift is made in complete surrender, in total submission to God's will and pleasure. Such is the extreme delicacy of Mary's heart. Her heart does not want to do anything that is not directly willed by God. Under the inspiration of the Holy Spirit, she understands that the best way to respond to the Father's mercy is to become increasingly more open to this mercy, not limiting it by human standards but yielding herself to it, abandoning herself to it. Thus this first consecration is really a consecration in surrender, or rather a consecration of surrender, for it wants nothing but a complete and total surrender without any restrictions either of matter or time. We yield ourselves to God's will and pleasure, bound hand and foot, and we promise Him that during our entire life we will consider this attitude as the most true and fundamental one. Such abandonment is characteristic of the creature raised to the supernatural order as son of God. Our Lord teaches us this very clearly.[42] For the most characteristic attitude of a rational creature who presents himself to God is to adore Him. It is the first act of the sons of man, Cain and Abel, that is revealed to us. A rational creature steps aside and disappears before his God. He cannot look at his Creator without trembling. And yet, the proper attitude of a son is to love his God and Father and to live in unity of love with Him. We then understand how the characteristic attitude of a rational creature raised to the dignity of a son of God is this filial, loving fear, blossoming into full surrender.[43]

---

42. Cf. Lk. 12:22: "Do not be anxious about your life, what you shall eat."

43. It would be interesting to compare the first act Scripture reveals concerning Moses, God's servant, with the first act given by Tradition concerning Mary, God's servant. "One day, when Moses had grown up, he went out to his people and looked on their burdens; and he saw an Egyptian beating a Hebrew, one of his people. He looked this way and that, and seeing no one he killed the Egyptian and hid him in the sand" (Ex. 2:11-12). Moses responds to the prevenient mercy of God who saved him from the waters of the Nile with an act of human justice—one could even say there were three successive acts of human justice, thus a fullness of human justice (Ex. 2:13-17). Mary responds to the prevenient mercy of God who drew her out of the waters of sin with a promise of surrender. This is the only appropriate response to divine mercy. For to respond to mercy by means of human justice is to reduce divine mercy to our human standards; it is to channel it within the bounds of our own reason and consequently destroy it. Moses is afraid of the consequences of his act when he realizes that Pharaoh has heard of it, so he flees to the land of Midian. Yet, to respond with a promise of surrender is to acknowledge the absoluteness of divine mercy, to want to live by this mercy as much as possible, to open one's soul to this

The little child falling asleep in his mother's arms is a good illustration of this attitude of perfect surrender. As a little one he trusts solely in his mother, having no other support than her arms. As a little one, he has no anxiety whatsoever; he does not even know what anxiety is. He yields himself so fully to his mother, he is so surrendered, that he quite naturally shuts his eyes and goes to sleep. This is only an image, but it can help us understand this essential demand of divine life in the heart of man. "Whoever does not receive the kingdom of God like a child shall not enter it" (Lk. 18:17).

This holy abandonment of the "little one" is not quietism, for it is the fruit of acts of faith, hope and love in God the Father's almighty and loving mercy. It is not psychological abandonment, consequence of a lethargic temperament often nonchalant and indecisive. It is above all a divine abandonment, preserving the soul in a state of total readiness to accept God's will. While we can compare this divine surrender to the

---

mercy so that it may take possession of everything. Instead of using God's mercy in a human way, one wants to be possessed by it, one wants to hide in it as completely as possible. One then becomes strong with God's strength. It should be pointed out that while Mary, thanks to the purity of her heart, abandons herself immediately in such a perfect way, this does not mean that her act is not a heroic one and does not require true death to human initiatives. A living being is one that "moves itself"; surrender requires that the lower living being agree to keep silent, to not "move itself," in order to allow the higher being to act freely, according to his will and pleasure. Surrender to divine mercy thus requires that the "Egyptian" (who represents the pagan, the one who obeys Pharaoh, the tyrannical human power) be put to death and buried in the sand. Moses' act is thus significant and symbolic. It sheds light both on the grandeur and purity of Mary's act—showing us the chasm that exists between justice and abandonment—as well as on that which this act of abandonment presupposes and implies: the death and burial of the "old self."

attitude of a little one falling asleep in his mother's arms, we must also compare it to the state of the servant who is awake and watchful for his master's return, anxious to receive immediately his beloved master's first order.[44] This spirit of abandonment is indeed the rational creature's fundamental attitude before his God; he knows that to serve God, to place himself entirely in His hands, to carry out His orders, is the greatest thing a creature can do. The proper attitude of the servant who loves God is to await the initiatives of Him to whom he has devoted himself body and soul, so that he may respond with the greatest diligence and in perfect joy. This divine surrender is thus a state of loving attention to God's will, so that one may receive this will as it should be received. The petition in the *Pater Noster* expresses this in a wonderful way: "Thy will be done on earth as it is in heaven." The rational creature must adopt heavenly customs in order to receive the Father's will in a divine way. All the delays and pauses proper to earth must be banished, and there must be a fundamental desire to receive this loving and eternal will immediately and with love.

Finally, to enter more deeply into what is so divine in this spirit of abandonment and to avoid all human imitation, we could also compare this fundamental state of the Christian soul completely surrendering itself to God the Father's will and pleasure, to the attitude of a father who keeps watch so that a thief not break into his house (cf. Lk. 12:39); to the attitude of a soldier standing guard at night; to the attitude

─────────────────────

44. Lk. 12:35-45: "Let your loins be girded and your lamps burning."

of a lone gunman on the alert for any indication of possible danger from cunning, underhanded attacks. It is no longer merely the basic attitude of a servant who awaits his master's orders; it is the attitude of one who is on the lookout and ready to fight. He knows that, while awaiting his superior's orders, he must watch out for the maneuvers of the enemy who wants to prevent him from receiving the orders and carrying them out. The Christian life here below is a militant life. The untiringly active adversary is always trying to turn the Christian away from the Father's will. St. Peter reminds us of this: "Be sober, be watchful. Your adversary the devil prowls around like a roaring lion, seeking someone to devour."[45] The devil's action is particularly strong and noticeable with respect to this beginning, this starting point, which is so important for all that will come afterwards. The first orientation is always what is most delicate, most sensitive, and also most important. The devil is too intelligent not to give it particularly vigilant attention. That is why the holy abandonment of the "little child," of the Father's son, is not only the attentive state of the loving servant (for the son always remains a creature who must serve God) but also the watchful state of the soldier totally engaged in battle, who knows that although the enemy may be hidden he is indeed present, ready to devour his prey at the slightest imprudent move. This Christian surrender thus requires extreme vigilance with regard to all that is not God or God's messengers. Moreover,

---

45. 1 Pet. 5:8: *"Sobrii estote, et vigilate: quia adversarius vester diabolus, tamquam leo rugiens circuit quaerens quem devoret . . ."*

this extreme vigilance is not the fruit of acquired human prudence alone which, however perfect, cannot detect the devil's trickery. We need the light of faith to detect his trickery; we need infused prudence aided by the gift of counsel, to be "prudent as serpents." This is the only prudence that enables the soul to be as "simple as a dove."

This consecration of abandonment in Mary's soul has all these divine dimensions: it hands Mary over totally to God as a little child abandons himself into his mother's hands; it places Mary in the position of a loving servant of God who expects everything from Him and is anxious to carry out His will and pleasure; it places Mary in a position of defense against Satan, her personal enemy. This consecration of abandonment is the best way for Mary to strengthen herself in God against any possible attacks from the devil. For in abandoning herself to the Father's mercy, she hides in this mercy and escapes the devil's notice. She flees into the desert. Satan knows nothing about Mary's first gesture. This is the first way Mary crushes Satan's head!

Indeed, this consecration of abandonment appears to be what fundamentally brings to bloom, in the most perfect way, her fullness of faith, hope and love, which she received with her privilege of being immaculate. Is this not the first fruit of the gifts of the Holy Spirit, her first cooperation with the Holy Spirit? Does the gift of wisdom not lead her to discover first and foremost God's exclusive and jealous rights? God wants everything; Mary gives herself without reserve. Do the gifts of fear and counsel not make her especially docile to God's absolute sovereignty? The fulfillment of God's will and pleasure is the only thing that has value in her eyes. What is essential is not the quality of the offering considered in itself, but the very fulfillment of God's will accomplished in this offering.

In order for the offering to be holy and acceptable to Him, it must be the living expression of His will. That is why, in order to consecrate herself fully and perfectly, she completely surrenders to God's will and pleasure, preferring His will to the consecration of her being: all her joy and strength are found in God's gracious will.

We can see the difference between Mary's act here and the first act that the Holy Spirit reveals to us about Eve, our mother according to flesh and blood. Eve's first act is an act of independence, of proud isolation, of frightful autonomy. Eve answers Satan's questions; she tells him God's secret and becomes his prey.

There is a constant struggle in us between these two first initiatives, which are as it were two heredities, one coming to us from Eve, and the other coming to us from Mary. In fact our initiatives waver between these two conflicting attitudes. To the extent that we are begotten to divine life, to this same extent our initiatives come closer and closer to this total consecration of abandonment. We live more and more by holy abandonment, understanding that the *ecce venio*[46] and the *in manus tua*,[47] which are at the beginning and the end of Jesus' earthly life, are the fundamental characteristics of the Christian attitude. Indeed, the in manus tuas is as it were the alpha and the omega of a disciple of Christ. Mary, the first among

---

46. See p. 55, note 39.

47. See p. 31, note 25.

Christ's disciples, the one who announces the evangelical law, is a model for us.

This first consecration of abandonment of Mary's soul to God remains completely hidden; a secret and intimate covenant is sealed between her and God. No creature witnesses it. She and God are the only ones who act in this. God takes the first initiative; she cooperates and responds to it. She does everything possible to love Him exclusively and above all else, as the sole thing necessary. This is normal, for abandonment must be hidden and reserved for God. When a soul truly abandons itself to God it is hidden in God, for it wants to live only for Him. This mystery of Mary's consecration, of her presentation, remains intimately hidden in the secret of Tradition, probably in order to lead us to understand the importance of this hidden modality. Every beginning must be reserved for God, must be exclusively His; He has a right to the first fruits of everything that is created.

Nothing has changed from the standpoint of the community. Life in the temple remains outwardly the same. Mary does not alter it in any way. People's glances could not discover anything. God alone knows how much Mary, in the midst of others, lives in a totally new way, according to more profound and divine demands, those of the evangelical law. The evangelical ideal must first be lived in Mary's heart in a very secret way in the shadow of the temple.

The first stone of the edifice that God wants to build in us—the divine temple in which the Holy Spirit is to live— must be as though buried in our inmost recesses, in the Father's mercy, without anything necessarily being changed on the outside. This is one of the demands of divine governance, which is so marvelously revealed to us by Mary's first response, in the mystery of the growth of her divine life.

First Communal Consecration

The secret gift made conditionally to God will be modified, or more accurately, will *blossom* thanks to Joseph. We do not know what happened when Joseph and Mary first met: whether Mary confided her secret to Joseph or whether the Holy Spirit Himself revealed to Joseph God's special love for Mary. The first hypothesis seems to be more in keeping with the laws of the divine governance, and it would unite Joseph and Mary more intimately. Joseph would have been the first one to receive Mary's trust and would thereby become the first beneficiary of her fraternal and merciful charity. For to confide to someone a personal secret that deeply concerns one's entire life shows very great trust in that person and constitutes an act of friendship toward him or her. Joseph would thereby have become Mary's first confidant and friend, as it were, from a spiritual point of view. Scripture tells us that Joseph is officially betrothed to Mary. By the simple fact that he agrees to consider her as his betrothed in the eyes of all while respecting her total gift to God, Joseph enables Mary's consecration to God to be more fully fulfilled. Joseph is as it were God's first merciful response to Mary's full surrender since, thanks to Joseph, there is no longer any obstacle that can prevent the realization of her total gift, body and soul, to God the Father. Joseph, the Virgin's guardian, is the one who hides the first work accomplished by Mary in the Father's mercy: her filial surrender. He actively and freely cooperates in this surrender by living it in his own heart and making it his life. This cooperation enables God's work to be strengthened and established in a communal mode of marriage, the most intimate and natural mode there is.

We should clearly see the progression of the demands of divine love in Mary. This love requires the total gift of herself: first, in a completely solitary and hidden manner—she alone lives by it—and then, the demands of love have to seize the heart of her nearest neighbor: Joseph. Together they must live by these demands of love. Fraternal charity and mercy at their summit immediately take hold of Mary's heart and bind her to Joseph in that extraordinary bond that only the gift of counsel can demand. Obviously, this is a bit crazy when viewed by our poor human eyes. It is wonderful in the eyes of divine wisdom. We might think that virginal consecration, by binding us exclusively to God, should separate us from fraternal charity. In reality, by uniting us more closely to the love of God, a virginal consecration enables us to love our neighbor more deeply, to love him with a totally divine depth and delicacy. It is very impressive to consider that Mary, so totally vowed to God, should at the same time give herself to Joseph in such bonds of fraternal charity. Her virginal heart loves Joseph in a completely divine and pure, yet very real and efficacious, way. It has nothing to do with a sort of distant, abstract, platonic love. Such love is not divine; love like that is always very latent with selfishness and superficiality. Fraternal charity leads us to love our neighbor as God loves him, with all the depth, realism and purity of divine love, which reaches everything that is, without itself being affected, in a totally selfless generosity. It is truly out of love for the other that we love him, wishing him every good and the most excellent good of which he is capable.

Mary loves Joseph with this divine love. She loves him because he is the neighbor chosen for her by God, who is to be her betrothed and husband. She totally conforms herself to God's choice. She chooses Joseph as her "travelling companion," her support, her leader, her confidant. She chooses him so that she can lead a very intimate communal life with him, the communal life of a household, of a family. Her trust in Joseph is such that she confides the secret of her soul to him: her virginal consecration to God. This is really the model of all fraternal charity, for this charity appears both so pure that it perfectly coexists with the highest demands of Mary's heart, immaculate and consecrated to God; and so profoundly human that this love implies a very particular mutual choice, a very absolute and faithful choice that will definitively determine the human orientation of their lives. Their choice is a promise of fidelity that cannot be officially re-nounced; Joseph and Mary are betrothed. This choice is very intimate, very respectful of mutual demands and very welcoming and trusting. We can even say that just as Mary totally surrenders to the Father's all-powerful mercy by consecrating herself to Him, so her trust in Joseph—the representative of the Father's authority over her—is so complete that she truly and completely surrenders herself to him with respect to everything that concerns communal life. She can have total confidence in the divine prudence of this just man (Mt. 1:19). Only Christian prudence completely divinized by the gift of counsel can direct the outward acts of such fraternal charity and order this communal life of Mary and Joseph, which is the dawn of the first Christian community.

Here again, let us consider this demand of divine governance: God wants what is initially very secret and hidden in our hearts to progressively take possession of our entire nature. First He wants our hearts to be totally His in what is deepest in them, and then also totally His in their relationships with other people. Charity must take possession of human friendship in its most excellent aspect, and it must transform friendship. Thanks to fraternal charity, God's mercy can overflow. It is no longer Mary alone who is totally consecrated to God; Joseph is also now consecrated, through his relationship with Mary. It is not Mary alone who is God's servant, but also Joseph who is God's servant by becoming the servant of God's servant. Joseph is a very poor servant whose principal role is to conceal. God needed him in order to hide His handmaid, and in this way He keeps her more closely for Himself. In His merciful governance, God likes to multiply His servants so that His mercy may be superabundant. He likes to unite them in a very intimate way, creating among them very strong bonds of fraternal charity, conditioning even the efficacity of the services rendered by one to the fidelity of the other. In the Old Testament, Moses and Aaron[48] can be taken

---

48. Cf. Ex. 4:14-16. It would be very interesting to compare the way in which God unites Joseph to Mary as the guardian of His servant, with the way in which He unites Aaron to Moses, since in both cases we witness a certain superabundance of divine mercy multiplying its instruments and uniting them to one another in order to carry out a joint work. But the way in which God unites Joseph to Mary is very different from the way in which He unites Aaron to Moses, just as the specific reason for their union is very different. Joseph is both far

as a prefiguration of what is realized between Mary and Joseph. Aaron is given to Moses to hide him. Aaron becomes Moses' official spokesman, "Moses' mouth." Moses will then be able to remain completely turned toward God. But we will not dwell on this. We can simply consider how God gives an immediate fruitfulness to this first consecration of abandonment. The true and divine abandonment of a soul totally consecrated to God overflows and engenders abandonment in the soul of one's neighbor.

This First Consecration: Model of Religious Consecrations

We can say that the consecration of the Most Holy Virgin to God is the model of all religious consecrations. Hence her consecration must show us what is essential and principal in all religious consecrations. Mary can only respond to God by giving herself totally to Him. This consecration is Mary's first joint work with God. It is the full divine utilization of her initial grace: the Immaculate Conception and the fullness of grace. Mary divinely responds to the Father's prevenient mercy that envelops her by totally surrendering herself to this mercy, body and soul. God gave everything gratuitously; Mary freely hands everything over to His will and pleasure. Such is

more united to Mary and far more separated from her; Joseph shares in Mary's secret by reason of her perfection. On the contrary, it is because of Moses' imperfection that Aaron is given to Moses to help him. This parallel can help us better understand what is so perfect and divine in this union that God realizes between Joseph and Mary and how, thanks to this union, God demands such intense fraternal love and much greater poverty from both of them.

her response to the Father's initial mercy. Such is the divine gesture that springs directly from the fullness of faith, hope and love of her totally pure heart. The consecration of virgins takes root in the mystery of the Immaculate Conception. It is in response to this mystery that it has come into the Church.

It should be clearly understood that Mary's consecration is first done in secrecy. There is nothing juridical or official about it. It is for God and for God alone, and for Mary and for her alone. That is why, if we want to be precise, we must say that Mary's consecration is the model for the spirit of all other religious consecrations, the model of what should inspire them and give them their divine character. And since the proper modality of Mary's consecration is that of abandonment, through the mystery of the Presentation, Mary teaches us that the spirit of every consecration is abandonment. The vow of abandonment, or rather, the spirit of abandonment is as it were the soul of the other vows; it is the essential element. Vows be-come rigid if they are not constantly revitalized by this spirit of abandonment. For this very reason, the mystery of the Presentation is not only the model of all religious souls; it is also the model of every Christian soul. The latter must always live by this spirit of abandonment even when, juridically and socially, God has allowed the soul to follow a different path than religious life. A Christian soul can never be exempt from living in abandonment, in total surrender to fraternal mercy; and thus this soul will live by the spirit of religious vows.

In the same way, we can say that the community established through Joseph is the model of every Christian community and especially of religious communities. But we must again point out that what Mary teaches us is not the juridical and social aspect, but the way to live in a Christian community. She shows us the spirit that must animate every Christian community.

Mary's virginal consecration to the Father in abandonment to His mercy and this pure, steadfast fraternal confidence that binds Mary to Joseph are as it were the ultimate fruits of the entire Old Testament. The entire Old Testament culminates and draws to a close in these two acts of divine love: one with regard to God, the other with regard to one's neighbor. With respect to God, Israel's expectation culminates in abandonment, since this is the most divine form of supreme desire. When supernatural desire reaches its paroxysm, if it wants to remain divine and avoid becoming material and human by turning into revolutionary impatience, it must be transformed into abandonment: one totally surrenders oneself to God's mercy. Thus all of Israel's expectation comes to bloom in the Presentation of Mary. With respect to neighbor, the relations of justice and charity that united the members of the people of Israel could not find a more perfect culmination than in the relations of justice and charity established between Joseph and Mary. They are both of the house of David. They are united in the bonds of marriage, which constitute close relations of justice; and they unite while mutually respecting each other's virginal consecration to God, which requires the purest and greatest fraternal confidence and hence an extraordinarily strong mutual love. Thus the entire law of the Old Testament actually culminates in these two acts of Mary, which are already beyond the law and prepare, in an ultimate way, for the New Law.

CHAPTER 4

THE ANNUNCIATION AND *FIAT:*
MARY'S SPECIFIC CALL

WITH the mystery of the Annunciation we come to God's specific plans for Mary. The period of preparation, of pure indeterminate expectation comes to an end and becomes more defined. The text of Holy Scripture is sufficiently clear. The angel's annunciation and Mary's response show us how she fully enters into the mystery of her divine motherhood, which implies a mystery of Christian contemplative life and a mystery of very humble and noble service rendered to God.

First Act of Christian Faith

With the mystery of the Annunciation, we are in fact presented with the first act of explicit Christian faith. Elizabeth tells us in the mystery of the Visitation that Mary's blessedness in this mystery is purely and primarily a blessedness of faith. She is blessed because she believed. Our Lord Himself tells us this in the Gospel: when someone says to Him: "Blessed is the womb that bore you, and the breasts that you sucked!" Jesus replies: "Blessed rather are those who hear the word of God and keep it!"[49]

In his treatise on virginity, St. Augustine states the following concerning these words of Christ: "Mary is more blessed in receiving the faith of Christ, than in conceiving the flesh of Christ. (. . .) Her nearness as a Mother would have been of no profit to Mary, had she not borne Christ in her heart after a more blessed manner than in her flesh."[50]

This act of faith of the Most Holy Virgin must not only lead us into the full mystery of her divine motherhood, which begins with this act of faith, but must also help us understand in an immediately practical way what our Chris-tian faith should be and how we must behave as believers receiving God's Word.

Through her *fiat* to the angel's words, Mary's spirit, in its deepest, most vital and intimate core, fully adheres to the words of God's messenger as God's Words for her. In this living and loving act of faith, Mary's spirit (St. Augustine speaks of her "spirit" and her "heart") touches the Word of God Himself in His personal mystery; or, more accurately,

---

49. Lk. 11: 27-28. In his commentary, Cajetan specifies that Christ thereby reveals "the common reason of blessedness for all the elect," which is true to the highest degree for Mary.

50. *Of Holy Virginity* in *Nicene and Post-Nicene Fathers.* First Series, Vol. 3 (Edinburgh: T&T Clark, 1993), Ch. 3, p. 418. St. Thomas, as a theologian, explains: "Since the spirit is closer to God than the body, it was not suitable for uncreated Wisdom to come to live in the Virgin's womb without the spirit of this same Virgin being resplendent with the lights of supreme Wisdom" (*III Sent.* Dist. 3, Q. 3, Art. 1, ad. 1um).

the Word of God acts upon her spirit, which totally surrenders to this divine hold over it. The Word of God imprints Himself on her spirit from the inside, so to speak, so that Mary's spirit is as though possessed by the Person of the Word. "Christ dwells in our hearts through faith" (Eph. 3:17). The Word of God Himself dwells in her spirit and possesses it.

We see here the wonderful divine control over her entirely pure soul. She listens to God's Word—*fides ex auditu* (Rom. 10:17)—and she touches the Person of the Word. The senses of hearing and touch help us express the realism of faith as well as its imperfect nature: the believer does not see, he hears. He hears God's Word. Since this Word is divine, it does not act from the outside like human words. It acts from the inside, which is why it has a unique realism and efficacity; it enables our spirit in its inmost depths to truly touch the divine Light, the Person of the Word, from the inside.

Mary listens to this Word and keeps it in her heart, letting it take root in her, letting it develop all its divine power, letting it take complete possession of her. In her intelligence and heart nothing resists, nothing opposes God's direct action; everything is surrendered to this action. In her, there is no reservation, no restriction or limitation to this fundamental gift of her spirit and heart. Thanks to her vow of abandonment, everything in her is divinely disposed for this direct hold of God's Word over her. Evangelical abandonment is directed toward receiving God's Word. It is like the plowing which enables soil to be "good soil" capable of receiving the divine seed, the seed of life. Without this surrender our souls are arid, turned inward, incapable of being open to God's Word.

Of course, it is in *non visum,* in obscurity and darkness, that Mary receives God's Word. She cannot see anything; she can only listen and touch. She allows God's truth to take hold even of the most vital depths of her intelligence. She joyfully accepts the fact that God communicates Himself in silence, in a very hidden, mysterious manner. She freely and lovingly accepts the fact that the "Light" and the "Word" are given to her in "darkness" and "silence." This is part of this mystery of the fullness of faith. Faith does not give light, but prepares and orients the deepest capacities of our intelligence for this light.

Although everything occurs in obscurity and darkness, it occurs nonetheless in certainty. Mary yearns to have the inmost depths of her spirit fully determined by the divine truth, the Word Himself. Her *fiat* accomplishes this in a marvelous way. It fixes her firmly in God and thereby separates her from all the changes and relativities of creatures. In this act of faith, her spirit acquires a new certainty, which enables her to stand firm, as though her spirit were able to see face to face Him who is given to her in an invisible way and in darkness, but who is more intimately present than ever.

Purity of Mary's Faith

To understand more clearly the wholly divine character of this act of faith of the Mother of God, of this act that makes her Mother of God, we must, following the example of St. Augustine, compare this Annunciation with the other annunciations related by Scripture, to consider their similarities and differences. In fact, all the other annunciations prefigure the Annunciation to Mary and offer sketches, so to speak, that are more or less similar to the latter.[51] We shall especially compare Mary's attitude to Zechariah's.

Zechariah, who was righteous before God, "walking in all the commandments and ordinances of the Lord blameless," lacks faith when confronted with the angel's message, which is so extraordinary and so unbelievable from a human point of view. He is too cautious in his faith, too rational, too human; he asks for a sign. To ask God for a sign when God demands an adhesion of faith is in fact to ask for some human aid, something that speaks to our reason, our prudence, something that is connatural to us. Our reason can indeed be terribly afraid of the absoluteness of the adhesion of faith; it often trembles before the divine abyss that the voluntary adhesion of faith digs in our souls. Our reason is frightened by the divine mystery that will take hold of us and become ours to the extent that we believe in it. So we instinctively ask for some sign so that our reason may reflect more clearly, verify whether or not all this is truly God's will. It is not necessarily because we lack good will and refuse to believe that we ask for signs, but in order to gain time. It is due to a lack of generosity. It is an excuse to give ourselves a little more time.

Christian faith indeed comes about in very different ways and very different situations: the faith of a disciple does not have the same demands as the faith of a servant or the faith of a child. The disciple can ask for certain signs, certain

51. Cf. Lk. 1:26 ff; Ex. 3:1 ff; Jdg. 6:11 ff.

rational grounds of credibility, so as to adhere to his master's actual words. As a "disciple," he seems to have the right to ask for such grounds for himself, to justify in the eyes of his own reason the foundation and legitimacy of his adhesion of faith. He can also ask for such signs for others, for those who do not believe and to whom he must bring the good news. Consider Moses. God sends him to Pharaoh with a very specific mission to fulfill. Now Pharaoh does not believe in Yahweh. So, to Moses' timid objection: "Who am I that I should go to Pharaoh, and bring the sons of Israel out of Egypt?" God replies: "I will be with you; and this shall be the sign for you, that I have sent you. . . ." (Ex. 3:11-12a).

St. Thomas tells us that signs are for unbelievers, for those who do not yet believe. A sign is like bait that will lure them, that will arouse their attention and curiosity. This is particularly the case when this sign is a punitive sign that afflicts them or a merciful sign that saves them. Pharaoh, confronted with the punitive sign of hail "such as had never been in all the land of Egypt," exclaims: "I have sinned this time; the Lord is in the right, and I and my people are in the wrong. Entreat the Lord; for there has been enough of this thunder and hail; I will let you go" (Ex. 9:27-28; 10:16-17). Consider Christ with the Samaritan woman. The moment our Lord appears to her as a prophet who knows what she is through and through, including the secrets of her private life, she becomes keenly interested; and she is on her way to faith. Similarly, we notice that God does not reproach Gideon when he asks for a sign so that his people may believe in what he will say in the name of Yahweh. Yahweh Himself gives these "miraculous weapons" to Moses so that Pharaoh may learn that "there is no one like Him in all the earth" (Ex. 9:14), so that Moses may be able to contemplate His power, so that His name may be proclaimed throughout all the earth (Ex. 9:16).

Under the guidance of the Holy Spirit, Mary adheres with the divine spontaneity of the Father's beloved little child. She adheres immediately, without asking for a sign, and the angel gives her one out of superabundance. The grounds for her adhesion are not this sign, as it is only a "figurative example," as St. Thomas puts it.[52] The true grounds for her adhesion are really expressed by her response to the angel: *Fiat mihi secundum verbum tuum*—"Let it be done to me according to your word"(Lk. 1:38). She believes in the fullness of God's Word because it is God's Word. She does not want to reduce the magnitude and depth of this divine Word to her human understanding of it, so she does not reply: "I consent to be the mother of God," but in point of fact: *fiat secundum verbum tuum.* She is one who receives God's Word as light, as that which is source and principle of all light and all knowledge. Her intelligence is totally receptive to this light, without restricting or diminishing it in any way. Such is indeed the filial attitude of the child welcoming the Father's Word as an absolute not to be contended, but rather received as a treasure.

One might object that Mary does not adhere spontaneously since, like Zechariah, she questions the angel and asks him the *quomodo,* "how can this be?" St. Augustine understood her objection quite well:

---

52. *Summa Theologica* III, Q. 30, Art. 4, ad. 2.

Concerning this question asked by Mary, *quomodo fiat istud,* if we wanted to speak ill of her, we might say that she too did not believe enough, while she was only trying to find out how this would be done, without doubting the power of God. And the answer she received—"The Holy Spirit will come upon you, and the power of the Most High will overshadow you"—could have been similar to the one made to Moses when he was worrying in the desert as to how such a large number of people could be fed: "Is the Lord's hand shortened? Now you shall see whether my word will come true for you or not" (Num. 11:23).

The angel could have replied: "Is this impossible for the Holy Spirit who will come upon you?" It is true that Zechariah, having said something similar, is reproved for his lack of faith and struck dumb in punishment for his sin. Why? Quite simply because God judges according to the intentions of the heart and not according to words; *nisi quia Deus non de verbis, sed de cordibus judicat.*[53]

---

53. Cf. *Book V on the Seven Books of the Four Questions on the Heptateuch.* Also, the *Sermon* 291, t. 18, 503: "By asking the angel this question, she wants to know how she is going to become a mother and raises no doubts about God's omnipotence: how will this be done? How will what you are announcing to me be accomplished? You are announcing a son for me, you find my soul fully prepared, yet tell me how this son will be

If we look at the intentions of Mary's heart, as St. Augustine suggests, the *quomodo* in Mary's heart is not at all a desire for justification in order to be sure of God's Word; it is not a reflexive attitude adopted to gain time. On the contrary, it is the *quomodo* of a child who does not understand and asks what she must do to fully enter into God's plans for her. Thus it is the fruit of obedient, fearful love—inspired by the gift of fear—which does not want to go astray or disfigure God's will.

The divine purity of this act of faith of a child who adheres to God's Word because it is God's Word clearly shows us the first quality of Christian faith. This first explicitly Christian act of faith is accomplished with such divine clarity and transparency.

We must not however believe that there is any disparagement or rejection of signs. So before considering the other characteristics of Mary's Christian faith in this mystery, it

born. This virgin might fear, or at least be unaware of God's counsel, i.e., by wanting to have a son, perhaps He disapproved of her vow of virginity? What would have happened if the angel had told her: be united with your husband? No, God could not speak in this way, for as God He had accepted her vow of virginity, and had received from her what He Himself had given. Do tell me, divine messenger, how can this be? The angel knows that it is the desire to be informed and not defiance that prompts her question, and because he knows the intentions of her heart, he does not refuse to enlighten her: 'Your faith is intact—and your virginity will be intact as well.' The Holy Spirit will come upon you and the power of the Most High will overshadow you. This overshadowing (*umbraculum*) is unaffected by the ardors of concupiscence. That is why you will conceive by faith; it is because you will become a mother through faith . . . that the holy one you will bear will be called the Son of the Most High."

would be helpful to try to specify, from a practical point of view, the role and precise function of "signs" and grounds of credibility as God seems in fact to reveal them.

Grounds of credibility, including divine signs, miracles and prophecies, must not be rejected or disregarded. God wants us to use them either for the infidel who always keeps watch within us, or for the unbelievers who live around us. Nevertheless, this does not mean that God wants us to ask for them.

What is certain is that God does not want these grounds of credibility, these signs, to become the specific reason for our adhesion of faith. God cannot want our faith to be measured by the reasonable and human knowledge we have of these signs, since then our faith, relying directly and essentially on human and experiential knowledge, would become human and would flow directly from our personal judgment as its normal conclusion. This is the case with the faith acquired by devils. It is no longer a divine and infused faith, the proper grounds of which can only be God's very Word. Divine faith must be directly and formally measured by the divine Word itself, as it is revealed to us. Hence the devil's tactics toward believers always consist in confusing the grounds of credibility with divine grounds. He increasingly emphasizes only the grounds of credibility with a view to progressively degrading the quality of the adhesion of faith to the point of destroying its divine character and retaining only the external and psychological aspect of one who adheres to God's Word because he thinks it cannot be otherwise. Thus we can clearly see two possible orientations for the imperfect faith of a disciple. Under the devil's influence, this imperfect but divine faith will gradually deteriorate until it loses its quality of divine faith and retains only its psychological behavior of natural faith or of a firm and stable opinion. Under the Holy Spirit's influence, this imperfect faith of the disciple needs to grow and aspire to a more divine and pure faith. God then requires that the believer really consent to his intelligence being captured by God's Word, to his intelligence becoming a voluntary prisoner of divine truth. The believer's intelligence must then be enclosed in its divine motive, so to speak, and must completely surrender to God's Word.

This then is the faith of "little children," the faith of those who do not reason but who, through the instinct of the Spirit, the instinct of Love, believe fully and entirely in God's message and totally commit themselves to the service of God who speaks to them: "Lord, your servant is listening, what do you want from him?"[54] It is faith that allows us to enter the kingdom of God.

He who loves no longer needs such signs, such grounds, such crutches, which are useful for a cripple but cumbersome for those who walk perfectly well. By taking hold of the believer's human intelligence, divine love enables him to adhere in such a way that his sole concern is to set no limits to the absolute demands of divine truth. So, if God gives a sign, if the gift of intelligence gives a very clear view of the grounds of credibility and the proper value of signs, one who believes like a "little child" does not refuse these signs, but he does not dwell on them either. Signs are no longer of any

---

54. Cf. 1 Sam. 3:9: "Speak, for thy servant hears."

interest to him, for he longs only to adhere to the mystery for its own sake, in its most divine and therefore most obscure, mysterious and transcendent aspect.

Such are the first purifications of faith brought about by the Holy Spirit. In Mary, these purifications have already been made. With Zechariah, we see them being realized. He asks for a sign while he should have been more confident, more daring in his faith. God expected something greater and more generous from him. God corrects him as a Father, for He loves him. He inflicts a punitive sign upon him; he is struck dumb. It is a paternal chastisement, a purification. Zechariah accepts this divine correction. He bears it with patience and love.

Realism of Mary's Act of Faith

The other characteristic of the act of faith of the Most Holy Virgin Mary in this mystery of the Annunciation is its realism. Through this act of faith, the summit of her intelligence adheres to God's living Word, to the Word who becomes incarnate in her and by virtue of this very fact Mary's entire human life is engaged in this adhesion of faith. The Word of God Himself is present in her, dwells within her, and takes hold of all the capacities of her intelligence, her heart, her sensibility. Her entire being is mobilized by God and for God. We must clearly understand the realistic character of this act of faith that transforms Mary's whole life and demands from her in one instant a profound, unreserved acquiescence to God's loving will for her. St. Thomas tells us that the object of faith is divine Reality, and that it is thus the most realistic knowledge there is. Hence faith determines not only our speculative intellect but also our practical intellect. Mary's *fiat* at the Annunciation clearly reveals the divine realism of her act of faith. We must not forget that while faith can very often appear to us as an abstract knowledge, this is due to the fact that it is realized in us in a way which is still too human, too much according to our connatural mode of knowing: an abstract mode of knowledge which is neither intuitive nor realistic. Through charity and the gift of intelligence, the act of faith should normally blossom into a loving experience of the intimate presence of God, of a Father-God who acts with love toward us, carrying our whole being in His efficacious power, imparting to us something of His own being and life.

Faith—Trust

Mary's act of faith, which blossoms in love, also blossoms in hope, which gives it a note of joyful fervor, of desire, of aspiration and surrender. This *fiat* implies the first explicitly Christian act of hope in the Word Incarnate. Mary hopes in the divine promise being fulfilled in her. From the presence of God becoming incarnate in her, she draws a wonderful support, a new impetus of desire and a new surrender. It is the silent hope of the Mother who draws from Him who is within her a new fervor for life and an ardent yearning to see God. Hope is really the efficacious desire to see God, a desire that leans on God's merciful omnipotence. Hope is a divine "anchor" that fixes us firmly in the heart of Christ and directs all our vital forces toward Him, making us lean upon His merciful omnipotence. In her *fiat*, Mary expresses this efficacious desire to reach God, to possess Him and to be possessed by Him, through total abandonment to the Father's merciful omnipotence. This desire and this surrender, in and through her Son, assume a far more simple, more familiar and gentle character, yet also one that is far more fervent, ardent and forceful, since the promise is fulfilled in her in such an intimate and close way.

We should also take note of the extreme poverty of this hope. This is where we touch upon its completely Christian character, for we understand how firmly she must lean upon God's infinite mercy. Mary hopes in her Son, in her little one. She relies on God's Might imparted to her in the weakness of the "little one," of Him who has not yet been born. She has no right whatsoever over Him who gives Himself to her out of pure grace and divine generosity, yet she must possess Him as her own Son, her own Child. She must give herself to Him who gives Himself to her as a little child expecting everything from her. The gift of fear enables the hope of Mary's heart to acquire this divine note: it is the hope of a Mother who hopes completely in her little one, without having any right over Him. Through hope that is very poor, Christian faith blossoms into an attitude of trust. Mary trusts in God's Word, which is for her a promise of life. Her abandonment is transformed into unwavering confidence in Him who is given to her, in Him who is to come.

Faith—Gift

This act of faith and this act of hope enable the charity of Mary's heart to blossom, in a divine way, into a gift. We know quite well that all purifications of faith and hope occur with a view to an increase in love. If the Holy Spirit demands such purity of faith, such poverty in hope and such trust, it is to enable Love to act freely, without being limited or diminished by human restrictions resulting from our way of judging, of assessing and orienting our lives.

The love of God needs a free hand to act according to its divine demands. For God can personally give Himself only if man freely agrees to give himself to God. Charity is a divine friendship, a mutual, reciprocal gift that can be realized only in mutual giving. God gives Himself to Mary only if Mary gives herself to God, and here we can grasp all the divine fruitfulness of this gift. For in giving herself, Mary gives all mankind to God. We are familiar with the very beautiful doctrine of the Fathers considering Mary's *fiat* as the consent of all mankind to the divine nuptials with the Word. St. Thomas takes it up again with respect to the motives that explain Gabriel's announcement to Mary: "[I]n order to show that there is a certain spiritual wedlock between the Son of God and human nature . . . in the Annunciation the Virgin's consent was besought in lieu of that of the entire human nature."[55]

In the *fiat* of the Annunciation, Mary gives herself to God. This more explicit gift unites her more divinely and more intimately to the Father, the Son and the Holy Spirit. This gift implies a clear, precise choice which demands everything without reserve. God gives Himself in His only Son. Mary gives herself as Mother of God. This is the new covenant realized in this *fiat* of love. This *fiat* requires perfect

---

55. *Summa Theologica* III, Q. 30, Art. 1 and 4.

docility on Mary's part. The angel says to her: "The Holy Spirit will come upon you, and the power of the Most High will overshadow you" (Lk. 1:35).

Faith—Contemplative Life

Through this *fiat* of faith, hope and love, Mary enters into a completely new intimacy with God, her Son. The Father conveys His secret of love to her and asks her to live from it with Him. The Son conveys His personal secret of love to her and asks her to live by its light, facing Him and for Him. The Holy Spirit requires perfect docility in love from her. Through this *fiat,* Mary penetrates into the mystery of the Holy Trinity to live by this same mystery. Consider the wonderful way in which the Father revealed to mankind His mystery as Father by asking Mary to be His Son's mother. One cannot reveal a secret to a friend in a more delicate way than by having him live from the same secret, by having this secret immediately become his secret so that he may live from it in the same way. Revealing His Son, His Word, the Light, to men who are so far removed from this light, the Father asks Mary to allow His only Son to become her only Son. He reveals His fatherhood by giving Mary this miraculous fruitfulness as a Mother. It is in Mary's motherhood that He reveals His fatherhood to us.

This *fiat* is really the origin and the source of all Christian contemplative life. Through this *fiat,* Mary enters first and foremost into a life of contemplation. She becomes the bearer of God, a living tabernacle for the Word Incarnate. She is the true temple of the Holy Spirit containing God's new covenant with mankind. St. Augustine, addressing Mary, expresses this in a striking way: "The Word becomes united with flesh, He makes a covenant with flesh, and your womb is the sacred bed on which this holy union of the Word with flesh is consummated."[56]

Thus she is truly God's house, "the house of prayer" and contemplation. Everything in her soul, intelligence and heart is directed toward the Word, toward subsisting Truth. Everything in her must be attentive to the loving presence, to the preferential love of her God and Son. In this *fiat* Mary truly receives the divine Word and keeps it, safeguards it, takes it into her heart and intelligence. Through this *fiat* God's presence is given to her; God takes up His abode in her, establishes His roots in her, takes hold of her whole life in the most intimate and realistic way.

Faith—Silence

In the mystery of the Annunciation, the divine purity of Mary's faith is again shown to us by the fact that this act of faith separates and isolates her from everything that is not God in order to hide her in God, in order to unite her to Him in a completely new way. There is a secret, a new covenant between her and God, hence her silence even toward Joseph. She had conveyed her first secret to him, the one which concerned her work shared with God. Here when God acts directly to share His personal secret with her, God asks her to be secluded, as it were, in this secret. This is part of this act of faith which divinely unites her to God in a very personal way. Faith draws us into God's personal mystery; it

---

56. Serm. 291, 111.

has us keep His Trinitarian secret in order to live from it. By orienting us toward the beatific vision, which encloses us in the Most Holy Trinity, it is natural that faith, in its most divine aspect, should have this same requirement. Mary must agree to be enclosed, so to speak, by God in a new silence. By sharing His secret with her, God wants her to keep it jealously in her heart, so that it may bear fruit in her. She must agree to keep silent, to say nothing, to be a "sealed garden" for God alone. After having accepted her consecration, God gave her to Joseph and entrusted her to his care. He takes her back again entirely for Himself in this mystery, in this secret. He wants her to live for Him; He wants this very secret bond to exist between her and Him, a bond that separates her from everyone. Through her divine motherhood, He wants her to enter into the most intimate aspect of His Trinitarian life.

We should take note of Mary's silence in the mystery of the Annunciation, which is the sign of her contemplative life and a safeguard for her divine solitude. This silence is the direct consequence of the secret covenant that exists between her and God.

Silence cannot vitally take hold of our lives and be-come an essential element of them except through love in its most proper aspect, i.e., when it concerns love of friendship which results in a friend confiding his secrets to his friend. Only a friend can receive his friend's secrets, and he has no right to confide them to anyone else. The sharing of a friend's secret to his friend is a proper effect of their friendship and neces-sarily produces silence, for the friend must not say anything to anyone else. He is hemmed into silence, so to speak. To the extent that the secret confided by a friend profoundly takes hold of our life, we become silent. We then live more and more intimately with our friend. This secret, however burdensome it may be, is at the same time a source of joy; and, as a fruit of love, it takes hold more and more of all one's intelligence and heart.

From a human point of view, secrets can never take possession of our entire human life, since secrets always concern practical and affective knowledge. There will always be possibilities of evasion thanks to the activity of our speculative knowledge.

It is different in the supernatural order since God, through a living faith, can take hold of our whole intelligence and heart. That is what happened with the Most Holy Virgin in this *fiat* that encloses her in God, as in a certain way God encloses Himself in her. God hides in her and Mary hides in God through this secret. She keeps silent in and through love, which enables her to be even more present, more attentive to God's loving presence. It is not at all a violent and forced silence, like Zechariah's silence (a punitive silence, a quarantine); it is a free and loving silence. One might say that when God's Word is addressed to us it always seems to demand silence. If we divinely adhere to this Word, it will hide us in its power and will render us silent in love; if we only adhere to it imperfectly, it will strike us dumb in order to correct us.

This silence, the sign and effect of the contemplative demand of loving faith, isolates Mary from Joseph. In this respect, it implies a certain divine trial for Mary and for Joseph. It is a divine means which intensifies the life of union with God and which at the same time separates one from all human community, however holy it may be. It should be observed that we said "from all human community" and not from God's instruments, in the precise sense of divine instruments, i.e., those who are sent by God and transmit God's message, like the angel Gabriel or a priest. Joseph only possesses authority with respect to the external forum. He belongs to this community as one who holds the authority. God wants Mary to keep His secret, even though it would have been so simple to tell Joseph the angel's words. It would have been more prudent according to our human perspective. Mary would thereby have shown more trust in Joseph, more respect for his authority. The Holy Spirit thought otherwise, so that both of them might be led along more divine and heroic paths. By accepting this silence, Mary shows Joseph even greater trust, the trust one shows someone when one can ask anything of him, even when one places oneself in a situation with him that outwardly seems to betray and deceive him. Heroic trust is needed in such a case. This is the kind of trust that Mary requires and expects from Joseph. She knows how much he loves her and that she can ask anything of him.

Joseph respects her silence without understanding it. He does not question her. But he wonders what he should do: "Her husband Joseph, being a just man and unwilling to put her to shame, resolved to send her away quietly" (Mt. 1:19). He does not doubt Mary's virtue, but he thinks he cannot keep her any longer as his betrothed. "But as he considered this, behold, an angel of the Lord appeared to him in a dream, saying, 'Joseph, son of David, do not fear to take Mary your wife, for that which is conceived in her is of the Holy Spirit;

she will bear a son, and you shall call his name Jesus, for he will save his people from their sins' " (Mt. 1:20-21). It is the angel who enlightens Joseph as to what he must do. Thus Mary can keep her secret, remain in silence and dwell with Joseph. Their union was put to the test, and to a terrible test, through the demands of God's secret; but, once beyond the test, their union becomes more intense and more pure. Joseph becomes the Mother and Child's guardian. He sees Mary in a new light; he looks at her through the angel's words and can thus have a divine knowledge of her. And Mary knows how much she can rely on his discretion, his respect, his love.

We have here principles that are extremely important for enabling us to have a clear understanding of the interweaving of contemplative life with communal life. In order to remain hidden from others, contemplative life originates in community, but it can last within a community only if it remains divinely separated and takes refuge in the intransigence of divine silence.

The Efficacy of Faith: God's Servant

It is important to note that while this *fiat* first commits Mary to a contemplative life, it commits her at the same time to a life of temporal service of God. For the *fiat* of living faith determines what is most intimate, not only in Mary's speculative intelligence, but also in her practical intelligence. Faith lies beyond the distinction between speculative intellect and practical intellect, thus any adhesion of faith transforms our speculative and practical attitudes. It must take concrete form in the obedient attitude of the faithful servant. Through her *fiat* Mary becomes the Mother of God, and through her motherhood she closely cooperates in God's governance of mankind. God asks her to accept in obedience this temporal and divine service of motherhood; her whole physical and sensitive life is, as it were, placed at the service of God.

No service is more humble, more constraining, more absorbing and at the same time more noble and beautiful than that of forming a human body for God, than giving God one's flesh and blood, giving Him all that one possesses in order to clothe Him with it. Being the Mother of God also implies a service of great poverty, for Mary must accept having no right whatsoever over her Son, which is the most trying and terrible renunciation for a mother's heart. A mother ordinarily has natural rights over her child, very strong and jealous instinctive rights. By consenting to be the Mother of God, Mary renounces all her rights over her Son. She understands that a creature cannot have any rights over God. For this very reason, she voluntarily renounces in spirit all thought of humanly possessing and claiming for herself Him who is to be her Son, Him who is to be so intimately dependent on her and obedient to her, Him who is to be the complete treasure of her life. Thanks to this renunciation, she becomes the poorest of creatures. The words that Gideon says in response to the angel announcing to him the mission that God is expecting of him—"I am the least in my family" (Jdg. 6:15)—would be even more true on Mary's lips, since Mary is to live and experience what no other creature will experience: divine poverty established in the inmost depths of her maternal heart with respect to Him who is everything to her.

It is really the service of a useless servant that God demands from her, while at the same time it is the service of a faithful servant, chosen in preference above all other children of men. For it concerns a service in which Mary is a secondary cause wherein she must give herself completely and unreservedly with everything that is most individual and personal in her: her life, her heart, her sensibility, her flesh and her blood. Her motherhood is a miraculous motherhood which directly depends upon God's omnipotence. It is a purely gratuitous gift from God to which Mary has no right, and it is at the same time a real motherhood, more perfect and more wonderful than all other motherhoods, of which Mary is the proper cause. We have here something unique in terms of excellence: Mary's motherhood is really the model of all other services that God may ask of men. Indeed when Yahweh chooses Moses to set his people free and orders him to speak to Pharaoh, "to let the people of Israel go out of his land" (Ex. 6:11), and when Yahweh orders Gideon to strike the Midianites, to pull down the altar of Baal, to build an altar to his God at the top of the stronghold (cf. Jdg. 6:16; 25-26). God invests His servants with new power, miraculously given to them out of sheer generosity. At the same time, He orders them to act on their own. God wants them to be both poor useless servants entirely surrendered to His will and faithful servants who do everything possible to carry out what God expects from them.

The same requirement in divine service is found over and over again, and it will be fully explained by Our Lord in His Gospel: a faithful servant uses the five talents that his master has entrusted to him to the best of his ability. He is

not content with just burying them in the ground for fear of
losing them. A faithful servant is not only someone who safeguards, who keeps what was entrusted to him, but someone
who turns it to good account and will be able to hand over to
the master twice the amount that he received, at the time appointed by his master. A faithful servant is thus someone who
works in a spirit of poverty; he keeps nothing for himself. He
is also someone who knows how to use intelligently and turn
to good account whatever his master has entrusted to him.
Among Christ's faithful servants, Mary is the first. Moses,
Yahweh's servant, is a magnificent prefiguration of Mary as
servant of God. The very grandeur of this great servant of
Yahweh and the divine omnipotence entrusted to him vividly
manifest the entirely new greatness of this little servant of
God, who renders Him a service that is more intimate, more
useful and greater still. In total and generous cooperation, she
allows God's omnipotence to take possession of all that
belongs to her. She will agree to keep nothing when the Master comes to take back the treasure He entrusted to her.

The Servant's Obedience

A servant cannot be faithful unless he perfectly carries
out the orders he has received in an intelligent and "non-
material" way. A faithful servant is one who lives in obedience. Obedience is a servant's essential virtue. A servant who
no longer obeys is no longer a servant. Let us try to understand the inner attitude of God's servant: her perfect interior
obedience to the will of God. Mary loves this divine will
more than anything; she completely abandons herself to it,
considering it as her sole light and her sole strength.

The Fathers of the Church strongly emphasized this *fiat* of obedience, which is the divine antithesis of Lucifer's *non serviam* and of Eve's act of disobedience.[57] St. Justin says:

> We have understood . . . that He [Christ] became man by the Virgin, in order that the disobedience which proceeded from the serpent might receive its destruction in the same manner in which it derived its origin. For Eve, who was a virgin and undefiled, having conceived the word of the serpent, brought forth disobedience and death. But the Virgin Mary received faith and joy, when the angel Gabriel announced the good tidings to her that the Spirit of the Lord would come upon her, and the power of the Highest would overshadow her: wherefore also the Holy Thing begotten of her is the Son of God; and she replied, "Be it unto me according to thy word."[58]

St. Irenaeus is even more explicit:

> Mary the Virgin is found obedient, saying, "Be-hold the handmaid of the Lord; be it unto me according to thy word." But Eve was disobedient; for she did not obey when as yet she

---

57. Cf. A. d'Alès: *Marie, Mère de Dieu, Tradition anténicienne,* Diction. apolog., III, c. 155 ff.

58. *Dialogue with Trypho* in *Ante-Nicene Fathers,* Vol. 1 (Peabody, Massachusetts: Hendrickson Publishers, Inc., 1995 (Second Printing)), Chap. C, p. 249.

was a virgin. And even as she, having indeed a
husband, Adam, but being nevertheless as yet
a virgin . . . having become disobedient, was
made the cause of death, both to herself and
to the entire human race; so also did Mary,
having a man betrothed [to her], and being
nevertheless a virgin, by yielding obedience,
become the cause of salvation, both to herself
and the whole human race. (. . .) [B]ecause
what is joined together could not otherwise be
put asunder than by inversion of the process
by which these bonds of union had arisen; so
that the former ties be cancelled by the latter,
that the latter may set the former again at lib-
erty. (. . .) And thus also it was that the knot
of Eve's disobedience was loosed by the obedience of Mary. For what the virgin Eve had
bound fast through unbelief, this did the virgin Mary set free through faith.[59]

This obedience of God's servant is realized in the greatest simplicity, humility and spontaneity, without any delay.
Mary has only one desire: to carry out God's order in a divine
fashion, so as to let God's order be carried out in her. Is she
not God's "soil"? This servant gives herself so that God may
use her, so that she may become God's "mold."

Just as the fidelity of God's servant shows us the divine
quality of obedience taking possession of her whole life, so

---

59. *Against Heresies* in *Ante-Nicene Fathers,* Vol. 1. Bk. III, 22, 4, p. 455.

her poverty and uselessness present us with the divine quality of the humility of her heart. Scripture reveals this humility to us when it shows us Mary's trouble at the angel's greeting. "Mary's trust in grace is so great and she thinks so little of herself that fear comes over her when she hears the angel's salutation. 'Mary,' the Gospel says, 'considered in her mind what sort of greeting this might be' (Lk. 1:29); meaning that she thought herself unworthy of being greeted by an angel and thought: 'How is it that an angel of the Lord should come to me?' "[60]

The way in which Mary accepts this divine service of motherhood for her Son must enlighten us with regard to the attitude God requires of us when He orders us to serve in a given way. Our *fiat* as servants must be obedient, faithful, generous and also carried out in a spirit of poverty. Otherwise, we shall no longer be true servants; we shall monopolize God's treasures and we shall prevent God from communicating them to us.

Poverty: Divine Link Between Contemplative Life and Active Life

Because of the fundamental poverty of Mary's heart, there will be no opposition between the demands of her contemplative, solitary and silent life and those of her active and absorbing motherhood, the latter necessarily placing her in communal life.

---

60. P. Aubron, S.J., *L'oeuvre mariale de S. Bernard,* Cahiers de la Vierge (t. 13-14), Editions du Cerf.

From a natural point of view and according to their proper structures, contemplative life and motherhood stand in opposition to each other and require an entirely different way of organizing one's life. Contemplation requires being concerned only with the sole necessary, while motherhood necessarily divides and takes root in the earth. In the mystery of her motherhood, Mary alone escapes this law, since her Son is her God. But this motherhood demands that she agree to have no right whatsoever over her Son and that she rather be possessed by Him.

Thanks to its poverty, this motherhood claims nothing and holds nothing back for herself. Mary can devote herself entirely to it; she remains free, her heart and intelligence adhering only to God's unique will for her, in and through the work God asks her to do. Spiritual poverty appears as the divine means that alone can combine and unite these functions which, from the perspective of our psychology, are so different and opposed: the function of contemplative rest and that of maternal activity.

To the extent that we become poor servants, hence useless ones, one thing alone takes hold of our intelligence and will: the desire to accomplish in the most perfect way possible God's loving will for us. Now, even when God demands a seemingly very active life from us, this desire to accomplish His will keeps us in His love and in His unity; and due to this very fact it can no longer be an obstacle for contemplative life. Indeed, under these conditions, the finality of active life no longer consists in achieving a temporal work. Its proper end is no longer human and earthly but in fact eternal: God's will, which we strive above all to accomplish. God's will is then the finality of everything; it actually determines our activity. Nevertheless, we cannot claim that all those who accomplish God's will as faithful and poor servants necessarily lead a contemplative life. Contemplative life requires something more, something that is proper to it and that gives its activity a particular and specific character. But we want to emphasize the fact that active life can be led in two ways: either according to its connatural mode—which inevitably conflicts with contemplative life—or according to a divine mode of poverty. This latter mode, far from conflicting with contemplative life, can serve it by becoming a sort of divine disposition toward it or, as it were, a visible overflow and manifestation of it which hides it from men and reserves it more entirely for God. This is in fact what happens in the mystery of divine motherhood. This miraculous motherhood hides Mary's virginity. The life of a Mother completely dedicated to the temporal care of her Child hides her silent contemplative life totally dedicated to God. On the surface, Mary leads the same life as all other mothers; deep down, in the eyes of God, her life has a unique quality of love. Moreover, her motherhood gives her contemplative life the wonderfully incarnated presence of God, which fosters a far simpler, more familiar and intimate contemplation. This same motherhood is also the proper fruit, so to speak, of her life of faith, hope and love, of her whole contemplative life. Such are the very intimate bonds that God in His wisdom willed to create between activities that are, from a human perspective, in such opposition.

It is very instructive for us to see that contemplative life, from its very beginning in the Church, went hand in hand with temporal and divine service. We have here a typically Christian form of contemplation on earth, which shows us both its divine superabundance—it must take hold of all our activities—and its hidden character reserved for God—it must escape the sight of men, it must not belong to this world.

Joy

The beginning of the Christian contemplative life in Mary, in her dedication as a poor and faithful servant, blossoms in a mystery of joy. The *fiat* of the Annunciation produces in Mary's heart a complete and absolutely pure joy, without the slightest trace of sadness.

Let us try to probe the mystery of this joy in order to understand more clearly how God, when He wants to work profoundly in a soul and raise it very high in His love, first opens it fully to His joy. This joy is an essential part of Christian life. Our Lord Himself wishes us to have it and asks the Father to give it to us: "that they may have my joy fulfilled in themselves" (Jn. 17:13b). So it is worthwhile examining joy at its starting point, in its first manifestation.

Considered in its profound structure, joy is the feeling we experience when we become aware of the full flowering of our own life potential. A man who leads his life as he wants, without any obstacle, annoyance or opposition, and who is fully aware of it, inevitably experiences a certain joyful euphoria. We see no reason for it to be otherwise. Think of all the joys in our lives: the joy of being reunited with those we love; the joy of having done a good job; the joy of having passed exams . . .

It is easy enough to understand—and experience shows it time and again—that there are several different varieties of joy that we can experience, each corresponding to the blossoming of our diverse modes of human life: intellectual, sensitive, vegetative. The joy of being in perfect health and of having a strong body is quite different from the joy of contemplation or from the joy we feel when we are reunited with a friend, someone we love dearly. We cannot go into all the various modalities of joy here; suffice it to say that we always find two elements in each of them: the blossoming of a given direction in our lives and the awareness of this blossoming.

If one of these elements is missing, there will be no joy. To be convinced of this, we need only analyze the opposite of joy: sadness. The latter is nothing but the feeling we experience when we are aware that our aspiration for something in our life is as it were crushed by some adverse force that hurts or stifles us. Sadness appears only if we are aware of the violent state in which we find ourselves; if we are not aware of this violent state, there is no sadness. So we see that sadness, like joy, requires a certain experiential knowledge of our state of life.

If we analogically transpose this analysis of joy to the level of supernatural life, it is easy to understand how supernatural Christian joy requires, on the one hand, the blossoming of our divine life of love and, on the other, the awareness of this blossoming. Or more accurately, we could say that—since our divine life is a life of friendship with God through Christ—Christian joy will spring from the experience of the presence of Christ in us and, in Him, the presence of the Most Holy Trinity. Christian joy is thus the joy of the presence of

Christ possessed as a friend, and in Him, the presence of the personal mystery of God's love.

In the mystery of the Annunciation, Mary experiences the fullness of joy. Mary knows in her faith that God is given to her in a very intimate way as a little one is given to his mother. The presence realized between God and herself through her *fiat* is both a spiritual and physical presence. It is a presence which is first of all spiritual. Mary chooses her Son or, more accurately, accepts being chosen by God to be the Mother of the Word Incarnate, of the Only Son of the Father. Thanks to this mutual choice, there is a perfect spiritual presence, and the quality and intensity of this spiritual presence spring directly from the quality and intensity of this fully lived reciprocal choice. This spiritual presence continues in a physical presence that is the most intimate mode of presence that can ordinarily occur on earth between two living beings: a child's presence to his mother when he is carried by her as an infant; and the mother's presence to the child when she carries him and keeps him alive, by transmitting to him everything she herself lives on. There is therefore a maximum vital dependence that establishes a very intimate presence. We must specify that, thanks to the gift of wisdom, Mary intimately experiences in her heart the efficacy of the choice of her God and Son concerning her. She knows how much her Son is given to her, entrusted to her, how much He depends on her in His physical life.

This joy is at the same time totally divine, very pure and profoundly human. It is the joy of the Virgin who is consecrated to God in a very special way and who draws life from His intimate presence. It is the joy of the heart of the Mother who draws life from her Son's intimate presence. Indeed, her Son brings her human life to bloom and is, as it were, its most exquisite flower. This joy is both the joy of her contemplative life and that of her maternal service; it is the joy of the Father's child and that of His lowly servant. These two joys are very different from the perspective of our human psychology. One can even say that they are the two most opposite and irreducible kinds of joy—one being deeply rooted in our whole human life, the other arising from what is most secret in divine life. Yet these two joys are united in Mary's heart; and, far from being in conflict, they, on the contrary, mutually intensify each other. Thus the primary characteristic of the joy of the mystery of the Annunciation is the perfect harmony between the demands of divine love and the demands of the blossoming of human life. This blossoming, however, is accomplished in a mode of divine poverty. Were it not so, human joy would overshadow divine, spiritual joy instead of being its fruit and its overflowing effect.

A second characteristic of Christian joy in the mystery of the Annunciation is its recollected, silent character: Mary must enjoy it alone. She must live this mystery in secrecy, so she must live this divine and human joy in silence. This recollection increases the fervor of her joy. She must keep it jealously for God. In a secret joy there is always a very special note of depth, interiority and intimacy. It is like a perfume carefully kept in a sealed bottle for fear that its fragrance might evaporate. For this very reason, there is a note of gravity to her joy. Mary must be joyful for the whole universe, which knows nothing. She must be attentive to the presence of God for those who are unaware of it.

Finally, this joy is very pure: it is its most intimate and divine characteristic. It is a poor joy in the sense that it does not cause Mary to withdraw into herself; on the contrary, it opens her heart more widely to divine love. For us, the danger of all joy lies in delighting in it, in lingering over it and in being entirely absorbed in it so that we turn inward in a feeling of completeness and satisfaction. The danger of complacency also exists in supernatural joys. Thanks to the very great purity of her faith and the poverty of her heart, Mary can intimately live from this divine joy of Jesus' presence without any risk of withdrawing into herself. On the contrary, through this complete, intimate and profound joy, Mary's heart can open up perfectly, can become more completely united to the love of her God and her Son. Her heart expands and becomes more and more welcoming and eager to love. If God gives this joy at first, it is precisely for this purpose. Like a wonderful educator, He begins by drawing a soul toward Him as much as possible, by broadening it with the joy of His love in order to demand staunch fidelity from it. He gives this joy at the beginning to steady the first steps and foster more spontaneous fervor. Since joy is the direct fruit, or "property" as it were, of love of friendship, it normally—or even "always" when it concerns divine joy—produces this expansion of our souls, this opening out and this steadfast trust which fosters new aspirations. Joy, being the effect of love, leads to a more perfect love. That is why it is natural that the first blossoming of divine love, in its most proper, most connatural and most profound aspect, should be joy.

The mystery of the Annunciation shows us the divine dimensions of Mary's soul. She is the one who receives God's

Word and keeps it in silence and obedient fidelity. This virgin's "conversation" is reserved for God. She is the one who is God's humble and poor servant. Her sole support is in God's will and promise. She is the one who is the loving Mother of her God. The virgin handmaid miraculously becomes fruitful, and this fruitfulness of love blossoms into joy. In this mystery, dawn of Christian life, Mary appears as the New Woman: the silent virgin, consecrated to God; the virgin, humble handmaid; the virgin Mother, fruitful in joy.

CHAPTER 5

THE VISITATION:
MARY'S FIRST INITIATIVE
IN COMMUNAL LIFE

AFTER the Annunciation, St. Luke recounts the mystery of the Visitation as follows: "In those days Mary arose and went with haste into the hill country, to a city of Judah, and she entered the house of Zechariah and greeted Elizabeth" (Lk. 1:39-40). In his divine message, the angel had given Mary not only the object of her contemplation but also a "sign," which she was to use to exercise her mercy: "And behold, your kinswoman Elizabeth in her old age has also conceived a son; and this is the sixth month with her who was called barren" (Lk. 1:36). The angel does not inform Mary about this extraordinary birth to no purpose. Nothing is superfluous in God's messages. Under the inspiration of the Holy Spirit, Mary will use this sign, given gratuitously to confirm her adherence of faith, as a divine food for her merciful zeal.

With the mystery of the Visitation, we see how Mary's silent, recollected and contemplative life and her condition as a servant totally consecrated to God do not in any way conflict with the generosity and spontaneity of her fraternal and merciful love. Quite the opposite: this total self-surrender to God prompts her to put herself at the service of her close relations, of her cousin Elizabeth who, because of her condition, needs Mary's domestic services. Indeed, Mary's plan is to go and put herself at her older cousin's service and to give her all the temporal and material help she probably needs. Mary prepares to do this quite cheerfully, "with haste," and is not afraid of distance and fatigue. "The love of Christ impels us" (2 Cor. 5:14), says St. Paul. It impels Mary's heart and asks her to transform all her bonds with the human community into bonds of mercy. In fact, as revealed in the text of Scripture, God uses this act of temporal mercy to bring about an act of divine mercy: the sanctification of the precursor John the Baptist and, through him, the sanctification of his mother. "And when Elizabeth heard the greeting of Mary, the babe leaped in her womb; and Elizabeth was filled with the Holy Spirit" (Lk. 1:41).

Let us try to grasp clearly this sequence of events that teaches us such a wonderful lesson. Mary teaches us temporal mercy here. We see her first communal gesture, which is in fact a gesture of temporal mercy toward her fellow creatures. This first gesture is made for someone who is very close to her by blood relation and by her divine life, and who needs her generous care.

Mary does not hesitate to devote herself to this task. On the pretext of her intimacy with God, of her silence and solitude, she could have spared herself from this gesture of mercy. She had a convenient excuse: had she not accepted a far more divine, urgent and personal service, one she must prepare for and which she must totally devote herself to? Having been chosen to be the Mother of God, it might have seemed natural and fitting for her to be exempt from carrying out ordinary duties that could be done by anyone. There is no need to dwell on all the well-known reasons that the devil so often puts in our imagination. Besides, note that no one forces Mary. By means of the angel, God did not require anything from her in this respect, and Elizabeth did not ask for help. So Mary could easily have refrained from going, in order to devote herself to what was certainly God's will for her.

The Holy Spirit does not let her dwell on such reflections. He wants this gesture of mercy to be made in a totally divine manner. Is God's mercy not completely gratuitous? Forced mercy is no longer mercy. The Father wants Mary to be merciful as He is merciful. That is why this first act of mercy must spring freely from her heart without any precept from God, without any call from a creature. There is only the call, the groaning of the Holy Spirit; there is only His prompting, more compelling to Mary's heart than any order. The Holy Spirit urges her to place herself humbly and "with haste" at the service of her cousin. It is Mary who undertakes the journey to go to Elizabeth. It is Mary who is humbly self-effacing with her cousin and greets her first. The order of social and family hierarchy is respected.

Yet while devoting herself to this merciful work, Mary does not forsake her contemplative life. She does not leave her God-Son. She carries Him, prays to Him and docilely obeys the Holy Spirit who is guiding her. Coming to Elizabeth to give her the aid of her hands, she brings her at the same time something infinitely more precious: God's real, physical and hidden presence. She really gives her God, without saying a word about the mystery which is her life. She keeps silent; she remains in her secret. Since Mary acts under the Holy Spirit's guidance, however, all her actions have a divine efficacy that goes far beyond the appropriate value of actions inscribed in a given, particular circumstance of time and place. This is manifested to us quite clearly here. The words of greeting uttered by Mary to Elizabeth are used by God to "make the babe leap for joy": "For behold, when the voice of your greeting came to my ears, the babe in my womb leaped for joy" (Lk. 1:44). John the Baptist is indeed the first person after Mary to receive through her the influence of Jesus' life-giving and salvific power. Thus he is also the first person for whom Mary—through Jesus' presence within her—exercises her role of divine motherhood. This action is carried out in an efficacious and mysterious way. Mary keeps silent. John the Baptist keeps silent but leaps for joy. This is the language of an infant. He is the first to have understood Mary's greatness. We must be "little ones" to recognize Mary's divine motherhood. Through John the Baptist, Christ's divine action in Mary reaches his mother Elizabeth who, as pointed out by Scripture, was then "filled with the Holy Spirit" (Lk. 1:41).

Take careful note of the joyful mode, so forceful and so gentle, of this twofold spiritual mercy. The Holy Spirit sanctifies Elizabeth through John the Baptist's exhilaration, and He sanctifies John the Baptist through Mary's greeting to Elizabeth. When it comes to sanctifying and transforming the heart of a mother, one cannot act more gently than by using her own little child still hidden in her womb, since there is nothing closer and dearer to a mother's heart than the little one she bears and to whom she gives life. But at the same time, one cannot act more directly, more efficiently, more powerfully, since the child is part of his mother. We can likewise say that one cannot act more gently on a little one's heart than by using his mother. In this first merciful gesture of Mary the predominant qualities of mercy clearly appear: mercy must be divinely spontaneous and be exercised generously and quickly (the poor do not have time to wait); it must be persevering ("Mary remained with her about three months"); it must be exercised with fidelity (it is not the capricious gesture of an amateur but a gesture of a totally different kind of gratuitousness); it must be exercised with humility so that it may be gentle and discreet, otherwise we can hurt the poor by making them too acutely aware of their destitution. The poor are fragile and vulnerable; they need to be treated with extreme gentleness.

Mary's humility when putting herself at the service of her cousin is wonderfully rewarded by God. Through Elizabeth she receives a new divine greeting following Gabriel's. It is the greeting of a mother who speaks as a mother, with a mother's language: "Blessed are you among women, and blessed is the fruit of your womb! And why is this granted me, that the mother of my Lord should come to me?" And going beyond this simple greeting, she proclaims the reason for Mary's blessedness: "And blessed is she who believed that there would be a fulfillment of what was spoken to her from the Lord" (Lk. 1:42-43, 45).

Before our Lord Himself proclaimed it in the Gospel— "My mother and my brethren are those who hear the word of

God and do it" (Lk. 8:21)—Elizabeth shows us Mary's true blessedness, that which really makes her a model for us and that which we can imitate in her.

Summing up the mystery of the Visitation, we see that it is an action of temporal mercy, an action of eternal mercy, a sanctification, a new revelation proclaiming the divine greatness of the one who is the handmaid of her Savior, of her family, of her people.

Mary responds to Elizabeth's greeting with the *Magnificat,* which reveals the grandeur of her soul and her wonderful magnanimity. She who comes to Elizabeth as a lowly handmaid listens to Elizabeth's greeting; and instead of behaving like those who are not humble enough to receive honors and who abruptly request silence from those who praise them, Mary on the contrary accepts the remarkable honor her cousin shows her. Mary does not reproach Elizabeth for the way with which Elizabeth greets her; rather, she receives this praise to turn it toward God. See how marvelously St. Bernard explains Mary's attitude:

> She then set out on a journey to visit her cousin Elizabeth, to whom the Virgin's incomparable glory was revealed by the Holy Spirit Himself; so that, over-awed by the dignity of Mary, she cried out, "Whence is this to me that the Mother of my Lord should come to me?" (Luke ii. 43). She also acknowledged the power of grace in the voice that saluted her, by adding, "As soon as the voice of thy salutation sounded in my ears, the infant in my womb

leaped for joy" (ibid. 44). And she commended the faith of Mary when she said, "Blessed art thou that hast believed, because those things shall be accomplished that were spoken to thee by the Lord" (ibid. 45). Magnificent eulogiums indeed! But the Virgin's devout humility would allow her to keep nothing for herself. All was referred to him Whose gifts were praised in her. "Thou dost magnify me, the Mother of the Lord," so she says in effect in answer to her cousin, "but 'my soul doth magnify the Lord.' Thou sayest that at the sound of my voice the infant in thy womb leaped for joy, but 'my spirit hath rejoiced in God my Savior' (ibid. 46, 47). Yea and if thy unborn infant, as 'the friend of the Bridegroom, rejoiceth with joy,' it is 'because of the Bridegroom's voice' (John iii. 29). Thou pronounces me blessed for having believed, but the one cause both of my belief and of my blessedness is the regard of the Sovereign Goodness, so that if 'from henceforth all generations shall call me blessed' it is only 'because He hath regarded the humility of His handmaid' (Luke i. 48)."[61]

Such is the wonderful, divine alliance between humility and magnanimity. Humility, in its purest and finest aspect,

---

61. "Sermon for the Sunday within the Octave of the Assumption" in *St. Bernard's Sermons for the Seasons and Principal Festivals of the Year* (Westminster, Maryland: The Carroll Press, 1950), pp. 275-276.

far from restraining the soul or closing it in on itself by depriving it of every ardent aspiration, puts it, on the contrary, in a state in which it can blossom, fostering nobility of soul and favoring divine audacities.

Proclaimed "blessed among women," Mary immediately proclaims God as Author of all these blessings whose value and truth she recognizes, but for which she does not want to take credit. God is their principal cause; He must therefore be paid all the honor of creatures.

The *Magnificat* is a prayer of praise, in which Mary's soul "magnifies" her Lord and her spirit exults with joy. This canticle is a sort of wonderful bouquet containing all the praise of the Old Testament which culminates in the *Magnificat.* It is the Old Testament's ultimate fruit and the dawn, as it were, of the New Testament.[62] For Christ is already present in it—hidden of course but divinely active. The presence of Christ gives Mary's praise a note of extraordinary joy: "My spirit rejoices in God my Savior." Her exultation, her overflowing joy cannot be contained. Her spirit exults with joy; the *heights* of her soul rejoice with a divine, totally pure joy. She rejoices "in her God," in the loving presence of her Savior, of the Savior who is *hers,* who belongs to her, since His whole body, by which He saves the world, is hers, totally hers, just as a little baby's body is part of his mother. This is indeed true Christian joy.

Under the inspiration of the Holy Spirit, Mary gives us the reason for this divine joy: "For he has regarded the low

---

62. Mary's *Magnificat* should be considered parallel to the two canticles of Moses: Exodus 15 and Deuteronomy 32, in order to better grasp what is completely original to Mary's song.

estate of his handmaiden." The real reason for her Christian joy is this loving gaze of God pursuing His creature, His poor creature, in her very littleness of being a creature, in her sorry, meager condition as a creature descending from Eve, made of mud and dust and being nothing by herself. God loved the weakness of His servant. He was well pleased with her, so much so that He willed for her to become His Mother, the Word Incarnate's living tabernacle. Moved by the gifts of wisdom and fear, Mary fully experiences her lowliness as God's servant, experiencing as well God's gaze of merciful love, of totally gratuitous predilection.

We need to understand clearly the intimate experience of the gift of fear that Mary reveals to us here with such simplicity. Through this gift she loves her own littleness, her own nothingness, so that all the glory may belong solely to God. She likes truly being the most little, the least important, in order to be more perfectly a servant, to be more dependent not only physically and socially but also morally. She likes to consider herself unworthy of any merit or virtue, knowing this to be the truth. By herself, without God's all-powerful mercy, she is nothing; everything is for God. When humility becomes wholly divine, it creates a complete void. It is no longer content with brushing aside the obstacles caused by pride or "bringing every mountain low"; it also creates an abyss of littleness in order to summon Love more efficaciously, to attract Love with greater force and audacity. It is this divine humility that draws God toward Mary's heart. According to the beautiful expression of St. Augustine: *"Facta est Mariae humilitas scala caelestis, per quam Deus descendit ad terras."*—"Mary's humility was the heavenly ladder whereby

God came to earth."[63] Littleness lived and loved for God is
at the root of all divine exultation.

Because she is so deeply rooted in humility, Mary can
recognize that "henceforth all generations will call me
blessed." The blessedness specific to a mother comes from her
children. Her greatest glory is to be honored in and through
her children. Based on Scripture we can say that while a wife
is indeed the glory of her husband, children are the glory of
their mother. The specific chastisement that God reserves for
woman is pain in childbirth, and her worst disgrace is to have
shameful, criminal sons. For Eve, the most terrible consequence of her sin and the one she felt most intimately was to
have a fratricide son upon whom the divine curse weighed
heavily: "And now you are cursed from the ground, which has
opened its mouth to receive your brother's blood from your
hand. When you till the ground, it shall no longer yield to
you its strength; you shall be a fugitive and a wanderer on the
earth" (Gen. 4:11-12).

Mary's greatest glory consists in being the Mother of
God's Son, of this first Son of man, Savior of mankind, the

---

63. Cf. St. Bernard: "Praises of the Virgin Mother," *Super Missus Est Hom.
I,* in *Sermons of St. Bernard on Advent and Christmas* (London: R. & T.
Washbourne, LTD., 1909), p. 29: "Upon whom shall my spirit rest, if
not on him that is humble and peaceable? (cf. Is. 66:2). He says not on
the virgin, but on the humble. If, therefore, Mary had not been humble
the Spirit would not have rested on her. If the Holy Spirit had not
rested on her, she would never have become fruitful. . . . Therefore,
as she herself testifies, in order that she might conceive of the Holy
Ghost, God the Father 'regarded the humility of his handmaid,' rather
than her virginity. And if by her virginity she was acceptable to Him,
nevertheless, it was by her humility that she conceived Him."

true Joseph who redeems His brothers who are guilty of betrayal and crime against Him. Through Jesus, Mary is also the Mother of the whole Church. At the foot of the Cross, Jesus officially establishes her as the Mother of the beloved disciple, who represents the Church. This is why all divine generations born of water and of the Spirit are her glory. They will all call her blessed.

It is interesting that the future tense is used here. It is a prophecy, something which is to come but which already now, *nunc,* at the present time, is being fulfilled, since John the Baptist's generation has already recognized Mary as blessed. The other generations of God's sons will continue calling her blessed until the end of time because she received the Word of God in her heart, in the "good soil" wherein the divine Word has borne fruit in plenitude. All other motherhoods can be sanctified and transformed through her divine motherhood; all other generations can acquire a new meaning through the Son of God's generation.

Inspired by the Holy Spirit, Elizabeth proclaimed Mary blessed because she believed. Inspired by the same Spirit, Mary asserts that all generations—not only Elizabeth—will call her blessed because God the "Almighty" has done great things for her and "holy is his name." Mary thereby completes what Elizabeth had proclaimed. While still on earth, her act of faith is what makes her blessed, yet this act of faith concerns her Son, the Word Incarnate. This is the reality on which her act of faith is based, and this reality is eternal. That is why Mary is eternally and universally called blessed by all generations.

God's omnipotence and holiness are invoked here, since the mystery of the Incarnation can only be explained by the intervention of this omnipotence and holiness. This wondrous, miraculous and holy event directly requires, on the one hand, an omnipotence for which nothing is impossible and, on the other hand, a holiness which is separate from all creation and elevated above all corruptibility and contamination. For a creature to give birth to her God, for a mere servant to be the Mother of her God, for a mother to remain a virgin in her motherhood: all this is wondrous and holy and is the direct object of divine contemplation.

It must also be understood that this generation of the Son of God, in the order of values, is the most perfect of all generations. Hence all other generations are necessarily relative to it; we can even say that in some sense they are measured and finalized by it. Indeed, the most wonderful natural masterpiece ever produced in our universe is Christ's holy humanity. This humanity is perfect, without the slightest flaw, the consummate image of God. That is why all generations will necessarily call this generation of God's Son blessed, and in and through it, His Mother. Throughout all generations, the whole physical universe recognizes her as blessed.

While omnipotence and holiness are inseparable and necessary to explain the admirable work of the Incarnation, mercy is necessary as well. Moreover it is this mercy that gives us the ultimate explanation, leading us to understand how near God is while still remaining almighty and transcendent, and how gentle His almighty action is. He is merciful and full of solicitude toward "those who fear him." This mercy is eternal; it endures "from age to age." Thus it never fails any creature; it is always present in all God's works.

But while God's mercy is always present and ready to be given, ready to save, it can be exercised efficaciously only with respect to "those who fear him." For one can be merciful only to those who recognize their poverty, i.e., those who fear God, knowing that they are nothing. Among these poor creatures, eager to receive mercy and requesting it, Mary is the first. She lives profoundly by this divine fear, having the sense of God's almighty majesty. This explains why she, more than any other creature, is capable of receiving God's mercy.

There is a connection here between mercy and filial fear. St. Thomas says that mercy is God's most proper attribute, i.e., the one that best characterizes the state of absolute superiority of God who depends upon no one and upon whom everything depends. This is why everything depends on His mercy and nothing escapes it. Divine fear is a creature's most characteristic attitude, the one that most profoundly distinguishes his or her condition as a creature before God. It is the state of someone who has nothing by himself and who at each moment receives everything from his Creator and his Father; the state of one who can be nothing but a beggar seeking God's mercy, since a creature as such has no right, in the strict sense of the word, with regard to his Creator. Fear of the Lord is thus the necessary condition, so to speak, for receiving God's mercy. It instills in us a receptivity and thirst, which spontaneously direct a creature toward the God of all richness and goodness. Fear of the Lord is, as it were, the measure of mercy for a creature. To the extent that we fear God, God has mercy on us.

After recounting God's omnipotence and holiness, Mary rightly goes on to tell us about His mercy and the fear that it requires. By considering this, she extends her praise to include all God's works. The *Magnificat,* which had begun with Mary glorifying God for the marvelous work He had accomplished in her, takes on a universal dimension: *"Non solum mihi fecit magna qui potens est,"* as the Venerable Bede puts it, *"sed et in omni gente qui timet Deum acceptus est illi."* "Not only has the Almighty done great things for me, but all peoples who fear God have received from Him."[64] Besides, this is normal since the mystery of the Incarnation, through the Redemption, is to have a universal efficacy and is to extend God's mercy to the whole universe. If all generations will proclaim Mary blessed, they will not do so from the outside, without entering into her own blessedness. On the contrary, they too shall receive God's mercy in their own way, just as Mary received it. In the light of divine mercy, everything is unified. Mary and those who will call her blessed have the same attitude; they all fear God.

This universal scope of the *Magnificat* invites us to consider a new aspect of this prophetic praise. We have said that the *Magnificat* reveals to us the magnanimity of Mary's soul —Mary, Mother of Jesus, handmaid of Elizabeth, and Mother of the Apostles. It is not surprising then that after directing to God all the honor that Elizabeth had shown her, she sings of all the wonders of divine governance. Indeed, the proper characteristic of Christian magnanimity is not only to glorify God profoundly for what He has accomplished in us and for the cooperation He expects from us,

---

64. *In Lucae evangelium expositio,* Livre I, ch. 1, col. 322 B et C.

but also for all that He accomplishes in the whole universe, for the marvelous cooperation He expects from His creatures. This indicates to us one of the differences that exists between the magnanimous man as shown by philosophers and the Christian magnanimous man. For Aristotle, the magnanimous man rises above honor and is not enslaved by it because of the greatness of his virtue and of the precise sense he has of its eminent value. Thus the magnanimous man always stands a little above the multitude, who are unworthy of him. For that very reason, he only undertakes great works and leaves all the little everyday activities to others. He picks and chooses among human, moral and political activities.

In a Christian context, magnanimity becomes the typical quality of the apostle, of the one who wants to live fully in the love of God and cooperate as closely as possible in His kingdom, to enable others to have access to divine life. The magnanimous Christian is someone who is totally committed to God's service, committed to carrying out all that His will expects from him, knowing full well that only what is willed by God is great and eternal. He cares little about the judgments of men who consider the value of realities from the outside, i.e., without considering their divine value, without immediately referring to God's will. On the contrary, for him the greatness of a given action directly depends on this reference. Fulfilling God's will even in the smallest of things, in the slightest detail, can always be a very great, a very noble thing if it is done with great love. For the magnanimous Christian, to serve God is to reign.

Thus the Christian who is magnanimous should no longer hold back and save himself for a paticular notable action. He is no longer the one who chooses; rather, God chooses for him. He must no longer separate himself, on his own initiative, from the multitude and place himself above communal life. His only desire is to conform more and more closely to God's plan for him and for all those around him, to become more and more Christ's faithful cooperator for the Father, in the conditions in which He has willed to place him.

With a magnificent greatness of soul, Mary accepted through her *fiat* this unique cooperation in God's governance, which places her in a highly privileged situation. Under the inspiration of the Holy Spirit, she reveals to us this sort of charter of divine governance, and thereby gives the Apostles the great divine principles which are to guide them and furnish the matter of their divine praise and thanksgiving.

These principles are very simple. On the one hand, they are the power of God who dispenses justice—the "Arm of God" appears to be at the service of His vindicating justice, so to speak. On the other hand they are His all forgiving and transforming mercy. "He has shown strength with his arm, he has scattered the proud in the imagination of their hearts, he has put down the mighty from their thrones, and exalted those of low degree; he has filled the hungry with good things, and the rich he has sent empty away" (Lk. 1:51-53).

This law of wisdom of divine governance is universal. It governed God's conduct toward the angels. To those who rose up in pride in the "imagination of their hearts," who preferred their own excellence to God's glory, who were too fond of their power and majesty, who considered themselves rich, lacking in nothing, God "has shown strength with His arm." He has scattered them, cast them down from their thrones and sent them empty away. He has exalted and filled with all His riches those who humbly yearned only for the glory of their Lord and God.

We find the same law in God's governance of man. Think of God's conduct toward Pharaoh (Ex. 7 to 12:42). However, a special characteristic appears here, which will become more and more explicit, since all God's conduct in the Old Testament occurs in view of the New. When justice and mercy meet in Christian wisdom, they meet in a different divine synthesis. This will be quite clear with the specific works of Christ, the Word Incarnate. Mary can already proclaim it, for everything in her is realized at its root, at its initial source. Under the inspiration of the Holy Spirit, she foretells the manner with which God will govern His Church.

In Christ, the Lord's Anointed, the Father "has shown strength with His arm" against the arrogant, the mighty and the rich: three forms of pride and self-satisfaction. And He exalts the humble and fills the hungry with good things.

The first work manifested by the divine power in the "Arm of God" is to scatter those who rise up in pride, just as one who is physically strong can scatter and push aside all those who strive to dominate him. So it is with things on a supernatural level. God pushes away from Him those who are full of pride and who think only of putting themselves higher than others. It is natural that the first work of God's divine power should be to push aside the proud, since pride alone among the human vices directly opposes God and tries to rise above Him. That is why He who seeks only His Father's glory must first of all bend the haughty heads which refuse to bow. It is a work of justice, since it is a question of rendering to God the first place, the place that He is due and that some want to usurp from Him.

This inner pride, hidden in the heart, often appears in concrete form in the pursuit of human power: political or social power. The advent of the King of Kings casts down the mighty from their thrones and exalts the humble. Think of Herod's anxiety when the Magi inform him of the mysterious birth of the King of Israel: "Herod was troubled, and all Jerusalem with him" (Mt. 2:3). Out of cowardly fear, Herod ordered the massacre of all those who might be this king. This is the only crime of these innocents. Think of Pilate's cowardice when he is facing the mob's shouts clamoring for the death of Jesus. Pilate is afraid of losing his position; he would rather become an accomplice in a crime, in a deicide, than lose his power. The "Herods" and "Pilates" of every age are actually judged and condemned by this Child-King and this Crucified One: "He has put down the mighty from their thrones."

Those in power are not the only ones who suffer from this madness of pride. Pride can rule anyone. Pride always has the same first fruit: putting into man's heart this perfect self-satisfaction which causes him to consider himself as being dependent upon no one, as possessing all riches in himself. For those rich in spirit and soul who are unaware of their dire poverty with respect to God's love, who think they are entitled to everything and consider themselves to be full of wisdom, justice is even more implacable: "the rich he has sent empty away."[65]

On the other hand, "he has filled the hungry with good things." Christ really came for those who "hunger and thirst for righteousness" (Mt. 5:6); He came for those who are aware of their weakness and misery and so ask for help. He fills all these poor, destitute people with His riches and good things. When John the Baptist heard from prison about the works of Christ, he sent two of his disciples to ask Him: "Are

---

65. It would be interesting to compare Mary's gesture of mercy in the mystery of the Visitation with Moses' gestures of mercy toward Pharaoh and his people. We must not think that the parallel is contrived. We only have to analyze the *Magnificat* to realize that while Mary in the mystery of the Visitation shows Elizabeth only extreme gentleness, she nevertheless proclaims and does not reject the "strength of the Arm" of God which has "scattered the proud"; "which has put down the mighty from their thrones"; which has "sent the rich empty away." Pharaoh is not absent from this mystery! The parallel between Mary's gentle mercy and the ten plagues of Egypt enables us to better understand how the Father wants Mary to be the dawn of evangelical mercy, whose primary characteristic is meekness. In the order of God's wisdom, Mary's first communal gesture as the Mother of God must be a merciful and totally gratuitous gesture which springs spontaneously from her heart and is carried out with extreme gentleness. To better manifest this gentleness, it appears in all its purity. Everything is gentle in this mystery.

Nonetheless, we should not think that strength is absent from Mary's mercy. It is present but surpassed. Absolute and excessive strength is needed to be truly meek. In her mercy towards Elizabeth, Mary is stronger than Moses in his merciful corrections of Pharaoh's hardness of heart. So we should not be surprised when Mary "visits" us—since there is still an "old man" in us whose morals are sometimes very similar to Pharaoh's. If we ask her to "maternally correct" us, to set free the "Israel" we carry within, we need not be surprised if she acts as forcefully as Moses, sending the ten plagues of Egypt to turn us away from our concupiscence.

you he who is to come or shall we look for another?" And
Jesus answered them: "Go and tell John what you hear and
see: the blind receive their sight and the lame walk, lepers are
cleansed and the deaf hear, and the dead are raised up, and
the poor have good news preached to them" (Mt. 11:4-6).

This is the fulfillment of Isaiah's prophecy which
announced the Messiah's reign in these words: "Then the eyes
of the blind shall be opened, and the ears of the deaf
unstopped" (Is. 35:5). "He has sent me to bring good tidings
to the afflicted, to bind up the brokenhearted" (Is. 61:1b).
The Messiah's governance is first and foremost a governance
of mercy that exalts the poor, the lowly, the wretched, and
this is what makes it so divine and praiseworthy.

In the Old Testament, wealth, power and an irre-
proachable conscience were often considered as signs of God's
benevolence, as the natural reward of the righteous. In the
New Testament, the poor take priority, a position that the
dispossessed rich are forced to give them. The disinherited,
the orphans and the weak come before the "mighty." Those
who have contrite hearts and are aware of their wretchedness
and acknowledge it are the only ones God looks at. In and
through Christ, the Father forgives, reinstates and exalts the
prodigal son, the publican, the sinner, the Samaritan; and
puts aside as it were the elder son, the Pharisees, the Levites,
the priests of the ancient law, who are more attached to their
own ritual justification than to mercy and love.

After contrasting and uniting three divine gestures of
mercy and justice, Mary's *Magnificat* concludes with a proclamation of God's merciful and faithful predilection for Israel,
His servant and His son: "He has helped his servant Israel, in

remembrance of his mercy, as he spoke to our fathers, to Abraham and to his posterity for ever." The mystery of the Word Incarnate is the great mercy granted in a special way to Israel. The fact that God chose a member of Israel's race to give the universe its Savior, to ennoble the whole of humanity in David's descendants, is a mercy *par excellence* shown by God to Israel. This mercy is the fulfillment of the promise made to the patriarchs; hence it has a particular mode. It is even more deeply inscribed in the chosen people, having been desired and implored by them for so long. Having prepared the coming of this ineffable mercy by a long period of expectation and prefigurations, God aroused a more parching thirst in the people of Israel and made them better understand their own weakness and helplessness when far from God's help.

All unexpected mercy that is given without preparation —apart from initial, prevenient mercy—cannot be as efficacious, since mercy can only exist with two parties: one that gives and the other that receives. The one who receives must be fully aware of his poverty to avoid limiting the giver's gesture. God did not need to wait to be prepared, but mankind needed it, to better understand the seriousness of its sin and all its consequences. Mary who, through her *fiat* at the Annunciation, ends this period of expectation, is even more thirsty than the patriarchs and prophets; for she understands better than they the gravity of sin and its grievous consequences. Her desire, which is so poor, and her virginal consecration of abandonment attracted God's mercy. This total abandonment was such a strong call for divine mercy that there was no further delay. Divine mercy came to settle in Mary in order to make her its dwelling, its temple. Ultimately, Israel is Mary. It is in her that the promise is fulfilled. Mary recognizes this and in her magnanimity, she glorifies the Lord for it.

The mystery of the Visitation shows us, on the one hand, how Christian mercy is the first fruit, so to speak, of Christian contemplation. This contemplation must blossom into works of temporal and spiritual mercy. On the other hand, the mystery of the Visitation shows us how liturgical prayer springs from mercy. Liturgy is the praise of the Christian community, formed by mercy itself. Indeed, the Christian community is directly founded upon mercy. No wonder then that the praise specific to the Christian community as such primarily proclaims God's mercy, since it is rooted in mercy. *"Misericordias Domini in aeternum cantabo."*[66] The *Magnificat,* like Moses' canticle, is first and foremost the song of God's servant, object of His prevenience, of His blessings, of His mercy.

---

66. Ps. 88:2 (Vulgate).

CHAPTER 6

THE NATIVITY:
MARY'S JOY IN THE
PRESENCE OF JESUS

B EFORE Jesus' birth, during the period of nine months of expectancy, Jesus is actually there, present for Mary: present in her contemplative life and in her heart as Mother and handmaid of God. But this presence remains an imperfect one. It is buried in Mary, so to speak. This presence asks her simply to be passive with respect to the power of the Most High. She has simply to obey the order of Gabriel who informs her that "the Holy Spirit will come upon you, and that the power of the Most High will overshadow you." Through her *fiat,* she draws life from this hidden presence of the Word who becomes incarnate in her.

With the mystery of her Son's birth, Mary enters a completely new phase in her contemplative life as well as in her life as God's servant. God gives Himself to her as a tiny baby is given to His mother, expecting everything from her. Mary is no longer to remain merely passive, allowing the Holy Spirit to work in her; she is to begin to take maternal initiatives. She is no longer to let herself be taken and consumed by Him, she must also give herself spontaneously and effectively to her little one in numerous gestures, actions and tasks. She must create a maternal milieu for Him in which His life as a Child can blossom and find protection.

It is extremely important to consider this if we want to have a clear understanding of how the Holy Spirit, after long periods of pure receptivity during which He is directly at work and requires from us only perfect docility to His action, can suddenly ask us to undertake totally new initiatives, without exempting us from the state of fundamental docility and dependence. He wants something more from us. He expects from us an effective gift expressed by certain attitudes and gestures, by certain responsibilities and commitments that are sometimes quite audacious, in which He wants us to take certain initiatives.

Moreover, with Jesus' birth, Christian community life will experience its first perfect realization. Jesus' hidden and invisible presence was not enough for this communal family life to flourish; His visible presence was needed. Thus the mystery of Christmas brings a very clear discernment of God concerning mankind: some refuse to receive Him. "He came to his own home, and his own people received Him not" (Jn. 1:11). Others are led to Him in a wonderfully gratuitous way.

Viewed in this light, we understand how Christmas is truly the mystery of perfect, divine joy. The angels clearly proclaim this to the shepherds: *Ecce enim evangelizo vobis gaudium magnum, quod erit omni populo;* "Behold, I bring you good news of great joy which will come to all the people" (Lk. 2:10).

Joy indeed implies the blossoming of our life and an awareness of this blossoming. Thus from a human point of view, there can be various types of joy, since there are various ways for our human life to blossom. Among these types of joy, the joy of friendship is both the most human and the most lucid for us. We are well aware of how sad our human hearts can be when we must accept separation and a friend's absence. His presence, on the other hand fills us with exultant joy. The joy of friendship is the one that can best help us understand the proper characteristic of divine joy, since the mystery of charity is a mystery of friendship with God, with the three divine Persons in and through Christ. Divine joy implies the blossoming of this friendship, as well as a certain experience of this friendship, i.e., the gift of God and our gift to God. This mutual gift results in a loving presence and a certain experience of this presence in living faith thanks to the gift of wisdom. The stronger and more intense the presence and the more this presence is lived and experienced, the greater and more intense the joy.

The mystery of Christmas is for Mary precisely this mystery of mutual gift: God given as a "little one" to Mary, His mother. No presence can be more intimate than that of a tiny infant with his mother, for the two persons are so close and so connatural to each other. No presence is more intensely lived and experienced than at the very moment of birth, the moment when this presence first appears. At that moment, this presence possesses a unique radiance. Christmas is God with Mary, God for Mary. And there is nothing aside from this fact, in all its novelty and purity. It is truly the mystery of great joy. At the Annunciation, God was indeed given to Mary and Mary to God, but this gift remained very hidden. The presence remained imperfect, for presence requires that the persons involved be perfectly distinct from each other, face to face; that there really be two individuals leading the same life. The unity of knowledge and love, even when this knowledge and love are divine, is not enough for a full presence, particularly with us who have bodies. We need a physical presence, a gaze which would reflect the living expression of this unity of knowledge and love. The specific feature of birth is precisely to bring about the perfect distinction of the child's body and his mother's, which enables the child to become present to his mother. This is why it is not joy that prevails at the Annunciation but silent desire pending the fulfillment of a promise. Perfect presence requires mutual action between two persons. In the mystery of Christmas, as Mary finds herself face to face with her little one for the first time, she must behave with Him as a mother, as someone who does not hesitate in the least to give Him everything, since He expects everything from her and totally depends on her.

Let us try to understand somewhat all the tenderness, love and respect that Mary pours into her first gaze upon Jesus, her first caress, her first kiss, her first maternal gestures. She "wrapped him in swaddling cloths" (Lk. 2:7), Scripture tells us. These gestures that other mothers make instinctively as an expression of what is most natural in their love are made by Mary under the Holy Spirit's guidance. For these gestures convey not only her maternal love but also her virginal love, her divine love for God who gives Himself to her in the weakness and smallness of a tiny child, totally surrendered to His mother. Prompted by the gifts of fear of the Lord, piety and counsel, Mary performs these gestures in a divine way. With chaste and loving fear, in perfect surrender to the Father's will, she presses her Child to her heart to warm the tiny, tender limbs of the Father's only Son.

The Virgin trembles as she receives her God in littleness and helplessness, knowing that God expects maternal initiatives from her. Just as the Son is eternally with the Father in an eternal and loving embrace, so the little Child Jesus is hidden in His mother's arms in a loving embrace on Christmas night. Mary's heart is for Jesus the living echo of the Father's eternal bosom. This divine trembling caused by the gift of fear does not paralyze the tenderness and love of her maternal heart but rather, on the contrary, enables them to blossom in a much deeper way. No mother has ever pressed her little baby to her heart with greater tenderness than Mary; no mother has shown more sensitivity and respect for his fragility.

The gift of fear does not harm in any way the profound demands of love or its bold endeavors. It does not make one scrupulous or fearful on a human level; rather it enables a person to flourish because the gift of fear is brought about in love. It attracts and purifies so as to enable love to go further, to carry out all its demands and aspirations.

In order to penetrate deeper into this mystery of presence and joy, let us pause a moment to consider the special circumstances revealed by Scripture in which this mystery takes place.

Mary and Joseph were compelled to leave Galilee to go to Judea, to Bethlehem, the city of David, since the decree of

Caesar Augustus required that each citizen be registered in his native city. Now it happened that "while they were there, the time came for her to be delivered. And she gave birth to her first-born son and wrapped him in swaddling cloths and laid him in a manger, because there was no place for them in the inn" (Lk. 2:6-7).

The mystery of the birth of Jesus takes place on the road, in exodus. Jesus was to be born neither in the temple of Jerusalem—God's house and the symbol of His own body (for He was to be born in an obscure and hidden way); nor in Joseph and Mary's house—they had to obey the imperial decree and render to Caesar what was Caesar's; nor at the inn—people having closed their door to Joseph and Mary's poverty. Refusing to receive Joseph and Mary and completely busy with worldly matters, mankind refuses to receive Jesus. "He came to his own home, and his own people received him not" (Jn. 1:11). There is no room for Him. Men do not want a poor King and God whose power has no exterior manifestation. There is nothing left for Joseph and Mary to do, rejected as they are by men, but to take refuge in a cave with animals. This is where Jesus was to be born. He is born for men, yet He is born far from their dealings and worldly structures, which prevent them from receiving Him.

In His wisdom, God uses this refusal from men to more fully realize His love and to manifest His joy and glory with greater splendor. The birth of Jesus takes place then in silence and the wonderful solitude of nature asleep. For this very reason, everything is reserved much more for Mary, everything is far simpler; there are no spectators, no intruders! Mary is alone to receive her Son and her God. This miraculous birth enables the mother to receive her Son immediately, to be fully attentive to Him immediately, to be truly alone with Him. No stranger's hands come between Mary's hands and the body of her little one. True, Joseph is there, near Mary and Jesus, but he is there to hide the mystery, to carefully safeguard the Father's secret.

According to the designs of God's wisdom, Mary, who has given birth to her firstborn, is to be alone with Him in the silence of the night, in order to experience the fullest possible blossoming of her love and joy. Since others rejected him and refused to receive Him, Jesus is present only for Mary and she for Him; therefore, this presence is all the more intense and pure. At the Annunciation, Mary was indeed alone with Him and He in her, but this refusal from mankind had not yet occurred, a refusal which almost violently thrusts Jesus back to His mother, since she alone accepts to receive Him.

Everything works together to deepen the mystery of this new presence in the solitude and silence of Christmas night, to make it more intimate and more divine. Joseph and Mary's outward poverty is as it were the guardian of this mystery. If Joseph and Mary had looked like rich people, if they had arrived as a lord and lady, people would have made room for them in the inn, due to Mary's condition. They would have turned out other less exciting guests; they would have found a way to keep them; and the mystery of the birth of Jesus would not have known this solitude and silence. It would have occurred in the midst of the hustle and bustle of an inn and would have even increased the commotion! This is not the way in which God visits our earth! On the contrary, poverty must prepare the way and push aside all those who seek only earthly riches and who think only of settling on earth.

When it comes to the mystery of the Word Incarnate's first visit to this world, poverty has done such good work that no one is left, except Mary and Joseph. It is in this solitude, fruit of poverty loved and accepted, that He comes to dwell, that he shows and reveals Himself in order to give Himself and hand Himself over.

In this silence and joy, Mary's contemplation can reach perfection. Through her faith in the mystery of the Incarnation fully accomplished in her, she can adhere to the Word who is present and who gives Himself to her in silence. God's living Word is given to Mary through a child (*infans*) who does not speak. God's dazzling Light is given to her in a little one who keeps His eyes closed. In her hope, Mary can lean on God's Strength, given to her in the very weakness of Him who expects everything from her. She can desire to live by the life of heaven, receiving God for herself alone in the person of her beloved Son. In her charity, she can experience God's love for her and for all mankind by settling down in the heart of her little one, by making His heart her sole resting place. Thanks to her little one's loving and silent presence to her, Mary experiences a new dynamism of contemplation, giving birth to a new demand for silence and solitude: a divine solitude and silence, steeped entirely in love, that do not prevent her from being perfectly mother or from being fully attentive to her tasks and maternal responsibilities. Mary's joy is like a living image of the Father's joy in the presence of His Son. Christmas is indeed the beginning of the mystery of the Holy Family. It is the first manifestation of the family character of divine life; it is thus the continuation for us, in our humanity, of the full mystery of the Most Holy Trinity.

Mary's virginal Christian contemplation is thus actualized in a communal family life which, since it is fully divine and extremely poor, remains a life alone with God. It is for this reason that her maternal actions toward her Son must be considered as the immediate shining forth of her contemplative silence. They have a liturgical value; and, viewed in this light, they show us the characteristic mode of Christian liturgy at its origin. The visible presence of Jesus gives birth to the whole of Christian liturgical life, which requires perfect communal life to be fully achieved. The mystery of Christmas shows us what is altogether typical of Christian liturgy: the practice of the virtue of religion informed by Christian charity under the direct motion of the Holy Spirit through the gift of piety. The *Magnificat,* as a song of praise, ends the Old Testament and opens the New; it is the dawn of the New Testament. At Christmas the "Sun" appears; He is present and already resplendent. Thus it is truly Christmas that should enable us to comprehend that which characterizes Christian liturgy in all its purity.

The liturgy of the Old Testament had successively chosen different places of adoration and praise: the high places where the vast expanse of nature was as it were invited to join the religious action; then Yahweh's Tent for the journey in the wilderness; finally, the temple of Jerusalem in which man's artistic genius guided by God had erected a divine dwelling. The high places, the tent and the temple required an ever more majestic and solemn liturgy. Since Christian liturgy is no longer merely a liturgy of expectation—one that symbolizes a reality which is to come—it has a much simpler and more realistic tone. Christian liturgy first appears gathered around the child Jesus, near the manger. God, coming to live with His own people, does not come to the sumptuous dwelling men had intended for Him. He is not born in the temple of Jerusalem but at Bethlehem in Judea, in a cave reserved for animals and poor homeless people, for vagrants. He wants His first visit to be really for the poor, for those who have nothing. He wants to rebuild everything starting from the nakedness of the manger. This is why the high places and the temple have been abandoned, and Bethlehem and the manger have been chosen as the place where the first gestures and acts of worship and praise of the Christian liturgy were to be performed. All the temple's majesty—which is a bit cold—is abandoned to be replaced by Mary's very simple and loving maternal gestures. The gift of piety is thus fully exercised and interiorly transforms the very exercise of the virtue of religion. The liturgy hereby assumes a familial quality which in no way eliminates the respect owed to the majesty of God but rather gives it a new character, consisting of intimacy, simplicity and tenderness.

Since the family character of this liturgy is divine, it is not exclusively and jealously closed in upon itself; the arrival of the shepherds, invited by the angels, attests to this. If Mary's contemplation and joy had been less divine, if her union with Jesus had kept a more human mode, she would have refused to welcome the shepherds. She would have asked Joseph to explain to them that they should not disturb a young mother at night when she has just given birth to her son. Mary could have given this pretext to cling jealously to her joy and silence in order to remain alone with Jesus.

Docile to the Holy Spirit, she behaves otherwise; she lets these poor strangers approach and contemplate her newborn Child. She makes this wonderful gesture of fraternal charity toward them. She gives them her most precious possession so that the fullness of her joy may be in their hearts also. She is truly the source of their joy since she shows them the Savior, allowing them to contemplate Him and draw life from His presence. These poor people who come in the name of God, urged by the angels, do not disturb her contemplative silence and immediately take part in this Christian liturgy. "And when they saw it," St. Luke says, "they made known the saying which had been told them concerning this child" (Lk. 2:17). Their praise is the same as that of the angels. They have none other; they are too poor. Through the shepherds then, this Christian liturgy has direct and explicit continuity with the angels' liturgy: the "glory to God in the highest and on earth peace among men with whom he is pleased" (Lk. 2:14) has become the praise of the "poor" who are the first to be evangelized and who expect everything from God's goodness.

Not only is Mary's joy and contemplative silence undisturbed by the shepherds, but they also give her new joy and peace. Is she not one of those "with whom He is pleased"? Mary, who has not turned these poor people away and has not considered them as inquisitive intruders, is rewarded for her merciful kindness toward them. For these shepherds not only communicate the angels' praise to her, this praise which

mysteriously surrounds the silence of the manger, but also
communicate to her what the angel told them about this
newborn child: "To you is born this day in the city of David
a Savior, who is Christ the Lord. And this will be a sign for
you: you will find a babe wrapped in swaddling cloths and
lying in a manger" (Lk. 2:11-12).

St. Luke adds: "But Mary kept all these things, ponder-
ing them in her heart."[67] The angel's words to the shepherds
confirm for her the Annunciation made to her by the angel
Gabriel, and specify the divine mission of her Son, Jesus: He
comes to save His people; He is the Savior.

Not only do these words confirm her faith in the angel's
message, but they also confirm her maternal attitude of tenderness and love toward her Son. Indeed the angel, inspired
by the Holy Spirit, uses Mary's first gestures with Jesus as a
"sign" whereby the shepherds will be able to recognize Him.
For her virginal heart, which in chaste fear had to take such
daring and tender initiatives toward God, these words from
God's messenger must have been extremely reassuring and
heartwarming. By behaving in such a maternal, loving and
tender manner, Mary had clearly carried out the divine charity she had to have toward her Son. All the tenderness, all the
love that a mother naturally has for her child, she had for
Jesus, but even more strongly; for the virginity of her heart,
far from diminishing her love for her Son, only intensified it
and enabled it to flourish in all its demands.

---

67. Lk. 2:19. Cf. Cajetan's *Commentary:* "She performed the office (*offi-
cium*) of contemplation by associating what she had been told with
what the shepherds were told."

Let us clearly understand this law of divine governance and see how God uses each and every person in a specific and original way to educate and form Mary's heart. First the Holy Spirit alone instructs her and shows her what she must do; then the Holy Spirit and the angel Gabriel; then the Holy Spirit, the angels and the shepherds. After this, as we shall see later, the Magi and Simeon; finally her Son Himself.

The angel Gabriel could have come to tell Mary explicitly how God wanted her to behave at Christmas. On the contrary, it pleased God for her to remain in the darkness of faith; and in this darkness, it pleased Him for her charity to have maternal initiatives toward God while remaining totally docile to the promptings of the Holy Spirit, silently accepting His indications, His gentle movements. To reward her for her docility, the Holy Spirit sends her the poor shepherds who reveal to her God's appraisal of her behavior, since the angel himself makes use of her gestures as a distinctive "sign." The Savior is the One who is wrapped in swaddling clothes, lying in a manger.

While the starting-point of contemplative life began due to an explicit intervention from God (the mystery of the Annunciation), here the intervention of the Holy Spirit seems to take place in an interior manner as if to intensify Mary's abandonment.[68] The visible sign appears only as a

---

68. St. Luke's Gospel clearly indicates the progression of Mary's contemplative silence; she responds to the angel with the *fiat;* she responds to Elizabeth with the *Magnificat;* she responds to the shepherds by carefully keeping all their words, by holding them fast in her heart. We should, moreover, clearly understand the extremely strong meaning of *conservabat—sunetêrei*—used here by St. Luke, as opposed to *retinent*

confirmation given out of superabundance. Mary did not need it out of necessity. But it gives her a new joy—the joy of a child who knows she is blessed by God and who finds that the angel himself makes use of her poor human gestures—and greater certainty concerning her actions as God's maternal servant. She must be Virgin entirely oriented toward God and consecrated to Him; she must be Mother completely directed toward her Son. This double order is but one in love. Far from being in conflict, the two aspects intensify one another. This double order, which unites her so closely to the Word Incarnate, does not isolate her from her fellow creatures but enables her to be extraordinarily welcoming toward all souls of "good will" whom God puts on her path.

Like every human birth, this mystery of Christmas is both an ending and a beginning. It is the end of every Advent, not only that of the nine-month waiting period but also the "Advent" or long wait of the people of Israel, ever since the promise made to Abraham, ever since the promise made to Eve after the Fall and their expulsion from Eden. At last, the Savior has come! As an ending, Christmas can be a mystery of presence and a mystery of joy—the presence and joy which demand an outcome, an accomplished feat. All the divine demands which had bloomed gradually in Mary's soul since

---

(Lk. 8:15) and to *custodiunt* (Lk. 11:28). Mary keeps God's Word in a unique way. She "keeps it like a secret," for it is entrusted to her; she is to safeguard it. Christ's other disciples are also to keep it—they ought not simply listen to it—but for them, keeping the Word indicates primarily being attentive to God's Word in order not to forget it. Gradually, with Mary's help, they too are to keep it like a unique treasure, like a secret of love.

the mystery of the Presentation are found in this mystery of Christmas, collected and unified, so to speak, in a joyful flowering. The demands of virginal consecration in abandonment and those of fraternal charity take possession of Mary's soul more deeply on this Christmas night. She is deprived of any human assistance except Joseph's. People refuse to give her shelter, to come to her aid. A desert of solitude builds up around her. She must abandon herself totally to the Father's almighty mercy, in order to receive help for herself and her Child solely from her heavenly Father and from His representative, Joseph. To abandon ourselves to God's mercy is nothing when we alone are concerned, but we need a superabundance of divine abandonment when it concerns surrender for the sake of Him who is our entire life, our favorite Child. This mother who is expecting her Child must totally abandon herself in very great poverty to the Father's mercy alone, and must at the same time, more than ever, trust Joseph completely in very simple fraternal charity, knowing full well that she can rely on him. This Jesus she is expecting, who is her Child, is expected by Joseph even more lovingly than if He were Joseph's own child, for everything that is Mary's is his; Mary knows this. Indeed, such is the supreme delicacy of fraternal charity which removes all trace of jealousy between those who love each other for God's sake. The silent *fiat* of the Annunciation then reaches a climax, as it were, in this final expectation of the birth. "He is coming," He who was promised and whom she carries and hides within her. Her desire to possess Him and to be entirely His has never stopped increasing and intensifying. Jesus' birth does not break the silence of her contemplation. She gazes at Him in a divine way, in the light of her faith, living her *fiat* even more divinely. Her maternal gestures convey the silence of her contemplation and express the generous and efficacious gift of her whole being, at the service of her little one.

The gratuitousness of her mercy is shown when welcoming the poor shepherds who need to approach their Savior. It is Mary who silently shows them the Savior's goodness. The angels' praise, respecting Mary's silence, proclaims the "Glory of God" in her name. It is the *Magnificat* of the Mother who, through her maternal gestures, praises God in silence, asking the angels to sing in her place.

While Christmas is an ending, everything also begins at Christmas. Christmas is the beginning of Christ's earthly life; it is the beginning of the great ascent to Jerusalem; it is the beginning of the separation. Mary becomes the one who will increasingly follow Jesus instead of being merely the one who carries Him and hides Him. To have a better understanding of these two major aspects of the mystery of Christmas, it would be helpful to consider what corresponds in Moses' journey to this mystery of Jesus' birth. Initially one might be tempted to say that in Moses' life there obviously cannot be any prefiguration of the mystery of Christmas, since this mystery is completely proper to the Gospel. Indeed, the Gospel begins with this mystery, with this "great joy": the birth of the Savior. Admittedly, viewed in this light, one should not look for any prefiguration of the mystery of Christmas but rather consider that Christmas is in some way a prefiguration of our entry into heaven, just as Advent is a prefiguration of our divine life here below, as we wait for our entry into heaven. However, after having emphasized the parallel that exists between the privilege of the Immaculate Conception and the birth of Moses, the Presentation of Mary and the first gesture of Moses, the Annunciation and Moses' calling, the Visitation and the ten plagues of Egypt, the *Magnificat* and the canticle of Moses, it may be worthwhile to continue. After Moses' canticle comes the entry into the desert, the beginning of this great adventure through the desert and through struggles of all kinds. Is this not a prefiguration of the other aspect of the mystery of Christmas which we have just emphasized? Christ's earthly life is indeed a journey through a vast desert.[69]

_____

69. Ex. 15:22: "They went into the wilderness of Shur; they went three
    days in the wilderness and found no water."

PART 3

THE MYSTERIES OF MARY'S PREPARATION FOR TRIALS

CHAPTER 7

THE PURIFICATION:
SORROW IS INTRODUCED
TO MARY'S JOY

THE mystery of Christmas occurs outside the temple, while the mystery of the Purification occurs in the temple. There is no opposition between the liturgical life of Christmas and that of the Old Testament; rather, one brings the other to completion. Christ's real presence in our universe renews all things and begins a new era. Yet His presence is not a revolution condemning what happened before with the people of Israel under God's guidance.

In His governance God renews while preserving. His boldest and most daring works are rooted in the tradition that He established for men. To the Jews who try to place Jesus' doctrine and gestures in opposition to those of Moses, Jesus replies: "It is Moses who accuses you, on whom you set your hope. If you believed Moses, You would believe me, for he wrote of me" (Jn. 5:45-46). Here again we touch upon one of the very profound laws of divine governance, a governance of wisdom which makes use of everything and never becomes rigid because it always remains directed toward the sole Good. It is very difficult for human governments to maintain this harmony, this equilibrium between keeping what is good—*conservatio in bono*—and moving toward the good—*motio ad bonum*—or if you prefer, the static and dynamic aspects, the formal and efficient ones. Human governments err constantly either by being too conservative or too revolutionary. They are either conservative to the detriment of renewal, or revolutionary to the detriment of tradition. God, in His wisdom, governs these two conflicting tendencies. He brings them into harmony so that each one may achieve all that may be achieved in view of acquiring the supreme good: blessedness.

The interdependent bonds linking the mystery of Christmas to the Purification, and the very originality of these bonds wonderfully manifest these principles. Nothing is more audacious than the mystery of Christmas in comparison with all that God had established in the Mosaic Law. We might even say that, compared to the legal formalism of that period—i.e., the manner in which the Law was put into practice—nothing is more revolutionary in its extreme gentleness. Yet equally, nothing is more deeply rooted in the Law than this renewal: the mysteries of the Purification and the Circumcision attest to this.

Let us try to understand how the mystery of the Purification will be a new stage for Mary in her contemplative life as well as in her liturgical life. This first return to the temple with the Child Jesus will be a source of great joy (joy for Simeon, joy for the people, joy for Mary) and at the same time it will be a source of a deeper and greater personal participation in God's plans through the prophetic announcement of suffering. In this mystery of the Purification, we must distinguish three complementary aspects: the Presentation of Jesus in the temple, the Purification of Mary, and the Appearance of the Prophetess, Anna.

Presentation of Jesus in the Temple

The law of Moses required that "you shall set apart to the Lord all that first opens the womb " (cf. Ex. 13:1-2, 11-16). This consecration was symbolized by the sacrifice of "a pair of turtledoves, or two young pigeons" (Lk. 2:24). Now the letter of the law did not concern Jesus, who was God's Anointed from the first moment of His conception through the mystery of the hypostatic union. Actually, the law applied only to every male child that naturally opened the womb— *"masculinum quod aperit vulvam, hoc ut matricem,"* as Cajetan points out in his Commentary—whereas Jesus miraculously came forth from His mother's womb, which remained virginal, *"clauso genitali membro matris, ita etiam clausa vulva est"* [the mother's generative part being shut, so also the womb was shut]. He was really above the law and His miraculous birth was, as it were, the sign of this fact. Nevertheless, God in fact wants Him to abide by the law, as He had already complied with the law of circumcision: "They brought him up to Jerusalem to present him to the Lord" (Lk. 2:22).

Indeed Jesus, as He will say later, is not sent to abolish the law, but to fulfill it. This law prescribing the offering of the firstborn commemorated the people of Israel's miraculous liberation from Pharaoh's tyrannical yoke. In the middle of the night, the Lord had struck down all the firstborn in the land of Egypt "from the first-born of Pharaoh . . . to the first-born of the captive who was in the dungeon" (Ex. 12:29). This law is fulfilled in the offering of the Firstborn of Mary and of the Father.

By complying with the law, Jesus was living fully and totally the common law of His people, the Law of all the children of Israel. His personal mystery remained hidden. He appeared officially as the "woman's son," while He too was carrying the consequences of Israel's common debt.

In the temple Mary and Joseph meet Simeon, a "righteous and devout man, looking for the consolation of Israel."[70] Not only was this man righteous according to the common law, but he lived in fear of the Lord and in hope for His mercy. He remained in a state of filial intimacy with the Holy Spirit: "The Holy Spirit was upon him. And it had been revealed to him by the Holy Spirit that he should not see death before he had seen the Lord's Christ" (Lk. 2:25-26).

This man, who had received the secrets of God's wisdom, "inspired by the Spirit came into the temple." He who fully belonged to the Old Testament, yet was faithful to its spirit, is led to the temple by the Holy Spirit. Mary, who fully belongs to the New Testament, but also to the Old from a material point of view, obeys the law by going to the temple with Jesus. We have here a wonderful ordinance of God's wisdom to bring together Simeon and Mary with the Child

---

70. Lk. 2:25: *"Et ecce homo erat in Jerusalem, cui nomen Simeon, et homo iste justus,*

     et timoratus, expectans consolationem Israel." ["Now there was a man in Jerusalem, whose name was Simeon, and this man was righteous and

Jesus. Simeon took the Child Jesus into his arms and gave thanks to God, saying: "Lord now lettest thou thy servant depart in peace, according to thy word; for mine eyes have seen thy salvation which thou hast prepared in the presence of all peoples, a light for revelation to the Gentiles, and for glory to thy people Israel" (Lk. 2:29-32).

Simeon's qualities show us quite clearly that he lives the expectation of Israel very intensely; he lives the expectation of the patriarchs and the prophets in its purest, most authentic form. That is why the Holy Spirit reveals to him first, before the others, the Messiah's presence in this tiny infant. After Mary, John the Baptist, Elizabeth, Joseph and the shepherds who are instructed by the angels, Simeon is instructed by the Holy Spirit Himself in the inmost depths of his heart and intelligence. It was in the midst of nature's silent expanse that the shepherds received the angel's message and set off on their way. It is in the temple, the house of God, that Simeon, docile to the prompting of the Holy Spirit, meets the Messiah. It is in the temple that Israel's desire is to be fulfilled.

Moved by the Holy Spirit, Simeon speaks on behalf of all people, as God's faithful servant awaiting the arrival of He who is to come as Savior. He recognizes that he is *right now* witnessing the fulfillment of the promise—"My eyes have seen thy salvation"—and for that very reason his mission is brought to an end. He has only to disappear to let the Savior act directly. The entire mission of Israel, bound to God by flesh and blood through the sign of circumcision, was to await the Messiah, the liberator of His people: "The scepter shall not depart from Judah, nor the ruler's staff from between his feet, until he comes to whom it belongs; and to him shall be the obedience of the peoples" (Gen. 49:10).

Simeon prophetically characterizes the mission of this universal Savior by means of two affirmations: "a light for revelation to the gentiles, and for glory to thy people Israel." Note the precision used here. As Savior—one who brings salvation—Jesus comes for all peoples. As Light—one who enlightens and manifests truth—Jesus comes for the Gentiles who have not yet received the divine revelation. His personal mission is to bear witness to the truth so that all men of good will may be able to receive the light. As Glory—one who brings to its ultimate completion a work already begun—Jesus is given to His people. He is its most excellent fruit, the One that brings all the perfections and riches of David's race into bloom. "He is like a tree planted by streams of water" (Ps. 1:3).

"His father and his mother marveled at what was said about him" (Lk. 2:33). Mary, who had kept the angel's and shepherds' messages in her heart, listens with admiration to Simeon's prophecy which explicitly reveals to her Jesus' universal salvific mission: her Son is the Salvation that God has prepared in the sight of all peoples; He is the Light sent by God to enlighten the Gentiles; He is the Glory of His people.

The mystery of the Presentation implies the offering of Jesus to God, an offering made by the priest. Without attempting to examine the question of whether or not Simeon was a priest, we will follow Cajetan's opinion which seems theologically valid. Cajetan considers that Simeon is a priest because Scripture tells us that "he blessed them" (Lk. 2:34). Now such a gesture can only be made in the temple by a priest whose proper function is to bless and offer sacrifices.[71]

The offering of Jesus by Simeon is the last act of the Levitical priesthood. After this it will disappear, for the reality is present and the era of symbols no longer has any reason for being. Simeon's *Nunc Dimittis,* which concerns the entire expectation of Israel, applies in a particular way to the Levitical priesthood.

Mary plays an important part in this final liturgical act of the Levitical priesthood. She is the one who presents Jesus to the priest; she is the one who gives Him to Simeon. It is from Mary that the priest receives Jesus to offer Him to the Father.

Mary therefore cooperates in this mystery which brings the Levitical priesthood to completion. Hers is a maternal cooperation that consists in presenting Jesus, in leading Him, in handing Him over to the priest's power. Through this cooperation, she divinely unites the Christian liturgy with that of the Old Testament. The maternal, intimate, and familial liturgy of Christmas assumes the legal liturgy of the temple by giving it a new significance. With the offering of the Child Jesus, first made by Himself in a completely silent and hidden way, then visibly by Mary and the Levitical priesthood, we witness the transformation of the Mosaic liturgy into the Christian liturgy.

Purification of Mary—Prophetic Annunciation

The Law of Moses required not only the offering of the firstborn, but also the mother's purification. Considered from

---

71. Cf. Cajetan's Commentary on Luke 2:34.

a material point of view, this law is not binding for Mary. She is totally pure; she has conceived and given birth to her child in a miraculous way. However, if we take a deeper look at the Law with respect to its application to Mary's soul, it culminates in mystery. A legal purification is transformed into a mystery of purification.

If Mary abides by the law, it is to remain hidden, so that her privilege may remain exclusively reserved for the glory of God. This is the attitude of the lowly servant of God who, by divine instinct, wishes to live according to the proper demands of the common law in order to remain hidden, in order to be inconspicuous. This is one of the signs of Christian humility as far as the social and communal life is concerned. It is the opposite of the tendency of the proud who seek every opportunity to attract attention, to be noticed by others.

Mary could have presented her privileges as a claim for exemption from the common law; she could have showed herself to be a soul privileged by God and called by Him to an extraordinary mission. Led as she is by this divine instinct of the gift of fear, however, she uses the common law to disappear unnoticed, without receiving any special attention. She understands that the glory of God consists in hiding His works.

This humility divinely prepares Mary's heart to fully receive God's Word, even if this Word will wound her heart. There is really a very close connection between faith and humility. Humility enables our intelligence to avoid setting human limitations to God's Word by adapting it to our natural needs. By keeping us in our place as creatures, it makes us realize our littleness and the limitations of our human perspective as compared to God's plans for us. It makes us capable of accepting a divine message which we may not understand and which at first even seems to conflict with everything we have been told before. Insofar as pride takes possession of us and exalts us, it closes our intelligence, which then thinks it is capable of attaining the fullness of truth. The proud man relies solely on his personal judgment. Hence he cannot submit to divine truth in its transcendence. Now, Mary has to be very poor and very humble to be capable of receiving this new prophecy from Simeon. Actually, Simeon not only reveals her Son's universal salvific mission to her, a mission of light and glory; but, even more directly, he reveals to her that this Savior is a "sign that is spoken against," that her fate as a Mother will be closely bound to that of her Son, that her Son's sorrows are to be her own sorrows.

The Scriptural text is quite clear: "Simeon blessed them and said to Mary his mother, 'Behold, this child is set for the fall and rising of many in Israel and for a sign that is spoken against (and a sword will pierce through your own soul also), so that thoughts out of many hearts may be revealed" (Lk. 2:34-35).

He who is the Salvation, the Light and the Glory is at the same time "a sign that is spoken against." He is really a "sign" because He signifies the fulfillment of all the prophecies; because He signifies perfect peace between God and mankind; lastly because He signifies God's immense grace imparted to the world. He is God's sign *par excellence*. But this divine sign is spoken against because the Jews will insist that He is neither a sign of the fulfillment of the prophecies, nor a sign of divine peace with mankind, nor a sign of grace granted to the world. This "speaking against," which will set Jesus in His teaching against the Pharisees, the scribes, and the chief priests, will lead to the Crucifixion. There Jesus will be more than ever "a sign of God" since there, everything will be accomplished. At the Cross He will be the "sign of God" *par excellence,* not only for Israel but also for the Gentiles.

As a "sign spoken against," He will inevitably stand for both the fall and the rising of His people, since the specific character of contradiction, or "speaking against," is to divide and to divide definitively. There is no possibility of taking an intermediary position; it is either acceptance or rejection. For those who receive Jesus as the Savior, as the One who comes to save and illuminate, He will be the cause of resurrection and life. For those who reject Him, considering Him as a blasphemer or a madman, He will be the cause of ruin on account of their refusal. Because of Him, many will refuse the light out of pride and will experience a darkness even more dark than if He had not come. Not only will they reject Christ, but they will also go so far as to reject God, to proclaim that God does not exist. St. John affirms that "the light shines in the darkness, and the darkness has not overcome it" (Jn. 1:5). He who is the Wisdom and Light of God for the believer is, at the same time, a scandal and a folly for the Jews and the Gentiles, for all those who refuse to believe in His mystery.

Mary's fate is intimately bound to that of her Son. That is why her soul must be pierced by a sword. Mary's soul must be tortured; it must experience the deepest and most acute sufferings. The image of the piercing sword clearly shows that it is not simply a superficial and transitory wound. It is a mortal wound that strikes what is most vital in her: her maternal heart, which must be pierced where it is most loving and vulnerable. In a prophetic way, Simeon tells Mary what is to happen to Jesus during His life. He reveals to her the diametrically opposed attitudes which will be taken with regard to Jesus and how she herself will be associated with this mystery and will have to drain the cup with Him to the dregs. That is why her soul must suffer this terrible wound. The sword that will physically pierce the breast and heart of her Son will mystically pierce her soul. All her suffering will be interior, hidden, reserved for God. Such is the special participation God has reserved for her and asks her to accept in her living faith. God makes this known to her. After asking for her *fiat* in the joy of the Annunciation, He asks her for this new *fiat,* which announces the sword. The mystery of the Incarnation is ordered to the mystery of Redemption and the Cross, while being distinct from it. It is not only a question of agreeing to live a joyful, divine motherhood in absolute poverty; God wants more. Mary, who was so closely associated with the mystery of the Incarnation, must also be associated with the mystery of Redemption. That is why He asks her to accept a bloody, crucifying motherhood so that she may be more intimately united to her Son's saving mystery.

All this must happen so "that thoughts out of many hearts may be revealed." Called by the Father to be so profoundly associated with her Son's mystery of Redemption, Mary becomes the new Woman, given as a Mother to John, the beloved disciple, and given through him as a Mother to all of Jesus' disciples.

The Redemption is so efficacious and so profound in Mary that she can cooperate with Him who redeems her. As a Mother, she can bring divine life to those who are saved by Jesus. Thus she is the Mother of the whole Christ. As Mother of the members of the whole Christ, she can receive the secrets of their hearts and keep them in hers. A child has nothing to hide from his mother. He tells her all the secrets of his heart; and, being a child, he can only tell them to his mother, for she is the only one able to understand them. Insofar as she is a mother, she can receive her children's secrets and keep them while hiding them. Mary, who is fully a Mother, who is a Mother in her whole soul, since her motherhood is divine, can receive the secrets of "many hearts" in her heart. It is really thanks to the divine wound of the sword that she can receive these secrets in her love, since it is through the wound made by this sword that she is intimately united to the work of Redemption and that she explicitly becomes our Mother.

Let us go back for a moment to the comparison of this mystery of the Purification with the mystery of the Annunciation, in order to better understand the order of divine wisdom. The Annunciation made by Gabriel was full of joy. The silence and poverty that it required were fully directed toward joy. The announcement made by Simeon is entirely directed toward sorrow and separation. The first Annunciation actually concerned divine motherhood with regard to Jesus and happened in secrecy, without witnesses. The second one focuses on the sorrowful motherhood—which will culminate at Calvary—with regard to all the "prodigal sons," all those who must be restored to favor and reinstated in the Father's house. It occurs in the temple; it is official and there are witnesses.

Thus it is perfectly normal that the first should come from an angel and the second, on the contrary, from a representative of men and in particular from a representative of Israel: a prophet-priest who, on behalf of his people and of all mankind, asks her to be the Mother of all poor sinners by accepting to have her soul intimately united to her Son's in His mission of Redemption and Salvation. It is normal that the first angelic annunciation should have taken place in secret. The mystery of the Incarnation had to be hidden from men's eyes so that Jesus would be able to lead the "common life" of mankind, so that the "King of Israel" would be able to serve by working hard, hidden from His own people for thirty years. It is normal that this second annunciation should be official: the mystery of Redemption is to be accomplished on the mountain, in the sight of all.

Mary had received the angel's joyful message in a *fiat* of faith, hope and love; she receives the prophecy from Simeon in a new *fiat* of faith, hope and love. This new *fiat* implies new demands and requires greater divine generosity. For although her *fiat* of faith at the Annunciation was pronounced in darkness, it gave her, nonetheless, the intimate presence of the Word Incarnate. Through this act of faith, Christ came to live in her. In the case of the second annunciation, this new act of faith forces her to accept a future separation. Through this act of faith, she experiences the threat of separation, a violent and bloody separation. This act of faith generates in her heart and soul a much greater poverty, which is that of a very sorrowful separation from Him who is everything to her, demanding a complete surrender to God's loving will. Without understanding, she must radically and fully accept this mysterious will of God for Jesus and for herself, preferring the complete accomplishment of this will—however painful and difficult it may seem to her—to the present possession, so wonderful and so divine, of Jesus. The more God lavishes His gifts on us, the more He demands from us this fundamental act of will, whereby we prefer Him, in His very will for us, to the gifts He has lavished upon us.

Simeon's prophecy requires Mary to live by Jesus' presence, which has just been given to her so fully by the Father, knowing that one day this presence will be snatched away from her in a terrible, violent way. Such is the very great interior poverty that God demands from her as Mother and as Virgin. The angel asked her for the poverty of a useless servant; Simeon asks her for another kind, that of a useless servant who must be completely devoted to her mission, knowing in her faith that from a human, exterior perspective, this mission will momentarily end in almost complete failure. This Savior "is set for the fall . . . of many in Israel." Since she is to cooperate in His work, since her fate is bound to His, she herself, as Mother, is set for the fall of many in Israel. Just as He shall be "a sign that is spoken against," so must she agree to be such a sign. For a Mother's heart, which knows only mercy, it is a terrible burden to bear. It is indeed poverty established in the inmost depths of her maternal and merciful heart: acceptance of the fact that her mercy will bring about a fall. She must accept being rejected herself one day, as her Son will be. She must accept being treated like Hagar, reduced to living in the desert, dying of hunger and thirst with her Son because people refuse to recognize His true dignity. He will be considered only as a slave, a slave's son, an intruder.

With this mystery, we witness the first encounter between Mary and the priest. This first encounter immediately assumes a character of holocaust and sacrifice. Mary's soul is prophetically immolated by the divine sword. But it has already been immolated by this other divine sword, which is God's Word, the Word that is addressed to her through Simeon and on which she lives through faith. This Word is her food, bitter food for her maternal heart. God's Word, which until then had always brought joy to her soul, suddenly becomes for her a crucifying Word that wounds and causes very hidden, very deep suffering. The journey through the desert really begins here, with this prophecy from Simeon. Now, the first incident mentioned in Exodus concerning this journey is when, at the end of a three days' walk without finding water, Israel arrived at Marah, but "they could not drink the water of Marah because it was bitter; therefore it was named Marah" (Ex. 15:22-23). This bitter water is like a prefiguration of Simeon's prophecy for Mary's maternal heart. But we know that Moses "cried to the Lord; and the Lord showed him a tree, and he threw it into the water, and the water became sweet" (Ex. 15:25). Simeon handed the little Child Jesus back to Mary. Mary clutched Him with greater love. She could now give Him not only the joy of her heart, but also this deep sorrow; she could offer

Him her soul wounded by the sword of the Word. Through
Jesus' presence, this wound, which was entirely for His sake,
becomes a source of new sweetness.

Simeon's prophecy, the last of the Old Testament, which
thus brings to a close all the prophecies of the prophets, is to
be buried in Mary's heart; it is to be kept hidden there like a
secret. Through this prophecy the entire Old Testament, in its
most divine aspect, comes to an end in Mary's heart, to give
her a divine wound.

All the prophecies of the Old Testament are in a sense
oriented toward this final prophecy, so that the weight of the
divine Word may be heavier, so that the sword may be
sharper. By accepting this prophecy from Simeon in faith, all
the prophecies of the Old Testament inundate her soul as it
were, and she accepts them in a completely new way.

*The Appearance of
the Prophetess Anna*

A widow "of great age" who "did not depart from the
temple, worshipping with fasting and prayer night and day"
(Lk. 2:37), moved by the Holy Spirit, begins to give glory to
God and to speak of the Child Jesus "to all who were looking for the redemption of Jerusalem." Before John the Baptist, who will be "the voice of one crying in the wilderness"
to announce the coming of the Messiah, after the angels who
glorified God in the highest, there is this poor widow in the
temple, who is the first to announce the good news. This
prophetess of the tribe of Asher is there as the representative
of all the other prophetesses of the Old Testament who bore
witness to God's merciful providence.

The mystery of the Presentation really brings together in the temple all that was living and true in the Old Testament. The Holy Spirit brings them together in God's house so that they may be able to receive this first visit of Christ to the temple, to share in His mystery by recognizing that the period of expectation has finally ended and that the Light appears and begins to rise.

This mystery shows us how the union of the Old and the New Testaments is found in Mary, how in and through her the Old Testament is assumed by the New without being abolished; the Old Testament is completely transformed. She is the woman who closes and completes the Synagogue and the woman who is the Mother and prototype of the Church.

This union is achieved through the mystery of the Cross, but Mary must first live this mystery in her faith, her hope and her love. This mystery must take complete possession of her soul before being accomplished outwardly in Christ's body. She must carry it in the inmost depths of her heart, and this is truly what constitutes this mystery of offering and purification, which is actually one and the same mystery. For every offering brings about a purification, and every divine purification must be an offering.

CHAPTER 8

THE ADORATION OF THE MAGI, THE FLIGHT TO EGYPT, AND THE HOLY INNOCENTS: MARY'S FIRST TRIALS

WITHOUT discussing the Magi's itinerary and without wondering who these men were or where they came from, we will simply consider what may clarify the present study and take us deeper into the mystery which directly involves Mary. Although this mystery still remains a joyful mystery, it already implies a struggle—certain separations and sufferings which are no longer purely prophetic, but which are immediately realized. Thus we have here the first struggles, the first attacks of the devil, the first separations and sufferings which come to wound Mary's heart and give her joy a particular nuance.

The Magi, who have come from the East after being miraculously instructed and guided by the star concerning the birth of the "King of the Jews," stop in Jerusalem to seek out those who know where the King of the Jews is to be found. After using the divine sign, the Magi must resort to more human means and seek help from acquired wisdom. But this recourse to human knowledge compels them to reveal their belief, to make known the purpose of their extraordinary journey. " 'Where is he who has been born king of the Jews? For we have seen his star in the East, and have come to worship him.' When Herod the king heard this, he was troubled, and all Jerusalem with him" (Mt. 2:2-3), Scripture says.

After consulting "the chief priests and scribes of the people,"

> Herod summoned the Wise Men secretly and ascertained from them what time the star appeared; and he sent them to Bethlehem, saying, "Go and search diligently for the child, and when you have found him bring me word, that I too may come and worship him" (Mt. 2:7-8).

As they leave Jerusalem, the star reappears to their great joy:

> And lo, the star which they had seen in the East went before them, till it came to rest over the place where the child was . . . and going into the house they saw the child with Mary his mother, and they fell down and worshiped him. Then, opening their treasures, they offered him gifts, gold and frankincense and myrrh (Mt. 2:9-11).

These outward gestures clearly manifest the inner feelings of admiration, veneration and adoration experienced by the Magi in Jesus' presence. These men of science had been so struck by the wonderful sign in the sky, the miraculous star, that they believed in God's very special protection over this royal Child as "sent by God." Thus they were not disconcerted to discover that nothing extraordinary was outwardly revealed. This King of Israel simply appears as the tiny child of poor parents. Given the Scriptural text, there can be little doubt that the Magi, in their hearts and minds, and with complete humility, adored the Child Jesus in spirit and in truth, recognizing Him as the One sent by God. "Whereas in a literal sense, the reason that prompted the Magi to offer one gift rather than another remains uncertain," Cajetan notes, "tradition has given them a certain symbolic value, since gold is suitable for royal dignity, frankincense for divinity and priestly dignity, and myrrh for His infant limbs and burial."[72]

Through their worship and offering, the Magi confirm for Mary what God had already told her through the angel Gabriel, the shepherds and Simeon. The miraculous star, as a divine sign in the sky manifesting this Child's wondrous birth, confirms for her His universal and divine royalty. In her heart Mary admires the attitude of these men who have come from a far distant country to adore her Son and pay homage to Him. What a striking, radiant manifestation of the Father's solicitude for His Son!

But there is something very particular about the Magi's adoration, as compared to that of the shepherds. The latter had been guided solely by the angels, without any intermediary.

---

72. Cajetan, *Commentary on St. Matthew*, II, 12.

Consequently, after their adoration at the crib, they went back to their usual occupations—inwardly transformed, certainly, but without any change in their outward life. The Magi, initially guided directly by God, were obliged to stop in Jerusalem to find out where they must go to find "the King of the Jews." The Magi's itinerary is not as simple as the shepherds'. They had to resort to human wisdom to get to Bethlehem, and this aroused bitter jealousy in Herod's and his followers' hearts toward this wonderful Child who had been announced as the ruler who would "govern my people Israel" (Mt. 2:6). That is why the Magi, as they were about to return to Jerusalem, were warned in a dream not to return to Herod. Thus, disregarding the latter's request, they returned to their own country by another route.

The Flight into Egypt

The Magi are not the only ones in this mystery who are instructed by the angels to flee. Joseph is warned as well:

> Now when they had departed, behold, an angel of the Lord appeared to Joseph in a dream and said, "Rise, take the child and his mother, and flee to Egypt, and remain there till I tell you; for Herod is about to search for the child, to destroy him" (Mt. 2:13).

Joseph arose, took the Child and His mother and set out that very night to take refuge in Egypt.

It is Joseph whom the angel warns this time, for the decision to be made concerns the head of the family as such, and Mary must have the full merit of perfect obedience.

What we have here is really a gesture of Christian communal obedience on Mary's part. She has already obeyed God more than once; she has obeyed His Word, His instruments. However, her obedience here concerns the external forum; it concerns obedience to Joseph as head of the family. This obedience affects the common good of the household, which is threatened and must be safeguarded at all cost. Let us consider the particular circumstances of this act of obedience to try to better understand the characteristics of Christian communal obedience as such.

This act of obedience is relative to the order given by Joseph to Mary, and through her, to the Child. They must leave Bethlehem immediately and go to a foreign country, to Egypt. This means expatriation and exile, for the life of the Child is in danger. They must go far away by night, without knowing exactly where or for how long. This order may appear imprudent at first glance. It may even seem sheer folly. The Child is still so small, and it will mean going on a long journey without any help or preparation. This order seems very sudden indeed and seems to be in such opposition to all that has just happened; the visit of the Magi seemed to reveal the Father's extraordinary solicitude toward this little Child! And then everything is changed at a moment's notice because of an apparition in a dream.

One can hardly think of a clearer, more precise, and more concrete order in more extraordinary yet apparently imprudent circumstances. Besides, does such an order not show a lack of courage? It means fleeing from an enemy who is still quite a distance away. Herod has not yet come. Could such an escape not have tragic results for others?

Mary accepts this order without question, in silence, as if it were the simplest, most natural thing in the world. Mary surely did not have to ask Joseph for an explanation to be certain that this was really prudent and in accordance with God's will. In her joy of being able to obey, she immediately carries out what she is asked to do. Indeed, the virtue of obedience consists in accepting the authority of a superior as a rule for any of our activities. Someone under authority freely receives his superior's order as the immediate measure of his act of obedience. The virtue of obedience regarding the superior's precept really pertains to the order of execution. This is why the quicker and more prompt the obedience, the more perfect it is, since the domain of execution naturally requires this promptness, unlike the phase of reflecting and seeking advice, which requires time.

The gift of piety, which transforms the infused virtue of obedience from within by putting it directly under the motion of the Holy Spirit, enables our acts of obedience to have a note of simplicity and filial trust. It is the obedience of a docile child to his beloved parents. Such obedience cannot tolerate the slightest objection or demand of our human reason against the authority of the one who gives orders or against the value of his orders. It cannot tolerate any human comparison or criticism that would diminish the authoritative and absolute character of the order received from the Father. It likes to carry out the paternal order with the utmost generosity and accuracy, knowing full well that in this way it efficiently cooperates with His will, with His reign. And for this very reason, we must surpass the tragic and dramatic attitude that obedience—particularly concerning the external forum—creates so easily in our psychological ego, since obedience always implies, to a certain extent, the death of our practical judgment. We must agree, out of our love for God, to completely disappear without making a scene. We must offer our holocaust without asking for spectators to praise or pity us, whether such spectators be within or outside ourselves. The gift of piety teaches us to die to ourselves in a very hidden way, out of love for God.

Moved by the Holy Spirit and by virtue of the gift of piety, Mary obeys Joseph's order in the most trusting, spontaneous, and divine way, since Joseph represents for her God's authority in all that pertains to family and communal life. Without the slightest hesitation or the slightest criticism, without wondering whether Joseph is prudent enough in giving such an order, she immediately carries out God's will for her, conveyed by Joseph. She does this lovingly and joyfully in the silence of the night.

This act of obedience maintains a joyful note; for although she must leave her native country and her Son's blessed birthplace to travel to Egypt, a place of captivity and exile, Mary goes into exile taking her Son with her. That is why this act of obedience, which requires her to be separated from certain external goods, from her country and relatives, actually unites her more profoundly to her Son. She must take Him away with her, since it is to save Him that she goes into exile. As on Christmas night, she is again completely devoted to Him, and their intimacy is even greater since imminent danger and peril bring them closer together. Mary's heart must become for her Child a rampart and a fortress, as it were, against the enemy who is threatening His life. This act of obedience, which surrenders Mary more profoundly to God's gracious will, thus brings a greater, more perfect fullness of joy to her heart, since His presence becomes more intense. Everything cooperates in the salvation of the saints; even God's enemies constitute an opportunity for joy to blossom in the sons of God.

The Slaughter of the Innocents

> Then Herod, when he saw that he had been tricked by the wise men, was in a furious rage, and he sent and killed all the male children in Bethlehem and in all that region who were two years old or under, according to the time which he had ascertained from the wise men. Then was fulfilled what was spoken by the prophet Jeremiah:
>
>> A voice was heard in Ramah,
>> wailing and loud lamentation,
>> Rachel weeping for her children;
>> she refused to be consoled,
>> because they were no more.[73]

The Magi's docility to the angel's message rescues the Child Jesus from death, but at the same time causes the terrible slaughter of these little children, very close to the Child Jesus in time and place. Such is the first sorrow that surrounds the coming of Christ on this earth. And this sorrow

---

73. Mt. 2:16-18.

must be suffered by these children and their mothers—all the children and all the mothers who, historically and geographically, are respectively Jesus' and Mary's contemporaries.

Considered from the perspective of the divine governance, we have here a Christian mystery which is, as it were, the first fulfillment of Simeon's prophecy. Christ's coming, however well-hidden in humility, immediately provokes terrible jealousy in the hearts of the proud who intend to rule over the earth at all costs and who fear being dethroned, for Jesus can come only as a King. Such men, who in their jealousy cannot tolerate the superiority of another, immediately desire to destroy Him and to do so using any means, even if it necessitates the slaughter of those who are innocent and whose only fault lies in being neighbors and contemporaries of the One they envy.

Since Jesus' Hour has not yet come, God protects Him from Herod's jealousy by putting Him out of his reach, through flight. Yet God allows Herod's jealousy to reach all those who, although unaware of it, are close to Jesus in age and by place of origin. Thus He makes them little martyrs, the first innocent witnesses of Christ's royalty, witnesses not by their words—they cannot speak—but by their deaths.

This divine permission may seem, in the light of human prudence, terribly unjustifiable to us. For if we go by our human prudence, we are always ready to agree with Caiaphas who advised that "it was expedient that one man should die for the people" (Jn. 18:14). Viewed with the eyes of faith, this divine permission is the work of Wisdom. It remains mysterious, yet we sense that it is actually divine mercy. It is a double mercy, protecting the Child Jesus' life on the one hand

and, on the other, delivering the poor little innocents to martyrdom, making them silent, involuntary yet patient and real witnesses of Christ's royalty.

In her faith and obedience, Mary adheres to the divine will. She takes these mothers' tears into her heart to offer them to Jesus. These human tears have not tarnished her joy, but rather have made it purer, more intense and more divine.

In this mystery of the flight into Egypt and of the slaughter of the Holy Innocents, there is a divine lesson we need to understand. First let us turn to a text by Louis de Grenade:

> Notice as well that no sooner has Christ been born than immediately a Herod rises up to put Him to death. Similarly, no sooner will Christ have been born in your heart than several "Herods" will rise up to kill him. The world with its persecutions, the flesh with its pleasures, false friends with their bad advice, the demon with his tricks, will vie with one another in tearing you away from your good intentions, i.e., in slaughtering Christ newly born in your soul. Like the woman in the Apocalypse, flee to the desert, seek solitude, avoid men, and especially those who might cause your ruin. Note that Jesus was safer with the Egyptians than with the Jews, in a pagan land than in the country of God's people. A Christian is often safer with pagans than in the midst of loose, sensual Christians. A public

enemy is to be feared less than a hidden traitor: a wolf is less fearsome, wolf though he is,
than when he is clothed with sheepskin.[74]

We must also point out that every act of Christian obedience, particularly one pertaining to the external forum,
which is exercised entirely under the motion of the gift of
piety, actually saves Christ's reign in us but often entails the
death in us of numerous innocent things, the slaughter of
which is psychologically very painful and causes tears and
groans. Do we not have many qualities, abilities and activities which are not bad or sinful in themselves and which we
would never have thought could become matter for sacrifice?
Christian obedience, which always unites us to the Cross of
Christ, very often asks us to sacrifice such things. And the
more perfect the obedience, the more numerous are the sacrifices it implies. So it is quite normal that Christian obedience, which prompts us to live by God's will and establishes
Christ's reign in us, should save Christ in us and at the same
time should be an occasion for sacrificing our own personal-
ity, our psychological ego with all its relations and external or
hidden ramifications.

These useless and unjustified slaughters cannot be
understood from the outside, and that is why we so often
weep over those who seem to disappear so uselessly and so
unjustly. In the eyes of someone who obeys, such slaughters
are necessary and serve as witnesses of the absolute primacy

---

74. *Memorial of the Christian Life. Complete Works of Louis de Grenade*
(Paris, Ed. Vivès, 1863), Vol. XII, p. 307.

of God's will and His love. God alone can act in this way, asking those who are innocent to bear witness to Him. By so doing He uses them and exalts them, and they cooperate with His love and acquire eternal merit.

CHAPTER 9

THE FINDING OF THE
CHILD JESUS IN THE TEMPLE:
THE FIRST SORROW
IN MARY'S HEART

THE mystery of the Finding of the Child Jesus in the Temple presents us with Mary's first separation from her Son. It is the first sorrow imposed upon Mary by God in His governance of wisdom. Yet this mystery remains a joyful mystery, for the separation is only a temporary one; it is a trial. This separation will foster a deeper union between Mary and Jesus.

This mystery must help us understand how, in the Christian life, there may be joyful mysteries implying great sorrows; how temporary trials prepare for the great separation of the Cross; how God can suddenly impose moments of Christ's absence upon us and enable others to enjoy His presence. Lastly, this mystery confides to us an intimate secret of Jesus' heart, His secret as an apostle, which Mary made her own and which helps us understand what characterizes the Christian community.

First of all, let us recall the circumstances in which this mystery comes about. St. Luke says:

> Now his parents went to Jerusalem every year at the feast of the Passover. And when he was twelve years old, they went up according to custom; and when the feast was ended, as they were returning, the boy Jesus stayed behind in Jerusalem. His parents did not know it (Lk. 2:41-43).

Ordinarily, the Child Jesus was to follow them with all the other children, forming a separate group in the caravan.

"Supposing Him to be in the company they went a day's journey" (Lk. 2:44). So it was only at the end of the first day's journey that Joseph and Mary realized He was not with them. "They sought him among their kinsfolk and acquaintances; and when they did not find him, they returned to Jerusalem, seeking him" (Lk. 2:44-45).

This sudden discovery at the end of the first day's journey must have been extremely painful for Mary, considering the intimacy which united her to Jesus and the fact that He had never left her before. This was the first break in her maternal heart, the first intimate and personal fulfillment of Simeon's prophecy: "A sword will pierce through your own soul."

This separation is all the more cruel because it was unexpected and unpredictable. Jesus had said nothing, had suggested nothing to that effect; and yet He, the perfectly obedient Child who "increased in wisdom," knew. Then He suddenly disappears without telling His parents. It would have been so simple to let them know. They would have been so understanding. God, in His wisdom, wanted something else. Because Jesus' absence is incomprehensible, it is all the more violently felt in Mary's heart. Since Jesus is still young, only twelve years old, do not Joseph and Mary seem guilty of a lack of attention and care for Him? Should they not have noticed His absence more quickly? They traveled for a whole day without Him!

One could not find circumstances more tragic in their simplicity to make this separation harder to bear for Mary's maternal heart. In their sadness and sorrow, Joseph and Mary make every effort to find Him, first among their relatives, then in Jerusalem. And this search lasted "three days," as if to show us that despite its limited duration, it seemed endless to Mary's heart. Was this trial not willed precisely by God as a preparation for the great separation of the Sepulcher, which will also last for three days?

Mary cannot hide these three days of agony, sorrow, and sadness from her Son. She says to Him, almost as a reproach as soon as she finds Him: "Behold, your father and I have been looking for you anxiously" (Lk. 2:48).

If we want to enter more deeply into Mary's soul during these three days of searching, we must remember what Scripture tells us in the Song of Songs concernirg the anxiety of the spouse searching for her beloved:

> I sought him whom my soul loves; I sought
> him, but found him not. . . . "I will rise now
> and go about the city, in the streets and in the
> squares; I will seek him whom my soul

loves." I sought him, but found him not. The watchmen found me, as they went about the city. "Have you seen him whom my soul loves?" (Song 3:1-3). I sought him, but found him not; I called him, but he gave no answer. The watchmen found me, as they went about in the city; they beat me, they wounded me (Song 5:6b-7b).

Louis de Grenade states in his *"Memorial of the Christian Life"*:

> God gave the patriarch Abraham three days after having asked him for the sacrifice of his son, so that this affectionate father might be able to think about the death of the son he loved so much and experience beforehand all the sorrow his death would cause. Mary was also given three days to drain to the dregs the bitter cup of Jesus' absence.[75]

"After three days they found him in the temple, sitting among the teachers, listening to them and asking them questions; and all who heard him were amazed at his understanding and his answers" (Lk. 2:46-47). It is in the temple that Mary finds Him among the teachers. He is in their midst, both listening to them and asking them questions. This is the humblest way to teach, the most merciful and the most suitable—on the one hand, for His situation as the Son of God, who has

---

75. Louis de Grenade, *op. cit.*, p. 311.

nothing to learn from men, but must teach them God's love for them and His infinite mercy toward them; and on the other hand, for His situation as a twelve-year-old boy who should normally be silent among these serious theologians.

Notice that this first teaching of the Word Incarnate is reserved for the teachers, the theologians of the time. It is they who receive the first fruits of Christ's doctrine. They are in some sense entitled to it because of their social function. Jesus respects this communal, ecclesiastical hierarchy of the Old Testament, just as He wanted to respect the law of circumcision. He, the Teacher *par excellence,* wants first of all to question the teachers in Israel. It is in the temple that this first teaching is given, in the Father's house, which is the house of truth, in which the tables of the law are kept as well as all the doctrine revealed by God since Moses.

While Mary was with Joseph in anguish, Jesus was among the teachers and was granting them this great grace: the joy of His presence and of His first teaching. Jesus' absence, which was so cruel and which Mary had to bear, would allow the teachers to enjoy the presence of Jesus as Teacher and to live this time with Him. He was there for them; He had left those who were dear to Him, Joseph and Mary, to come to them.

When they found Him in this place and in such company, Mary and Joseph were "astonished." And yet Mary could not help telling Jesus what was weighing so heavily on her maternal heart: "Son, why have you treated us so? Behold, your father and I have been looking for you anxiously."

This is the most natural question of a mother who has suffered because of her son and who does not understand

how her beloved son could have behaved in such an unexpected way! She does not scold Him, since she is merely
God's handmaid, but she questions Him sadly.

This question that Mary asks Jesus is the first question
that the Holy Spirit has revealed to us. This question is a
prayer which expresses her soul's deep sorrow. It springs forth
like the direct fruit of these three days of suffering and
anguish. While it expresses the sorrow of Mary's heart, it
shows us even more deeply Mary's ardent love for her Son
and reveals somewhat the mystery of their intimacy which is
so strong. The intensity of sadness due to separation directly
depends on the intensity of love. Mary cannot tell us the
intensity of her love for Jesus; she cannot tell us the quality
of her love for Him. When we love with such intensity, we
keep silent. But once we have suddenly been freed from an
agonizing sadness, we can finally express how overcome we
were, and this reveals indirectly what is most intimate in our
hearts. In expressing how much we suffered, how broken our
hearts were, we show how much we love. Only a wounded
heart can show how much the heart loves.

Jesus does not give a direct response to His mother's
question, but rather questions her in turn and shows the intimate relationship of His life with the Father: "How is it that
you sought me? Did you not know that I must be in my
Father's house?"(Lk. 2:49). Jesus' first reply to Mary, the first
that the Holy Spirit has revealed to us, directly corresponds
to Mary's first question to Jesus. Now, His response is not the
usual reply a child gives his mother when she has shown him
all the sorrow he has just caused her and requests an explanation. His reply can only be a divine reply, that of the

Father's beloved Son who wants to instruct Mary. It is really the first teaching Jesus gives to His mother. After giving the teachers the first fruits of His teaching, He can then turn to His mother and authoritatively communicate to her God's Word, for her in particular. He had taught the teachers of the Law by questioning them. It is the only kind of teaching that teachers can receive. He teaches Mary directly, with authority. He knows she is capable of receiving from her twelve-year-old Son such clear and seemingly harsh words.

When Jesus says, "How is it that you sought me?" He is not reproaching His mother. Mary has done the right thing in making every effort to find Him for three days. She did what she had to do. But Jesus does not want her to stop at His visible presence with her. He wants to take her further in her contemplative life; He wants her faith to become even more pure. Indeed, for her faith, visible presence matters little, which explains why He really is addressing one who is blessed in her faith when He questions her instead of answering her: "How is it that you sought me?" Addressing in fact the Father's little child, He wants to reveal to her primarily the substantial bonds that exist between Him, the Son, and His Father: "Did you not know that I must be in my Father's house?" The Son, as Son, is necessarily entirely with the Father, and He cannot be anywhere else. For Him the only authority is the Father. "My food is to do the will of him who sent me, and to accomplish his work" (Jn. 4:34). He came for that purpose. This is why whatever the Father wills is really His good, His food.

"And they did not understand the saying which he spoke to them" (Lk. 2:50). Mary receives this first divine instruction in faith. She divinely adheres to it, but her maternal heart cannot understand it. "And his mother kept all these things in her heart" (Lk. 2:51). She keeps these words of her Son in her heart as God's Words for her, accepting the fact that she does not understand their full meaning. Mary's wholly divine attitude should not go unnoticed. She keeps God's Word in her heart. She keeps it as God's Word. So it really does not matter whether she understands it or not! She knows quite well that this is not what is essential. "To understand" or "not to understand" obviously completely modifies the psychological perspective and transforms the subject's behavior, while faith in its objective aspect goes beyond such a perspective and such behavior. Faith requires that God's Word be kept intact whether it is understood or not, whether it gives us joy and expands our hearts or whether it wounds and crushes us. We can never understand the sword that wounds. We can accept it and live by it, but we cannot understand what crushes us. To adhere only to what we understand reduces God's Word, in one way or another, to our human manner of knowing. In such a circumstance, the natural order would become the measure of the supernatural order.

Mary's faith is very pure, very divine; she keeps all the objective demands of the revealed mystery intact. She thus allows her soul to be, as it were, beyond the demands of her human intelligence.

"And he went down with them and came to Nazareth, and was obedient to them. . . . And Jesus increased in wisdom and in stature, and in favor with God and man" (Lk. 2:51-52). To obey His Father, Jesus had left His mother without saying anything and had remained in Jerusalem without her knowing about it. Again, to obey His Father, He goes back with Joseph and Mary as if nothing had happened. He returns to Nazareth and continues as a very obedient Son. He "was obedient to them."

Apparently life in Nazareth, this life of hidden work, will resume as before. But it will in reality blossom in a completely new way. For, to Mary and Joseph, Jesus is no longer merely the Child entrusted to their care and whom they must bring up, but also the Child who has revealed Himself with all His authority as the Father's Son. He is the One who has just revealed the true meaning of this family community, its true orientation, its proper principle: it must be totally occupied with the Father's affairs.

Jesus lives in this light; Mary receives this same order from Jesus and lives by it in her faith. And Joseph accepts it as well. This principle is really the charter of the Holy Family. It enables us to see that this community is the model of all industrious families that work out of love for God and out of fraternal love for their members. And this community is also the model of religious life, lived for the glory of the Father. Such a community remains a contemplative community in which each of its members are directly bound to God, to the Father, as one of His faithful servants receiving paternal instructions from Him. And for this very reason, within this close-knit community, there is a mystery of solitude which is even more radical and profound.

In light of the Child Jesus' words, we can easily grasp the difference that exists between the Christian community as such and the human community. The latter is entirely ordered to the immanent common good: friendship, *concor-*

dia among its members. Each person, as a member of a community, is ordered to the common good of the community. Of course we know that man can, through some of his activities, go beyond this finality and turn toward the absolute separate good. But then, to that same extent, he is also beyond the community and becomes a solitary. The members of the human community as such lead an active life; the contemplative, as a contemplative, is no longer a member of the human community. But, in some way, he finalizes it.

Based as it is on charity, the Christian community is both community and solitude, since the common good of this community can only be the whole Christ. The whole Christ is both God in His personal mystery and God communicating Himself to men to save them; He is the only Son and the Savior. These two aspects are inseparable and indivisible. This is why every Christian community implies a mystery of solitude, even amidst the very close and deep communal relationships of its members. Christian solitude is no longer the solitude of a philosopher who cuts himself off from the human community in order to better attain his separate end. Christian solitude is a mystery of solitude rooted in divine love. In order to live by that love, a Christian does not leave the Church—on the contrary: the more he lives in solitude, the more present he will be to the Christian community and the more he will be an essential and necessary member of this community. While outwardly, the hermit, the solitary, has to live far away from others, we should understand that he lives far away from the world yet in close communion with his brothers, carrying all of them in his love and enveloping them all, as it were, in his prayer.

Thus while these two elements of community and solitude exist in the Christian community, they are completely transposed and transformed. This transformation, far from abolishing their proper natures and turning them into a kind of mixture, enables the community to be, on the contrary, much more itself, and the solitude to be much more itself as well. There is no greater solitude than that of the Christian contemplative, since he lives the very mystery of divine solitude. No one is more a member of the community than he, since it is the same love that encloses him in God and gives him to his brother. The Christian community brings about the unity of life of its members, a unity analogous to that of the Holy Trinity: "that they may be one, even as we are one."

Life in Nazareth offers us the prototype of the Chris-tian community, and the mystery of the Finding in the Temple tells us its divine secret. In fact, in the liturgy for the feast of the Holy Family, the Church proposes the passage from St. Luke relating the mystery of the Finding in the Temple as the Gospel. At first glance, this choice may seem surprising. A mother who might have experienced an analogous event with one of her sons would not recall it as an event capable of showing us the perfection and holiness of her family. In fact, Jesus did not ask His parents' permission. He apparently disobeyed. We might even say that, humanly speaking, these three days spent away from His parents without permission seem very much like an attempt to run away. While it is true that afterwards He becomes the perfectly obedient Child once more, this event does not seem to show us the model behavior of a son toward his parents. According to the customs of our earthly families, we would take good care to forget such an episode, especially since everything was straightened out afterwards.

The Church and, before the Church, Mary, both under the inspiration of the Holy Spirit, think otherwise. They recall this episode from Jesus' childhood and keep it as a mysterious, extraordinary event that shines with singular radiance amidst the silence that envelops the rest of Jesus' hidden childhood. So we must be very attentive to what the Holy Spirit wants to teach us here.

First of all, He shows us that Jesus owed obedience, in the strictest sense, only to His Father. He owed obedience to His Mother and Joseph to the exact extent that it pleased His Father. Jesus was right in acting as He did. He did not disobey, since, on the contrary, He was obeying His Father. Jesus, as the Consecrated *par excellence* (through the mystery of the hypostatic union, He is the Father's Anointed), is essentially relative only to His Father, who alone has authority over Him. No man can have a natural authority over Him, no creature, not even His Mother. Jesus enjoys the supreme freedom of the Father's only Son with regard to all creation, since no creature can have any natural, proprietary right whatsoever over a divine person. Yet out of love for His Father, He freely submits to those that the Father proposes to Him.

Mary accepted this great poverty in her heart: the poverty of being a Mother without having any right over her Son. When the angel asked her to be the Mother of God, she spontaneously declared that she was the Lord's servant. This is why she does not rebuke her Son when she finds Him in the temple; she only conveys to Him her astonishment, her anguish, and her suffering.

Hence, this escape by the Child Jesus was a mystery of obedience to the Father. As He Himself explains to His mother, it was in order to be entirely absorbed in His Father's affairs, "to bear witness to the truth" before the teachers, before those whose specific duty was to seek the truth and who, for this very reason, were in some way entitled to be the first ones to receive it.

Thus this attitude of the Child Jesus shows us concretely, in particularly revealing circumstances, both His fundamental docility with regard to the Father and His freedom, His unflinching autonomy with regard to creatures, even with regard to His mother. He who submitted to the Law is above the Law, for He is God, the only Son of the Father. He respects the Law of Moses because He wants to teach us to respect it. This Law comes from His Father and if He sometimes seems to free Himself of it, it is to show us the relative character of the Law with respect to its end, which is the Father's will, the Father's love.[76] The purpose of the Law is to enable us to be entirely absorbed in the Father's affairs, to act with Him and according to His will. We always tend to materialize the Law, to make it a goal, an end, which is always contrary to love. In His first teaching to Mary, Jesus shows her the primacy of love.

As the Father's only Son, as His Messenger, Jesus not only teaches His mother in this mystery, but He also educates her, and He particularly educates divine poverty in her. He

---

76. When the Jews were scandalized by the cure of a paralytic on the Sabbath, Jesus affirmed: "My Father is working still, and I am working" (Jn. 5:1-18).

asks her in effect to exercise the poverty of her maternal heart
in a totally divine way. He wants her to be ever poorer in her
divine motherhood; so she must possess this poverty even as
the one who is supposed to be the educator. Outwardly she
must act toward Him like all other mothers who, after giving
birth to their children, must raise and educate them and give
them something of their own heart and intelligence. Inwardly
however, Mary must be a mother who is totally poor in her
educational activity. Jesus possesses all the virtues that Mary
could impart to Him. He possesses in His heart all the treasures of love that she could transmit to Him. He even possesses them in a more perfect way. However, the Father wants
her to keep her place near His beloved Son; He wants her to
be there, exercising her educational motherhood toward her
Child, appointed as it were by Him. He wants her to exercise
it fully and more perfectly than any other mother, knowing
in her heart that she is only an instrument, that she cannot
do anything on her own.

Whereas poverty in motherhood is liberating and joyful, poverty in maternal education, while remaining liberating and joyful, already implies certain separations that are
sorrowful and painful. This mystery shows this quite
clearly: Mary accepts without understanding, like a true,
poor servant. She accepts first with anguish, then with joy,
but still without understanding. When divine poverty takes
hold of our works of spiritual mercy, as is the case here with
maternal education, it requires holy ignorance. It requires
that we exercise mercy as a useless servant, without being
concerned with the results that can be obtained but considering only the Father's will. This is what Jesus teaches His

mother, and He wants her to live the beatitude of "the poor in spirit."

Jesus acts this way in this mystery precisely because He is prompted by the Holy Spirit with a view to accomplishing what He is sent to do: to bear witness to the truth and to be occupied with the Father's affairs. He bears witness to the truth before the teachers, the rabbis, in Israel first, to explain Scripture to them in a divine way; then before Mary and Joseph by explaining His mission to them. It is the first time that Mary is confronted with Jesus as Priest. It is the first time that Our Lord speaks to His mother with authority, using divine words which are like a sword to her maternal heart. It is the first intimate fulfillment of Simeon's prophecy in Mary's heart.

Let us understand how God, in His wisdom, wanted this teaching to be completely fruitful. He prepared Mary's heart in a very special way, with three days of separation and anguish. These three days plowed Mary's heart, so to speak; they made it extremely sensitive. Anguish, sadness, then the great joy of seeing Him again, placed Mary's loving heart in a unique disposition, which makes it particularly vulnerable. It is at this precise moment that Jesus addresses to her these first words, so mysterious and hard, which wound her maternal heart that yearns for a gesture of tenderness and understanding. These words must have completely taken hold of Mary's heart, bruising and expanding it, turning it toward the Father, ridding it at once of all the anguish and anxiety, to consider only the Father's affairs, His paternal will. There is something extraordinary about this, for it shows us how Jesus could rely on His mother's fidelity, how He could trust her, knowing that she would be strong enough to accept everything with love.

Through this teaching, Mary's heart knows new divine demands. Thus this mystery takes us more deeply into the mystery of the Holy Family. It gives us, moreover, the bright light which will help us understand it. This family is divine; all its members must be directly bound to God, and this bond is made through Christ, through Christ's priesthood, through His priestly action. It is in Him and through Him that Mary belongs totally to the Father.

That is why this true family community implies Christian solitude. Christ is more given to Mary than before, for He is given to her not only as a Son, but also as a Priest, with His intimate and divine secret, with His relationship with the Father. Precisely because Mary is poorer, she can receive Jesus in a more divine and absolute way. The presence is therefore greater, and the joy as well. Moreover, this presence is lived with sharper awareness and in a more divine and poor way. For the momentary separation from Jesus gave Mary a more accurate notion of the value of this divine presence; she realized how much it is the food and meaning of her life. This separation made her realize more clearly that this presence was a free gift, a pure grace that God could hold back and remove when and how He wanted. From then on Mary lives by it far more intensely, with even more loving attention. This momentary trial was willed by God so that Mary might live even more deeply by the wonderful gift He was granting her, so that she might become more sharply aware of it. This is what God often does in our lives: He momentarily deprives us of a particular favor, a particular privilege, so that we may more thoroughly understand its value and so that our gratitude may be more manifest when He gives this same favor back to us.

So this trial was willed by God so that the teachers might receive Christ's visit and benefit from His teaching. This is yet another general law of His governance. He asks for certain mortifications from the souls He loves, periods full of divine sadness, periods of dryness in prayer, in order to merit for others visits from Christ, moments when He passes by. That is why, when we experience such separations—if our conscience does not accuse us of any infidelity, any lack of fervor, any lukewarmness—we must not worry about it but must make every effort to find Him anew. We should not immediately think that God acts in this way to punish or chastise us. Sometimes it is only to purify us and take us further in His love and intimacy; sometimes it is to prepare us for a more divine teaching; sometimes it is so that we may merit graces of intimacy for others.

These sorrowful separations must not deprive us of our objective attitude. Like Mary, we must keep our eyes on Him alone. We must above all avoid dwelling on our sadness, considering it in all its aspects and relishing it. As Blessed Louis de Grenade says:

> After the Holy Virgin's sorrow, consider the diligence with which this tender mother set out to look for the jewel she had lost and to inquire everywhere. The evangelist tells us that she looked for Him particularly among her relatives and friends and did not find Him. Nor will you find Christ in the affections and pleasures of the flesh and blood, but in mortification and in renouncing all such

pleasures. "Whom will He [the Lord] teach knowledge," exclaims the prophet Isaiah, "and to whom will he explain the message? Those who are weaned from the milk, those taken from the breast" (Is 28:9).[77]

Sadness that is divinely accepted must implant charity into our soul and thereby deepen it, making it more virile. But this divine virility—which excludes any infantile behavior, any human indulgence, any psychological childishness which prevents us from acquiring true autonomy—must not be confused with psychological virility. Divine virility implies divine littleness, divine poverty, a spirit of radical dependence upon the Father's will. To be an adult in the divine life implies a perfectly accepted and fully lived divine littleness, whereas adulthood on a psychological level means being weaned from maternal milk and everything related to it. This distinction is essential; otherwise, like Nicodemus, we would not be able to grasp the divine meaning of this divine birth according to "water and the Spirit," a birth which keeps recurring more and more profoundly. We would no longer agree to return to the maternal womb, the womb of Mary and the womb of the Church. On the pretext of virility and full awareness of our rights, we would refuse this new birth, this state of evangelical littleness, this dependence upon the Mother who is given to us.

---

77. Louis de Grenade, *op. cit.*, p. 311.

CHAPTER 10

LIFE IN NAZARETH: MARY'S CHARITY IN WORK

S T. LUKE tells us: "When they had performed everything according to the law of the Lord, they returned into Galilee, to their own city, Nazareth" (Lk. 2:39). And St. Matthew affirms as well: "Being warned in a dream he [Joseph] withdrew to the district of Galilee. And he went and dwelt in a city called Nazareth, that what was spoken by the prophets might be fulfilled, 'He shall be called a Nazarene' " (Mt. 2:22-23). Without considering the differences between St. Luke's and St. Matthew's narratives or the reasons for these differences, we will simply focus here on the fact affirmed by both evangelists: the communal life lived by Jesus, Mary and Joseph at Nazareth in the family household.

We have here the first part of what we call Jesus' "hidden" life. There is nothing extraordinary in the eyes of men about this simple, industrious life; yet it is so rich and so full in the eyes of God because everything is ordered to the accomplishment of the divine will, down to the slightest details of everyday life. We are presented here with the model of Christian life, industrious, generous, simple and loving, taking place in the most intimate environment possible, the family environment. Christian grace and charity are then manifested to us as capable of assuming all the demands of this communal family life, of inwardly transforming them, of giving them divine, meritorious value and thus of enabling them to become food for the growth of love.

It is not the intrinsic value of our activities that gives them their divine value, but the supernatural love with which we perform them. Such is the difference in value judgments made by a philosopher and a Christian concerning our human activities: the former judges our activities according to their intrinsic and objective nobility. He has his scale of values for human activities in accordance with his conception of human nature. A Christian, as a child of God moved by the Holy Spirit, judges the value of his human activities according to their conformity with the divine will and their conformity to the degree of love that prompts him. The merit of an action is not directly derived from the difficulty we had in performing it or from the more or less important value of that action, but from the love and the intensity of love we put into it.

This first period of Mary's hidden life with Jesus presents us with that mystery of divine love which seems sometimes— and often in fact during the long periods of formation—to prefer expression in very small gestures, in very ordinary, even very banal, activities. Nothing is more ordinary than the activity of a good mother raising and taking care of her son, doing the cooking for all the members of the household and taking great care to make her household joyful, attractive and pleasant. Divine love, and especially Christian love, truly likes to hide in order to be more pure and to rule more completely. When love inspires heroic human actions—very beautiful, grand actions—it can seldom take hold of everything and assume everything. It must often accept compromises with human glory and honor. Love can be altogether pure when it inspires very humble and very hidden human gestures. Human activity can then very easily be merely a "sign," a testimony of love, drawing all its significance, all its proper value, from divine love. It can then be clothed solely in an intense love of God.

This explains why divine wisdom—after the great events of the Nativity, the adoration of the shepherds and the Magi, the Purification, and the exodus and life in Egypt—reserved for Mary this quieter, simpler, more hidden period in her life. It was not that Mary needed rest and relaxation; it was to enable her to love in a purer and more intense way, and to ensure that everything in her was really prompted inwardly by love.

It is in this light that we must understand how Christian charity requires, here below, not only a blossoming within abandonment in contemplative life, in a life of fraternal charity and mercy, and in liturgical life, but also a transfiguration of work, in the very simple life of one who must work by the sweat of his brow to earn his daily bread. Charity then takes hold of this state proper to man, a social animal involved in a community, using his practical intelligence and all his energy to preserve and develop his life and the lives of those whom Providence has entrusted to him. In such a case, charity is more than ever the leaven that causes the dough to rise.

For without it human work, which became difficult, humiliating and truly punitive due to sin, always runs the risk of being rejected as an evil that we cannot accept, as a burden that is too heavy, that we can only carry while grumbling and with a desire to be rid of it as quickly as possible, by any conceivable means. Then work is no longer part of our authentic human life, and we come to consider it as an enemy that bullies us and does violence to us, that bruises and chokes us, and which we are allowed to evade and cast off as completely as possible. Such is one of the excesses to which we are almost inevitably driven when human work is considered solely as a punishment due to sin.

We must point out another excess, however, which is diametrically opposed to this one but has the same results practically. This excess no longer stems from the austere, tedious character of work but from its profound connaturality with our human nature. Considered in itself, purely as a means of acquiring wealth, as a mere sign of social and political domination, work and technology always run the risk of monopolizing all our human powers, faculties and horizons, to such an extent that we become enslaved by this type of work. Instead of using work as a means of livelihood, man is dominated and tyrannized by his work. After allowing himself to be trapped by this brutal and inhuman tyranny, he will often be ready to accept anything to escape and be freed from this work.

The only way to humanize work is to transform it by charity into something punitive that chastises man, of course, but one that also purifies him by becoming a means of being both more human—for all work demands a constant struggle and effort—and more a son of God, by requiring from him a more pure and generous love capable of bearing punishment with joy and of offering it.

It should be pointed out that this transformation of work by charity should be considered as something completely different from the transformation brought about in the virtue of religion. Actually, we must be aware that the exercise of the virtue of religion will remain in heaven, while the exercise of work will not, since it is essentially earthly. Religion is not punitive but rather is based on the demands of human nature as such. Work, with its characteristic of arduous labor, is punitive, a consequence of original sin based on human nature found in the particular conditions that were imposed here below after the initial fall. The exercise of the virtue of religion is totally and intrinsically transformed by charity in such a way that this exercise truly possesses a new form and structure. Work can only receive a new and extrinsic motivation from charity: work is done out of love for God, to manifest to Him our dependence on Him and to eradicate our pride. The essential nature of work cannot be changed, however. It remains what it is. While special techniques can help to improve work, it retains its proper demands. For although work belongs to the moral sphere as regards its usage, in and of itself it belongs to the sphere of the *factibile,* of what man "makes." Now the *factibile* cannot be directly transformed by charity, for it only concerns a particular end, the useful good or the beauty of a work, which belongs to the sphere of the exemplary cause. The *factibile* thus has no direct connection with the ultimate end. Only in its exercise, in its usage, will it be possible to connect it with the ultimate end, and this not by virtue of the finished product as the end of work, but by virtue of the end of the one who is working.

The mystery of the hidden life, from the return from Egypt to the Finding in the Temple, is a model of the humble and simple sanctification of the manual work of Mary, as mistress of the household in Nazareth. Scripture gives us no details concerning this period whose predominant characteristic is to be hidden and to live according to the common law of mankind. It simply states: "And the child grew and became strong, filled with wisdom; and the favor of God was upon him. Now his parents went to Jerusalem every year at the feast of the Passover" (Lk. 2:40-41).

It is this progress of the Child-God—physical progress ("he grew and became strong") and moral and spiritual progress as regards experience and manifestation—that the Holy Spirit wanted to point out so as to bring it into full light. In correlation to Jesus' physical and experiential progress, there occurs in Mary's heart a wonderful ascent in love. The very hidden work previously mentioned, which is totally directed toward God and totally at the service of fraternal charity, is as it were the daily food that enables this ascent in charity to be realized in such a divine and simple, but also steady, way. While, on the one hand, charity transforms work by ordering it to God and neighbor, thus giving it a new meaning, work accepted out of love is, on the other hand, a sort of fuel which keeps the divine fire of love burning. It offers love some human penal matter to be burned, to enable this fire to be ever purer and brighter in the sight of God, yet ever more hidden, as though covered in ashes, in the sight of men.

It is in this light that we should understand how charity transforms all the tedious labor connected with the duties of our state of life, and how this labor enables our divine life to remain more hidden and pure, clothing it in the "ashes" of punishment due to sin. God likes to plunge the souls he loves into the common and banal duties of mankind for a long time, so that they may progress and become stronger in their humble love, so that the grace of God may penetrate them more and more deeply.

This entire period remains a mystery of joy. Jesus is present. No matter how tedious and difficult, labor becomes joyful and a source of joy if Jesus is there and the work is done for Him. For human labor keeps the family community closely united and enables it to experience a new intimacy, that of common work accomplished together with a view to reaching the same goal. And in this way, it is really a source of joy and blossoming in fraternal charity.

After the mystery of the Finding in the Temple, the Gospel states: "He went down with them and came to Nazareth, and was obedient to them; and his mother kept all these things in her heart. And Jesus increased in wisdom and in stature, and in favor with God and man" (Lk. 2:51-52). Apparently nothing has changed. This second period of the life in Nazareth is a continuation of the first. Christ continues to progress in physical and spiritual growth, as does Mary in her life of charity and work. However, we must not forget what we pointed out concerning the mystery of the Finding in the Temple. After the mystery of the Finding, Mary outwardly resumes the same life, yet deep within there is something new. Christ's words are a loving light for her which shows her how to live this communal life in an ever more contemplative way. She must become increasingly poorer, increasingly surrendered solely to the Father's will. By His sole concern to accomplish God's will, Jesus teaches her how to surrender more and more to this holy will; He teaches her the divine way to bring an increasingly deep peace to her heart. Her heart had already experienced how piercing and sharp the sword of the divine Word was and how it could bring about a cruel and divine separation. In this experience that remains present, Mary realizes in her faith even more clearly the absolute demands of the Father's will. Nothing whatsoever is stable, fixed or certain for her apart from the constant conformity of each moment to this will alone, since everything may be taken from her at any moment according to the Father's will and pleasure. In such poor abandonment, so "impoverishing" for her maternal heart, she must continue doing everything as though all were stable and certain. She must do everything with all the more care and generosity, since everything is done as though it were the last time and as though Jesus were to disappear again and be taken away from her. Such are the characteristics of this second period in Nazareth, which is very similar to the first and yet requires an even poorer abandonment, an even more selfless fraternal charity, an ever impoverished labor of a useless servant, an even more demanding contemplative solitude. The more Jesus grows up, the more Mary disappears in this self-efface-ment, this very poor surrender, so as to make way entirely for Jesus. John the Baptist's attitude with respect to Jesus is even more true for Mary: "He must increase, but I must decrease" (Jn. 3:30). Joseph's very death enables Jesus to be more fully

Mary's sole support, the sole authority given to her by the Father. Accordingly, after Joseph's death, Nazareth is more and more the Father's house, a house of silence and solitude, a house of contemplative life entirely reserved for the Father, hidden in the very humble daily work of poor servants. In this family milieu which is so poor and so consecrated to the Father, all the gestures, actions, words and silence of Jesus are reserved for Mary and belong to her. These really make up the sole nourishment given to her by the Father. The more she accepts being nothing, recognizing the Father's sovereign rights over Jesus and herself, the more Jesus is given to her and the more Jesus is present.

PART 4

THE MYSTERIES OF SORROW:
ROOTING OF MARY'S CHARITY

CHAPTER 11

THE WEDDING AT CANA: MARY'S COOPERATION IN JESUS' APOSTOLIC LIFE

SCRIPTURE tells us nothing about Joseph's death. No one knows when and how he died. But he most certainly died before Jesus and Mary. Only Mary is invited at Cana. She will also be alone at the Cross.

Following Joseph's death, Jesus would become the head of the family. He is the breadwinner; and, as priest, He has authority regarding not only the external forum but also the internal forum. The intimacy between Mary and Jesus at Nazareth becomes even stronger; it becomes very simple and divine, since Jesus holds full authority with respect to Mary. Now Mary only needs to love and to obey with filial devotion. The Christian community is thus a contemplative community, very silent and very hidden by the humble task of earning a living. This contemplative life—in which Mary is at the school of Jesus—unfolds within the framework of a close-knit human community, held by the bonds between a beloved mother and her beloved son.

In order to be fully receptive to her Son's teaching, Mary had to live alone with Him as a mother, as a disciple, as a "little child." This long, silent, recollected, joyful and peaceful preparation was necessary to enable the sorrowful mysteries to take place with all their bloody brutality. It is like a long advent which prepares her for the supreme and sorrowful gift.

The Cana wedding feast to which Mary is invited actually constitutes a sort of transition between the joyful mysteries and sorrowful mysteries.

> On the third day there was a marriage at Cana in Galilee, and the mother of Jesus was there; Jesus also was invited to the marriage, with his disciples. When the wine failed, the mother of Jesus said to him, "They have no wine." And Jesus said to her, "O woman, what have you to do with me? My hour has not yet come." His mother said to the servants, "Do whatever he tells you." Now six stone jars were standing there, for the Jewish rites of purification, each holding twenty or thirty gallons. Jesus said to them, "Fill the jars with water." And they filled them up to the brim. He said to them, "Now draw some out and take it to the steward of the feast." So they took it. When the steward of the feast tasted the water now become wine, and did not know where it came from (though the servants who had drawn the water knew), the steward of the feast called the bridegroom and said to him, "Every man

serves the good wine first; and when men
have drunk freely, then the poor wine; but
you have the kept the good wine until now."
This, the first of his signs, Jesus did at Cana in
Galilee, and manifested his glory; and his disciples believed in Him (Jn. 2:1-11).

Jesus' apostolic life, inaugurated by the baptism in the
Jordan, the forerunner's official testimony and the choice of
His disciples, is about to begin. The Cana wedding feast to
which Jesus is invited with His disciples and His mother will
provide the opportunity for His first miraculous sign, hence
for the first public manifestation of His divine power.

The amount of wine planned for the feast was in fact
insufficient. In the motherly mercy of her heart, Mary notices
the steward's embarrassment. She then says to her Son: "They
have no more wine." She addresses Him with a tone of
maternal pleading in her voice, to show Him the difficulty
of these good people and induce Him to intervene on their
behalf, if such is His and the Father's good pleasure.

According to St. John's Gospel, this is Mary's first
request to her Son, the first that the Holy Spirit willed to
communicate to us. If we combine John and Luke, we must
understand this request as Mary's second intervention with
her Son. Jesus no longer responds as a submissive and docile
Son, but in a mysterious way: "O Woman, what have you to
do with me? My hour has not yet come."[78]

---

78. Cf. St. Augustine: *Tractates on the Gospel of John,* VIII: "It is because of
an indubitable mystery that He appears not to acknowledge His mother,

In his book entitled *Mother of God's People,* Father Braun remarks:

> Some commentators have tried to take the sharpness out of this remark. According to them there is no question of a refusal in this answer. They concede that the term "woman" is a little solemn, but not so solemn as to prevent a young Jew from using it when

from whom as the Bridegroom He came forth, when He says to her, 'Woman, what have I to do with thee? Mine hour is not yet come.' What is this? Did He come to the marriage for the purpose of teaching men to treat their mothers with contempt? (. . .) Beyond all doubt, brethren, there is some mystery lurking here. (. . .)

"Our Lord Jesus Christ was both God and man. According as He was God, he had not a mother; according as He was man, He had. She was the mother, then, of His flesh, of His humanity, of the weakness which for our sakes He took upon Him. But the miracle which He was about to do, He was about to do according to His divine nature, not according to His weakness; according to that wherein He was God, not according to that wherein He was born weak. But the weakness of God is stronger than men. His mother then demanded a miracle of Him; but He, about to perform divine works, so far did not recognize a human womb; saying in effect, 'That in me which works a miracle was not born of thee, thou gavest not birth to my divine nature; but because my weakness was born of thee, I will recognize thee at the time when that same weakness shall hang upon the cross.' This, indeed, is the meaning of 'Mine hour is not yet come.' (. . .) Now as she was not the mother of His divine nature, whilst it was by His divinity the miracle she asked for would be wrought, therefore He answered her, 'Woman, what have I to do with thee?' 'But think not that I deny thee to be my mother: Mine hour is not yet come; for in that hour I will acknowledge thee, when the weakness of which thou art the mother comes to hang on the cross' " (*Nicene and Post-Nicene Fathers,* First Series, Vol. 7 (Peabody, MA: Hendrickson Publishers, 1995 (Second Printing), §5, p. 58-59; §9, p. 61). See also F. M. Braun, *Mother of God's People,* trans. John Clarke (Staten Island, NY: Alba House, 1967) p. 53).

addressing his mother. To prove this, they point out that Jesus on the point of death speaks in the same way to His Mother. The expression: *ti emoi kai soi* (literally, "what is there between me and thee?") is interpreted: "Let me do it." As for the "hour" of Jesus, this is the time fixed for the working of miracles. Presented with such light nuances these explanations do not hold up under critical analysis.[79]

Without dwelling here on all the discussions concerning scientific exegesis, we shall simply mention Father Braun's conclusion, which helps us enter more deeply into the meaning of this mystery:

Christ's answer rings out clearly. It meant: "What is there between us at this moment that you ask me to intervene?" Though softened, perhaps, by the tone of His voice, it was still a refusal. . . .

The public life of Jesus had begun during which He is to be totally subject to His Father's will. Mary is invited to withdraw. Jesus makes her understand that the ties of blood, close as they are, are for the time being suspended.[80]

---

79. *Ibid.*, p. 49-50.

80. *Ibid.*, p. 58.

The attitude of Jesus here toward His Mother is thus quite similar to His attitude at the Finding in the Temple, but the outward circumstances are different. The scene is in Galilee at a wedding feast. Jesus is no longer a twelve-year-old Child but an apostle beginning His mission. Mary's request no longer concerns Jesus' personal behavior toward her but is simply meant to call Jesus' attention to a humanly delicate and difficult situation. It is a plea from Mary on behalf of those who are in a predicament, a very human predicament!

After Christ's words at the Finding in the Temple, Jesus is given back to her. He returns to Nazareth with her and is obedient to her; whereas after this episode, after this injunction from Christ, Mary will disappear, so to speak. She will hide in a new solitude; she will no longer be mentioned, except to affirm the fact that the bonds uniting her to Christ are primarily divine. The Synoptic Gospels actually report this fact at the beginning of Christ's apostolic life. No sooner have they returned to Nazareth than the crowd pressing around Him announce to Him: "Your mother and your brethren are outside, asking for you. Jesus replies at once: 'Who are my mother and my brethren?' And looking around on those who sat about him, he said, 'Here are my mother and my brethren! Whoever does the will of God is my brother, and sister and mother.' "[81] And this passage from St. Luke: "A woman in the crowd raised her voice and said to him, 'Blessed is the womb that bore you, and the breasts that you sucked!' But he said, 'Blessed rather are those who hear the

---

81. Mk. 3:31-35. Cf. Mt. 12:46-50; Lk. 8:19-21.

word of God and keep it!' "[82] He proclaims the absolute superiority of the spiritual bond established by faith in God's Word and by faithful obedience to it.

The Finding in the Temple was only a trial so that Mary might live in greater poverty and enjoy in a more divine way the physical presence of Jesus given to her. At Cana, however, it is no longer merely a question of a temporary trial but of a new stage which Jesus asks her to enter, a stage of separation which will end at the Cross and the Sepulcher.

This stage will last throughout Christ's apostolic life until the coming of His Hour. "My hour has not yet come": this reference to the Passion manifests both an ending to the separation and an ending to Christ's apostolic life; and it also indicates that, when the hour has come, Mary will have to be present again. This further clarifies Simeon's prophecy. The Son's Hour will be that of the Mother's. Both will be united in a very special way at that moment. Their intimacy will experience something entirely new, and Mary will then be fully entitled to ask Him for whatever she wants; she will be able to present to Him all the needs and misfortunes of mankind.

As at the Finding, and even more profoundly than at the Finding, Mary must accept to be separated from Him, so that, as the Good Shepherd, He may be able to seek out the lost sheep. She must accept a physical absence so that Jesus may teach, no longer the rabbis, but rather the twelve Apostles,

---

82. Lk. 11:27-28. Cf. Cajetan's *Commentaries:* "He does not really deny what was said . . . but affirming it, He adds the formal common reason of beatitude."

and converse with the rabbis. Mary accepts all the sufferings brought about by this separation for the sake of Christ's apostolic work. As a Virgin, she follows the Lamb wherever He goes, spiritually and divinely, yet she accepts all the separations willed by Him, as He wills them.

That is why the silent and loving acceptance of these separations is meritorious and efficacious for us. In a certain way, it enables Mary to already play her role as Advocate and Mediatrix. When, in the purest and most absolute poverty, Mary relinquishes her intercession for these good people, she merits for them Christ's miraculous action.

In the mystery of the Finding, without understanding and without asking for an explanation, Mary in fact keeps silent after Christ's response because she alone was concerned, together with Joseph. In that case it was more perfect to keep silent and to believe. Here she is no longer the only one involved. Thus, accepting in her heart the words that separate her from Christ, accepting them with love, she wants to live entirely by this new order; she wants to hide and remain silent. But as this silence is a silence of love, full of trust in Jesus' infinite mercy and love, instead of humanly turning to the servants and telling them somewhat sadly and bitterly as we do when our request has not been granted, "I am sorry, but He does not want to do anything; His Hour has not yet come, so there's nothing I can do for you," Mary says to them, "Do whatever he tells you." She immediately obeys Jesus; she gives up all her desires for intervening or altering her Son's plans. But this renunciation is the fruit of love and thus is fecund. She wants to help them understand how good it is to surrender totally to Him; she communicates to them what she is living at that moment. She wants this total submission to His will, which is her true joy, to be their joy as well. It is the best thing that she can give them. She began by interceding for material goods, the wine that she could not give them. Jesus' refusal obliges her to communicate to them the only thing she has and which to her is more than everything else: this boundless docility to His gracious will. In this way, she puts these good people directly in contact with Jesus. By withdrawing and stepping aside, she will push them forward so that they too may obey whatever He tells them to do.

Here Mary teaches us the completely divine attitude we must take in prayer of petition. She shows us the divine boldness we must have to "knock at the door," an even greater boldness due to the fact that prayer is a form of mercy, the highest and most efficacious form of mercy that we are to exercise toward our neighbor when he needs it. Mary takes these good people's interests in hand; she suddenly considers their trouble as her own. In her heart, she takes their embarrassment upon herself with motherly mercy, without intending to pass judgment on it. Mary could have made them realize that the shortage of wine did not matter. Was the problem not merely about a surplus of temporal goods? Such goods were nothing as compared to the divine and infinitely superior good that they possessed in Jesus' presence. As a mother, Mary marvelously adapts to the feelings of those she loves and whom she wishes to lead to her Son. Experiencing their embarrassment and experiencing it more intensely than they do, she no longer hesitates, and she points it out to Jesus with complete confidence, however extraordinary her request may appear. Her confidence is in no way diminished by the unexpected answer she receives.

We comprehend here the divine transformation of the virtue of religion through charity and the divine mode of exercising it under the influence of the gift of piety. The request assumes a note of familiarity, of confidence, of totally divine simplicity; and, for this very reason, it can extend to very human realities which concern all those whom the Lord puts on our path as our neighbor. The gift of piety must enable us to act toward Jesus as Mary does. We can ask for anything if we really remain in a spirit of complete filial confidence and abandonment; precisely in the sense that, if Christ does not respond to our call, if He even seems to be uninterested, if He seems to keep at a distance and turn away, we must nevertheless have confidence and lovingly accept these silences, these rejections, this separation, and not interpret them in a human way or lose confidence. Christ is Love; everything we ask Him to do interests Him: "Not one hair of your head shall fall . . ." We must have this complete confidence and do everything as He wills it; we must remain attentive to whatever He wills.

Mary's confidence and loving obedience touch Jesus' heart, so much so that He answers her prayer beyond what she requested. For her, Jesus anticipates and advances His divine action; because of her, He works His first miracle.

Many have wondered in fact whether it would have been possible to obtain the wine required for the wedding feast by natural means. It seems that it would have been possible. In any case, the magnitude of the miracle is quite clearly disproportionate with Mary's original request. Not only is there plenty of wine, but people also marvel at its quality, which is understandable since this miraculous wine is the direct fruit of God's omnipotence. St. Augustine notes that what God brings about directly by Himself must not be inferior to what nature brings about, since God is the author of this nature. The striking magnitude of the miracle is intentional. It manifested the glory of Jesus; it was His first miracle. Simeon had predicted to Mary that Jesus would be the "glory" of His people. It was normal that Mary should have the first fruits of this glory, since she was to be so closely united to His Passion.

By manifesting His glory to her, Jesus glorified her as well through this miracle, accomplished for her and because of her. He was truly the glory of Israel, thus the glory of Mary. Through this miracle, Mary understood more clearly all the greatness of her Son and how much God's omnipotence dwelt in Him. She had believed in it ever since the angel's words, but now she herself was a witness of this almighty power. It is her Tabor, the manifestation of Jesus' glory. It consisted of only one stage in Jesus' life, the stage that was reserved for her, the stage during which He had wanted to lead the daily life of mankind in its fullness and during which she had to exercise fully her motherhood by remaining so close, so intimately united to her beloved Son. But that stage was coming to an end. Now a new phase in His life was going to begin, during which He would have to be the faithful witness of the Father's love, during which He would have to manifest His glory, to teach and form His disciples, to struggle against all those who refuse to follow Him. He will be "a sign that is spoken against." The prophecy will be fulfilled in its entirety. During this period, Mary must keep silent, remain hidden and carry in her heart all these struggles and all this glory. She must accept being the hidden Mother of Him who is treated as a madman and of Him who is exalted. She must accept being separated from Him and agree to let Him act according to the very demands of His mission, because this full, loving acceptance is fruitful, more fruitful than any outward activity.

With the mystery of the wedding at Cana, Jesus asks Mary to renounce all human activity, however noble and great, and to abdicate her role as His Mother at His side, in order to live solely a hidden, contemplative life, the life of the Mother of the Apostle and Good Shepherd. Jesus asks her to believe that this hidden contemplative life will be even more fruitful than the very exercise of her physical motherhood toward Him, and even more loving than the holy and perfect communal life that she had experienced with Him. In her faith and love, Mary must receive this new divine teaching, which shows her that loving acceptance of these separations enables her to cooperate divinely in Jesus' apostolic life and hence to know an even deeper and more complete intimacy with Him. Cooperation in a friend's profound work means being conformed to his will and living in union with his heart. The more perfect this cooperation is, i.e., the more it comes under the realm of spiritual complementarity, the more faithful an attitude it requires; thus the unity that it brings about can be perfect. Nothing is more complementary to Christ's apostolic life than the solitary, contemplative silence of Mary. The very symbolism of this miracle shows this. For we must not forget that, like almost all the miracles reported by St. John, it has a spiritual meaning; it is a divine sign. Mary's first activity, her activity as Jesus' Mother, was to be transformed into this new divine activity as Mother of the souls that Christ was coming to save. It is the transformation of water into wine.[83]

---

83. St. Augustine, speaking of the water of the first jar, the one that for him symbolizes the first age, that of Adam and Eve, recalls the symbolism of the Apostle (Eph. 5:31): " 'Therefore shall a man leave his father and mother, and cleave to his wife; and they two shall be one flesh' (Gen. 2:24)." Now, if Christ cleave to the Church, so that the two should be one flesh, in what manner did He leave His Father and His mother? He left His Father in this sense, that when He was in the form of God, He thought it not robbery to be equal with God, but empties Himself, taking to Him the form of a servant. In this sense He left His father, not that He forsook or departed from his Father, but that He did not appear unto men in that form in which He was equal with the Father. But how did He leave His mother? By leaving the synagogue of the Jews, of which, after the flesh, He was born, and by cleaving to the Church which He has gathered out of all nations. Thus the first water-pot then held a prophecy of Christ. . . . (§10, p. 66).

We could speak of Mary instead of the synagogue and the separation at the Cana wedding feast would be all the more clear.

This symbolism, which primarily concerns Mary, concerns the whole Church as well. The water contained in the stone jars set out for the Jewish rites of purification would signify the old regime of the Law. This legal regime is over; it is to be transformed into a more divine regime: the "new wine" of the Gospel, the regime of love and the Spirit. This is the explanation given to us by St. Augustine concerning the mysteries hidden in this miracle:

"In the ancient times there was prophecy, and no times were left without the dispensation of prophecy. But the prophecy, since Christ was not understood therein, was water. For in water wine is in some manner latent. The apostle tells us what we are to understand by this water: 'Even unto this day,' saith he, 'whilst Moses is read, that same veil is upon their heart; that it is not unveiled because it is done away in Christ. And when thou shalt have passed over,' saith he, 'to the Lord, the veil shall be taken away' (2 Cor 3:14-16). By the veil he means the

Not only is Mary the first beneficiary of this work of divine transformation, of transubstantiation, but she also cooperates in this work in a very special way by interceding in a very poor fashion, i.e., by accepting the rejection her intercession meets, by agreeing to do nothing and leave all the glory to Jesus. She intercedes as a useless servant, all the more confidently and boldly since she lovingly accepts this uselessness so as to completely make way for Jesus. This intercession has a divine efficacy: Jesus acts at once with divine omnipotence to achieve more than Mary, with all the boldness of being just a poor servant, would have dared suggest to Him.

The proper and intimate fruit of this first miracle, in which Mary cooperates in such an unobtrusive way and

covering over of prophecy, so that it was not understood. When thou hast passed over to the Lord, the veil is taken away; so likewise is tastelessness taken away when thou hast passed over to the Lord; and what was water now becomes wine to thee. Read all the prophetic books; and if Christ be not understood therein, what canst thou find so insipid and silly? Understand Christ in them, and what thou readest not only has a taste, but even inebriates thee; transporting the mind from the body, so that forgetting the things that are past, thou reachest forth to the things that are before (Phil. 3:13)" (*ibid.*, §3, pp. 63-64).

Speaking of the disciples of Emmaus, St. Augustine writes: "[T]he disciples were called irrational by the Lord, because as yet they [the Old Scriptures] tasted to them as water, not as wine. And how did He make of the water wine? When He opened their understanding, and expounded to them the Scriptures, beginning from Moses, through all the prophets; with which being now inebriated, they said, 'Did not our hearts burn within us in the way, when he opened to us the Scriptures?' For they understood Christ in those books in which they knew Him not before. Thus our Lord Jesus Christ changed the water into wine, and that has now taste which before had not, that now inebriates which before did not" (*ibid.*, §5, p. 64).

which manifests Jesus' glory to His disciples, is the disciples' faith in Christ. The disciples already believed, of course; otherwise they would not have been "disciples," but they needed to believe in Him in a more divine way.

This miracle is thus intended and ordered by God to manifest the glory of Christ by divinely granting His Mother's request because of her perfect obedience to His will and because of her very humble prayer as a useless servant. The miracle is also meant to increase faith in the disciples' hearts. It is Jesus' second epiphany as it were. The one that occurred at His baptism, through the dove and the mysterious voice, manifested His divine sonship: "Thou art my beloved Son; with thee I am well pleased" (Lk. 3:22). The one at Cana manifests His divine mission, His omnipotence, and the mysterious bond uniting Him to Mary, or rather uniting Mary to His mission. When it comes to the manifestation of His capacity as the Son of God, Mary does not intervene; when it concerns the manifestation of His sorrowful mission, of His Hour, Mary cooperates in her own way.

We can also note with St. Thomas[84] this mystical interpretation of the wedding at Cana, which signifies the spiritual and divine wedding of our souls with Christ. Mary is invited to this wedding; she is present and she has a part to play as *conciliatrix nuptiarum* because it is through her intercession that our souls are united to Christ through grace.

Thus with the wedding at Cana we come to an even more mysterious and divine aspect of Mary's life. It is really a sort of annunciation of the sorrowful mysteries, an annunciation

---

84. Cf. St. Thomas, *Commentary on the Gospel of St. John,* II, §343.

made directly by Jesus, who speaks to her of His death, of the part she will have to play at that time, and finally of what God expects from her in the meantime. This annunciation plunges her into a new advent, an advent of separation, of surrender, of prayers and tears, completely different from the first Advent of joy. During these three years which prepare her for the great sorrowful mysteries, Mary must keep Jesus' word, like good soil, to enable it to bear divine fruit. She accepts in silence and with love the fact that others apparently live closer to Jesus and receive His teaching more directly; she accepts the fact that other holy women devote themselves to Him and take care of His material and temporal needs. She accepts the fact that among the children of Israel some oppose His doctrine out of pride and reject it as too hard or erroneous, considering Him to be a blasphemer, an usurper and a traitor to the Judaic and Mosaic traditions and to the political authorities. Does He not regard Himself as King of His people and Son of God? His mercy is excessive and no longer respects the justice of the Law. Mary carries in her loving and faithful heart all these increasing and treacherous oppositions toward Him who is her Son and her God.

This advent required by divine wisdom will be completely silent and hidden. The grain of wheat must fall into the earth and bear fruit. The soil must be well-tilled so that the divine seed may be divinely received. It is an advent that prepares for the great heroism in love, and, for that reason, it is necessary to be recollected in love.

CHAPTER 12

THE AGONY IN THE GARDEN:
MARY'S SORROW IN
STRUGGLE AND SOLITUDE

CHRIST'S Passion—His Hour—begins with the mystery of the Agony in the Garden. In His priestly prayer following the institution of the Holy Eucharist, Jesus, praying to the Father, affirms, "Father, the hour has come; glorify thy Son that the Son may glorify thee" (Jn. 17:1). Let us try to penetrate the mystery of Christ's agony and see how Mary lived it, how the Spirit willed for her to live it; let us try to see the particular and unique dimension this mystery brings to her divine life; finally, let us try to see how we must live it through her.

Scripture emphasizes that once He arrived in Gethsemane, Jesus withdraws from His disciples about a stone's throw away to pray in solitude. Beforehand, He had recommended that they pray: "Pray that you may not enter into temptation" (Lk. 22:40). But the disciples, tired as they are, fall asleep "for sorrow." Jesus has to wake them up: "Why do you sleep? Rise and pray that you may not enter into temptation" (Lk. 22:46).

Jesus is therefore alone in His agony; the disciples did not enter into it despite Christ's entreaties and exhortations. They are weighed down by sorrow.

St. Luke, the evangelist of the Virgin's joyful mysteries, not only reveals to us, like Mark and Matthew, Christ's prayer during His agony—"Father, if thou art willing, remove this cup from me; nevertheless not my will, but thine, be done" —but he also reveals to us the mysterious presence of an angel and the sweat of blood: "And there appeared to him an angel from heaven, strengthening him. And being in an agony he prayed more earnestly; and his sweat became like great drops of blood falling down upon the ground" (Lk. 22:43-44).

In this terrible solitude of the Agony, there is an angel who is a witness and who watches with Jesus, who enters into His agony and who comforts Him, *confortans eum.* Scripture tells us nothing about Mary. She is not mentioned. Apparently Mary is not there; her physical presence will be indicated only at the Crucifixion. Nonetheless, the Most Holy Virgin certainly lived this mystery of the Agony in a divine manner, since it was the beginning of Christ's Hour and hence the moment when she, as mother, should remain very close to Him. As Virgin, moreover, is it not her duty and her right to follow Him even in His most solitary and perilous retreat? The Virgin "follows the Lamb wherever He goes" (Rev. 14:4). Nothing is excluded from this. There where the Apostles do not enter, out of lack of love and generosity, the wise Virgin is to enter alone. She who waits throughout the night for the Bridegroom's coming is the only one able to live this mystery of the final night, the night of Jesus' agony, a night which is reserved for her, so to speak.

Mary, the Virgin *par excellence,* the Virgin of virgins, divinely entered into this mystery.

Should there still be any doubt concerning this, consider that the practice of the Church attests to it. Among the mysteries of the Rosary—which show us the various mysteries of Mary and Jesus—there is the mystery of the Agony, the first of the sorrowful mysteries. Moreover, it would be difficult for us to understand how Mary could have escaped this mystery alone of Christ's earthly life, when it has been revealed to us and when we must try to live by it. Thus we can say that this mystery revealed and communicated to us by St. Luke is in fact revealed and communicated to us by Mary herself, she being the only creature to have divinely entered into the very heart of the mystery.

What immediately strikes us is Mary's physical absence and the angel's presence. At the Crucifixion, on the contrary, Mary will be physically present and there will be no further mention of an angel.

The Agony is indeed a mystery of sorrow. "My soul is very sorrowful, even to death," Jesus says. It is His soul that is sorrowful, His soul that can take no more. This sorrow is deadly, excessive. It plunges Christ's soul into agony and His whole body is shaken by it. This sorrow is lived in struggle, a struggle that reaches a paroxysm. It is proper to agony to involve a struggle leading ordinarily to death, an extreme, ultimate, final struggle. This struggle is part of the divine sorrow of His soul and gives it an acute, violent character. Yet in order for the Agony to be perfectly agony—a struggle in its paroxysm of sorrow—it was necessary for Jesus to be alone, physically separated from all His friends, His disciples, and

His Mother. It was necessary for Him to be alone before God, before His Father; and for Him even to be as if rejected and forsaken by His Father. "My God, My God, why hast thou forsaken me?" Due to this complete and divine solitude—a kind of divine duel, one might say, prefigured by Jacob's struggle with the angel—the Agony could be fully and completely realized. If Mary had been physically present, the Agony would no longer have known this acute paroxysm, which is reached only in isolation. The presence of the comforting angel does not put an end to Jesus' solitude, for it is an angel who enters into this mystery and he enters as a pure contemplative. He is there as God's messenger, the Father's messenger, not to eliminate the struggle and the weight of sorrow, but to "comfort" Jesus' soul, to sustain it by renewing His strength, enabling Him to persevere to the end.

Mary penetrated this mystery more than the angel did, for she is the Queen of angels; she lived this mystery in unison with Jesus' heart as His Mother and His Aide. She experienced the singular sorrow of His afflicted heart; and the divine struggle in the garden of Gethsemane extended into her soul and was, as it were, completed there. In order to be closer to her Son's agony, she too had to live the mystery of sorrow and struggle in the absolute solitude of the night. It was necessary for Jesus to be alone before His Father's merciful love, as well as His wrath and justice. It was necessary for Mary herself to be alone before this same mystery that was being lived in Jesus' soul. Christ's solitude produced a similar solitude in Mary's soul, which directly echoed His own.

If Mary had been physically present near Jesus, she would not have lived the mystery of the Agony with such intensity and force. She would have left this mystery of absolute sorrow, this utter collapse, this sort of prostration into which her Son's agony plunges her. To live truly in unison with the heart of her Son in agony, to experience the ultimate demands of the Father's love, in this deadly sorrow—far from the eyes of men, alone with Him, and, in a certain sense, even without Him—Mary had not only to respect Jesus' solitude, but hide herself in it and be, like Him, totally secluded in this excess of love.

Both of them are, as it were, recluse yet united in the same mystery. They obviously live it in completely different external surroundings and, from a psychological perspective, with different insights and knowledge. Jesus remains in His beatific vision. However, by God's permission, this beatific vision does not prevent His human nature, in its most natural aspect, from feeling all the horror of imminent death, of the violent death that His human nature cannot accept in its natural and instinctive love. As a man, Jesus trembles to the very core of His being when faced with this imminent death whose iniquitous circumstances are well known to Him. His human honor, in its natural foundation, cannot tolerate such insults, derision, degradation. His human heart, in its natural love for men, cannot tolerate this betrayal by a friend. More deeply still, His human heart, in its spontaneous love for men, cannot accept that His death should be the cause of terrible sufferings for His Mother, for John the beloved disciple, for the holy women, for all His disciples. From a purely natural point of view, there is something revolting for this man—who is more a man than any other, who is the new Adam, the new head of humanity—to be the One who, through His death, will lead all His disciples into a crucifying mystery of death. The natural generosity of His will would have accepted a violent death with all its infamy if at least His brothers, those who belong to the human race and for whom He came, were all saved and delivered from suffering. In His agony, He lived what was most profound and radically natural in the messianism of His people. We must go even further: His infinitely pure, immaculate heart cannot bear the horror of sin, of evil as such, as an offense and affront to the honor of His God. His human heart, in its purest, most profound and loving aspect—its natural love for God—cannot accept the mass of iniquities, from the first sin to the last, which are going to descend upon His heart and clothe it in iniquity. Actually, it is the terrible weight of the sins of mankind that provokes the sweat of blood, the infinite, unfathomable sadness, which is an unbearable weight that causes His soul to groan three times.

The reason why God, in His wisdom, allowed Jesus to experience all these naturally good and intimate demands of His human heart, despite His beatific vision, was so that Jesus might sacrifice them and offer them to the Father in full awareness; so that before the bloody and visible holocaust, there might be this other bloodless and invisible holocaust, which is all the more profound in that it lays hold of Christ's human soul in its most human, most radically natural character. Jesus consents to take upon Himself the entire mass of the world's iniquities. He consents to appear before the justice of His Father as being responsible for all these sins, as the scapegoat which bears all these evils. Jesus' prayer revealed to us by Scripture reveals the depths of struggle, separation and holocaust, which are accepted out of love for the Father. "Not my will, but thine."

Mary lives this same mystery in her faith, hope and love. In the darkness of faith, she accepts this mysterious struggle, this sorrow, this heartbreak of her Son. And at this point, her faith knows a completely new darkness, characteristic of the sorrowful mysteries. This darkness comes from the quasi-contradiction that exists in the Agony, in this infinite sadness that overwhelms the Son of God and reduces Him to nothing. He—the Mighty God, the God of Peace, the Father's beloved Son—struggles in front of His Father; He struggles in seemingly great weakness, and in a kind of duel in which His whole life is at stake, and in which there can be no compromise whatsoever. This struggle, which tends to separate and oppose in Jesus' heart, at the very core of His will, the deepest demands of His human nature and those of His divine life, is something of a scandal and folly for the human heart and intelligence. Is it not contradictory that the Beloved Son could fight against His Father? For the Mighty God to appear as though exhausted and crushed? For the God of Peace to be engaged in a terrible duel? This agony is a terrible trial for Mary's faith, she who fully adheres to the mystery of her Son and to the purpose of His redemptive mission. Nevertheless, this quasi-contradiction does not cause her to doubt for a single moment. Mary remains firm and steadfast in her faith; the certainty of her faith increases in her heart, despite the opaque darkness of the night.

This faith breaks her heart, for it is a living faith that is fully informed by love. This adhesion of faith thus implies a total commitment: accepting to live mystically in her maternal heart all that her Son lives and accepting to consider this mystery of the Agony as her own. She must adhere to the psychological death of her Son, to this death in sorrow and solitude, to this intimate offering of His "psychological self" in view of the demands of the Father's imperative will. She must live her Son's agony in her heart as mother and virgin. This is the sword that begins to pierce her heart.

Love always demands that the beloved be in the one who loves, present *as* the beloved, with all the proper modalities of a beloved. The fullness of love of Mary's heart for her Son demands that her heart be more and more in harmony with Him, that she live in unison with His agonizing heart by carrying in her heart the same weight of sorrow, of destruction, of struggle. She must consent to bear with Him the mass of the world's iniquities and, with Him and through Him, to take on the sins of all mankind; to be through Him a merciful Mother toward all sinners, all criminals, all the damned, who caused her Son's agony; to be through Him the one who fully accepts the Father's will for her Son and for herself. Mary's only prayer is the prayer of Jesus during this night of solitude. Having no other sorrow in her heart than Jesus' sorrow, Mary can be totally receptive, wholly attentive to this divine sorrow. She can receive it in very great purity, without altering it in any way. Mary has no agony of her own; she lives only Jesus' agony.

Here we touch upon one of the consequences of her privileges as the Immaculata. Since she is without sin, she has a very great objectivity with regard to sorrow. She can live it in a completely pure love, and thus really live the same mystery as Jesus.

As for us, because of the consequences of original sin, we carry numerous and diverse sorrows in our human hearts; we have our personal little agonies. Of course, we can and we must make them divine by uniting them to Jesus' agony, but it is very rare for our sorrows to be totally transformed by love because their character is often so deeply personal. It is by living this mystery in a plenitude of pure love that Mary mystically and divinely comforts the heart of Jesus in His agony. This is what can help us understand one of the characteristic properties of Christian hope, of which Mary is the model.

When we are sad, the mere fact of knowing that someone is living the same sorrow we are living, that this person accepts it in his heart out of love for us and wants to bear it with us in order to be closer to us, using this sorrow as a means to become more closely united to our heart, this fact alone comforts us and alleviates to some extent the terrible burden of this sorrow. Comforting the afflicted is an act of mercy, for sorrow is in itself an evil; it is an inner misery which can stifle us inwardly, completely cutting off the most intimate aspirations of our hearts.

In His agony, Christ is certainly the most miserable of men, the One who knows the most agonizing sorrow and lives it in the most lucid, conscious and most psychologically acute way. Yet He does not need comfort because His love for the Father and for our souls is so great that it gives Him a divine strength, enabling Him to bear everything with infinite nobility of soul. Moreover, because such is His Father's will, Christ wants His Mother to penetrate into His mystery of sorrow, into His agonizing heart. He wants Mary to live what He lives and for that very reason He accepts being comforted by her. The angel both expresses and symbolizes in a divine way this efficacious and mutual solitude. Jesus leads Mary into the solitude of His agony, and she follows Him. She lets herself be attracted by the depths of sorrow, and, at the same time, she comforts her beloved Son's heart. Through her Chris-tian hope, Mary leans upon her Son's heart. She leans upon Him who is in agony for her, and she draws from Him the strength to bear the terrible burden of His sorrows. This divine strength of love enables her to sustain and help Him who cannot go on anymore and who thus begs for her divine strength as a mother and virgin.

By consenting to be comforted by Mary, Jesus shows us how He thirsts to communicate His love to her as much as possible and how He thirsts to receive her love. By accepting to live this same mystery, Mary shows us the desire of her heart to be closer and closer to Him: one with Him in His mystery of Redemption. Here we can see how, in these sorrowful mysteries, the union between Jesus and Mary intensifies and knows a new mode of even deeper cooperation. Not only is Mary the one who, through her faith, can give the Word of God a human body; not only is she the servant who gives God her flesh and her blood; she is also the one who, through her faith, hope and love, can efficaciously cooperate in His mission as the Savior of mankind. She becomes the helper, the assistant, the new Eve of this new Adam, enabling Him to perfectly accomplish His specific work, the work for which He came.[85] She enables

---

85. See Pseudo-Albert, *Mariale,* Q. 42: "At the Cross, Mary is not vicar of Christ, but she is His assistant and associate [*non vicaria sed coadjutrix et socia*]."

Him to go to the end of this mystery of sorrow, to penetrate it more deeply than if He had lived it alone since, thanks to her faith, her hope and her love, this mystery of sorrow can overflow, as it were, into her heart and take complete possession of it.

We ourselves will only be able to penetrate, in turn, into the mystery of Christ's agony and the agony of His members—the current agony of the persecuted and betrayed Church—to the extent that Mary will help us enter into it. Without her, we will fall asleep, even if we are very good apostles, weighed down by human fatigue and sadness. Without her, we will not penetrate into this mystery. As a Mother, Mary can enable us to participate in this solitary and secluded mystery, which is one of the great means for us to know the mercy of Jesus' heart, to know the unfathomable depths of His heart's sorrow, to understand how much He took upon Himself all the sorrows of humanity, how much He Himself lived them. He made them His own, to the point of dying from them interiorly and psychologically. His agonizing heart is really the homeland of all sorrows. In this way we shall also know how much Mary is our Mother, she who took all our sorrow by taking Jesus' sorrow and by living this mystery of the Agony with Him and through Him.

CHAPTER 13

THE CRUCIFIXION:
MARY JOINS HER SON IN SUFFERING

STANDING by the cross of Jesus were his mother, and his mother's sister, Mary the wife of Clopas, and Mary Magdalene. When Jesus saw his mother, and the disciple whom he loved standing near, he said to his mother, 'Woman, behold, your Son!' Then he said to the disciple, 'Behold, your mother!' And from that hour the disciple took her to his own home" (Jn. 19:25-27).

St. Ambrose comments on this passage in this beautiful text:

> Mary, the mother of the Lord, stood by her Son's Cross; no one has taught me this but the holy Evangelist St. John. Others have related how the earth was shaken at the Lord's passion, the sky was covered with darkness, the sun withdrew itself; that the thief was after a faithful confession received into paradise. John tells us what the others have not told, how the Lord fixed on the Cross called to His

> mother, esteeming it of more worth that, vic-
> torious over His sufferings, He rendered her
> the offices of piety, than that He gave her a
> heavenly kingdom.[86]

The evangelist makes three very clear statements: Mary's presence near Christ Crucified; the words Christ addresses to His Mother and to John; John's new attitude.

Mary's Presence Near Christ Crucified— The "Stabat Mater"

During the mystery of the Agony, Mary and Jesus, faced with the Father's imperative will, lived the same mystery of agony and solitude yet in very different ways. At Calvary, they continued to live the same mystery; again, in very different ways, as we shall explain in more detail. However, what is specific to this mystery of the Crucifixion is Mary's physical presence; she is there, next to Christ Crucified.

When did Mary join her Son? Was it at Calvary or during the carrying of the Cross as traditional devotion likes to present it? Scripture mentions only her presence at the Cross, and this is sufficient.

From the scourging to the Crucifixion, Jesus' body has been bruised incessantly in a thousand ways. After the inner sorrow of the soul come the physical, violent sufferings. They lacerate His whole body, slashing it, without respecting any part. Not an inch of His body remains intact. Everything

---

86. *Letter LXIII to the Church of Vercellae* in *Nicene and Post-Nicene Fathers,* Second Series, Vol. 10, §109, p. 472.

must become a sign and an instrument of love, in and through blood. To these physical torments is added a climate of insults, blasphemy and disgrace. All possible deaths must come and take possession of His human nature in the most violent way. Jesus retained nothing of His human nature; everything that could be offered up was offered. It is indeed the perfect holocaust, in which everything is burned; everything is consumed for the glory of the Father and the salvation of souls. We must always maintain these two aspects of the same mystery: holocaust of love to glorify the Father; salvific mercy for souls. Love allows for a unification of that which, without love, could not be unified.

In order for the holocaust to be superabundant, Mary had to be there, present. In His wisdom, God willed it so. Actually, Mary's presence next to Christ crucified both increases and soothes His suffering. St. Ambrose notes that from the Cross, Jesus "received indeed the affection of His mother, but sought not another's help."[87] Mary is truly the joy of Christ Crucified. She is His glory. She who keeps His word, she who receives His blood, she who has kept the sword of the word, she who receives the Cross. She is the complete victory of His sacrifice, the first fruits of His royal priesthood. Mary's presence also brings an extreme sorrow in Christ's soul. She is there as a witness to all His sufferings, degradations and insults. And she is there as a Mother: she is the Mother of He who is condemned to death, of the One who is rejected as a despised slave. It is terrible for the heart of this beloved Son to be the cause of such a spectacle, to cause His own Mother such sufferings! As a

87. *Op. cit.*, p. 473, §110.

beloved Son, He would have wished in His human heart for her to be absent in order to spare her such sorrow, such dreadful sorrow! But the Father willed that the cup be drained to the dregs. Jesus accepted everything.

Mary takes all these sufferings into her maternal and virginal soul. She lovingly makes them her own, as she made all the sorrows of the Agony her own. Mary shares in all these sufferings. She suffers them with Jesus out of love for the Father and for us; she suffers truly as He does. This mystery of compassion is divine and absolutely pure. For Mary was not supposed to have suffered, just as she was not supposed to have experienced sorrow since suffering is a consequence of original sin. She truly suffers out of love, in order to follow Jesus wherever He goes and in order to cooperate in His specific work, which is to bear witness to the truth and redeem our souls.

Mary indeed bears all Christ's sufferings, without any exception. She takes them all into her heart and soul, since Jesus asks her to complete in her heart and soul what "is lacking in Christ's afflictions." We must make quite clear what we mean by "complete" and "lacking." There is nothing lacking in Christ's Passion. It is perfect and hence does not need to be completed as though it were an unfinished work. Jesus can, however, ask Mary to let the mystery of His Passion overflow in her. Of course, Jesus does not ask her to shed her blood or have her body crushed. No, Mary's body must remain intact; it is the body of the Virgin. But her soul must consent to complete what Christ Himself cannot accomplish and so accomplishes through her. For Jesus evades sorrow and sadness in the summits of His soul, His intelligence and His will, since these summits are illuminated by the beatific vision. In order for the whole of human nature to be offered up as a holocaust and consumed for the glory of the Father and the salvation of souls, Jesus needs His Mother who, as the new Eve and the all-pure Virgin, can live this mystery of the Crucifixion and death of her Son in faith, hope and love, thereby offering to God the holocaust of the summits of her intelligence and will.

We already emphasized this for the Agony, but here everything becomes even more explicit and clear. In the mystery of the Cross, Mary's faith knows a sorrowful mode, which violently immolates her intelligence. This faith focuses on the mystery of Christ Crucified. In this mystery there are as it were certain apparent contradictions for Mary: Is Jesus not the Son of God who is to reign over the house of David forever, as she was told by the angel Gabriel? She has kept these words addressed to her at the Annunciation in her heart, and now Jesus presents Himself to her as the Crucified one, the one accursed by God and men. Does Scripture not say "a hanged man is accursed by God"? (Gal. 3:13; cf. Deut. 21:23). Jesus thus appears as One rejected by God; and, not only does He appear as such, but He Himself exclaims: "God, my God, why hast thou forsaken me?" (Mt. 27:46). He, the Beloved Son, "with whom the Father is well pleased" (Mt. 3:17) is now the One who is forsaken and who is to endure this state of anathema and separation.

This brutal opposition crushes Mary's intelligence in its inmost depths, since this quasi-contradiction concerns Him who is her Truth, her Way, her Life and also her beloved Son. If Mary were to listen to the demands of her human intelligence, she would immediately have rejected part of this apparent contradiction. She would either have given in to despair—thinking that the angel had deceived her—or she would have refused to accept the Cross—wanting to keep and consider only the angel's words. Under these conditions, there would have been a human choice; there would have been a heresy, dividing in a human way what was "united" in God's wisdom. In the name of the demands of human reason, she would have chosen only part of God's message, instead of keeping it in its entirety.

In a heroic act of faith, the bride's act of faith, the *sponsabo te mihi in fide*[88] of Hosea, Mary adheres to the Father's will for His Son. This act of faith, under the motion of the gift of understanding, goes beyond formulas—the visible expressions that are almost contradictions and hence intolerable—to adhere to the *res* [reality]: the Father's loving will for His Son.

Already in the mystery of the Finding in the Temple, her faith had to go beyond all the exterior circumstances that were so difficult for her to understand, in order to adhere to the Father's will for His Son; but this very pure adhesion remained joyful. Jesus was given back to her for this very reason. Here, the fact that her faith goes beyond external circumstances leads her to follow her Son in His mystery of holocaust and violent, bloody separation.

By adhering in all her purity to the Father's infinitely loving will for His Son and for her, Mary enters much more deeply into His intimacy; for unity is then achieved in the Father's will, in the Holy Spirit. Mary actively cooperates in Jesus' work. The Cross takes hold of her intelligence, which, in this heroic act of

---

88. Hos. 2:22: "I will betroth you to me in faithfulness."

faith, is as though totally offered up and immolated. Consider Elijah's holocaust, a wonderful prefiguration of the sacrifice of the Cross. The fire of heaven consumes the victims, the altar and the water! It is truly the faith of the Bride who believes in her Bridegroom's love for her even though exterior circumstances seem to deny and contradict it. This faith is completely silent, for it implies the very holocaust of the intelligence. The intelligence can no longer say anything—it understands nothing; it is no longer able to understand anything. That is why even the *quomodo* of the Annunciation is no longer asked. Mary must be completely passive, completely surrendered, abandoned to the Bridegroom's gracious will.

This faith is fruitful since it allows for the divine cooperation with Christ in His mystery of Redemption. Through this act of faith, Mary becomes the Mother of all our souls. She gives birth to us in her faith. We can see this fruitfulness as being prefigured by the blessing God gives to Abraham after his acceptance of the sacrifice of his son. Abraham's faith, rewarded by God, is indeed a prefiguration of Mary's faith. We say a prefiguration, for the reality is lived by Mary. Abraham did not really have to sacrifice Isaac, the son of the promise, whereas Mary really had to sacrifice her Son. In Isaac's stead was the ram designated by the angel. Jesus was both the Son of the promise and the "scapegoat" offered for the salvation of His people. That is why Mary's faith is far more engaged, far more realistic and divine than Abraham's. She must go further than her ancestor. Not only does God ask her to accept a trial, as He asked Abraham; He asks her to accept an irremediable fact in its absolute character: the ignominious death of her only Son, the Son of the promise. The promise made to Abraham is completely fulfilled only in and through Mary.[89] Such is the wonderful fruitfulness of this heroic faith, which calls for such a holocaust, such a death! It is truly what is most vital and intimate in Mary that is sacrificed. It is normal then that a wonderful divine fruitfulness should result from this. Since Mary's faith is fruitful, this faith separates her from all that is not her crucified Truth. Already through her *fiat* at the Annunciation, Mary had experienced a very great solitude and deep silence. At the Cross, Mary experiences a new solitude and a new silence in the midst of the turmoil and human agitation through a *fiat* of faith in the Father's will. Alone among all the others, she remains very firm in her faith. She still adheres to God's Word, to Him who is the Word of God, regardless of the fact that appearances have changed, that men have totally changed their attitude toward Him.

What we have just said about Mary's faith, in her mystery of compassion, we must also say about her hope. Mary also effectively cooperates in the mystery of Christ through her hope. She is wedded to Jesus in divine nuptials also with respect to her hope, for she offers Jesus the immolation of what is noblest and most elevated in her human will, her human appetite as such. That which Jesus cannot sacrifice because He possesses full happiness, He sacrifices through Mary. At Calvary, Mary's hope knows a mode of bloodstained

---

89. "By myself I have sworn, says the Lord, because you have done this, and have not withheld your son, your only son, I will indeed bless you, and I will multiply your descendants as the stars of heaven and as the sand which is on the seashore. And your descendants shall possess the gates of the enemies, and by your descendants shall all the nations of the earth bless themselves, because you have obeyed my voice" (Gen. 22:16-18).

poverty. Not only is her hope divine and very poor, but it possesses a mode of such utter impoverishment that her heart, her will, is divested, so to speak, of all direction in life, of all human desire, of all human strength. At Calvary, Mary must hope in the Cross, in her crucified Son, against all human hope. For a mother, the death of her only beloved son is really cause for the deepest despair. The death of her only son deprives her of all *raison d'être*. Does this death not entail the very elimination of the exercise of her maternity? When this only son is at the same time the Father's only Son, His death instills in His Mother's soul an infinite annihilation, an abyss as it were of solitude and abandonment. God asks Mary to hope in the very death of her only Son and her God, to hope in His Crucifixion, and to consider it as the greatest reason for hope. Mary must lean upon the weakness of the crucified Christ, upon His ignominious death, to have the totally divine hope of the compassionate Bride.

This helps us understand somewhat the divine poverty of Mary's hope. We grasp how the gift of fear purifies in a divine way this Christian hope by allowing it to lean only upon the very strength of God, which is the Father's love—as He wills to manifest it—with respect to His crucified Son, and through Him, with respect to Mary. This will demands the complete and total holocaust of Jesus, which overflows through the holocaust of his Mother's heart. Mary's hope must then lean upon her Son's holocaust to be completely pure and divine.

Theological hope leans upon God's merciful omnipotence to obtain beatitude, eternal life, from Him. Christian hope leans upon God's merciful omnipotence manifested in Christ to obtain from the Father entry into the paternal house. In order for this hope to be efficacious, it must be divinely poor, for one can only rely on mercy if one is poor. God can only be merciful to the poor, to those who recognize they have nothing and receive everything from Him. There is an essential connection between mercy and poverty. Mercy takes possession of someone to the extent that he is poor. At the Cross, Mary's hope must rely on the Father's merciful omnipotence, manifested in the crucified Christ, to obtain eternal life from the Father for herself and for us. The Father's mercy is manifested in a completely divine way in His crucified Son, although it seems, apparently, to abandon Him, leaving Him alone in His misery, like poor Job. Mary's hope must therefore not stop at appearances; but rather, contrary to appearances, her hope must penetrate into the mystery of the Father's infinite mercy for His Son and, in Him, for her and for the entire human race. But she can penetrate into this mystery only through the narrow gate: she must relinquish all judgment, all human desire for messianism, all maternal ambition however noble and beautiful, any proprietary right whatsoever, and consent to be clothed in Christ's blood, in all His disgraces, all His insults, all His ignominy, all His opprobrium. She must consent to be the Mother of Him who is truly considered as a blasphemer, someone accursed, an usurper. To enter into the Father's mercy, one must have a Christian poverty that is bloody, humiliating and even outwardly and socially degrading.

This hope of the bride, hope in the Cross, thus requires from Mary's soul every possible renouncement, down to the deepest, most profound roots. This hope allows her to live in unison with Christ's completely impoverished heart and enables her to enter into all the depths of His wounded heart, to "take root" in it and to explore all its divine dimensions.

"Today you will be with me in Paradise" (Lk. 23:43). If these words are true for the good thief, they are all the more true for Mary. Through her hope, a divine "anchor," she is "fixed" in the heart of Jesus Crucified and enters into the most intimate depths of the mystery of the Father's mercy. This hope in the Cross thus places Mary's soul in a state of more perfect unity with God's mercy. It is the *sponsabo in misericordia.*

This mercy is so divine that it overflows and communicates a new fruitfulness to Mary's heart. For this hope of the bride, totally surrendered in its very poverty, gives her heart a new dynamism of love, a new *sursum corda,* in which she carries us all along with her. While her mother's heart really must consent to die at the foot of the Cross, her heart as the new Eve, in contrast, begins to beat. In her mystery of compassion, Mary truly hopes on behalf of the entire Church.

All of these deep demands of Mary's faith and hope come from love and are essentially ordered to a more divine blossoming of charity. The demands of faith and hope, which require such impoverishment in our human will and intelligence, are always directed toward love. They are carried out through love and their end is love. Love thus completely envelops them.

Christ on the Cross is a holocaust of love; He wants Mary to be a holocaust with Him. All the demands of this holocaust of the intelligence and desire that we have just examined arise from love. In order for Mary to give Jesus all that she can give Him, just as He Himself gave all that He could give her, it was necessary—from the standpoint of love's demands—that she offer Him, through her heroic faith and hope, all the vital forces of her intelligence and appetite. Otherwise, Mary would have been holding something back for herself. Thus it is truly divine love, in that which is most itself, that demands all these bloody, painful purifications. Love alone can demand such purifications. Divine love alone can require a human intelligence to abdicate radically its right to judge and to see things clearly. Divine love alone can require a human will and a mother's heart to abdicate its most deeply rooted rights: the rights of a mother with respect to her child's life. These purifications are ordered to love and allow divine love to take hold of everything. The fire from heaven will be able to consume everything.

Through Mary's silent *fiat* at the Cross, Jesus can offer the Father a complete "host": the consumed holocaust of human nature in its entirety.[90] Christ's holocaust is obviously perfect in itself, from the standpoint of the intensity and perfection of love. Its merits are infinite, and it does not need to be completed by another holocaust. But this holocaust can overflow in superabundance. It can have a specific action on Mary's heart and thereby acquire a new extension and a unique splendor. It can take root in humanity. Just as Mary's *fiat* at the Annunciation was the *fiat* of humanity freely accepting, in faith, this new convenant of God with mankind that is realized

---

90. Cf. Arnold de Bonneval, *De laudibus B.M.V.*: "Doubtless there was one will between Christ and Mary, and both at the same time offered to God one sacrifice, the one in the blood of her heart, the other in the blood of His body" (Quoted by M. J. Scheeben in *Mariology,* Vol. Two, p. 218).

in the mystery of the Incarnation, the *fiat* of Mary at the Cross is once again the *fiat* of humanity freely accepting in faith this bloody convenant of God with mankind, accepting the fact that the sacrifice of the Head is to be that of its members, that Christ's holocaust is to be the holocaust of mankind.[91]

Here again, only the excessive love of Jesus' heart can enable us to understand both the superabundant character of the mystical holocaust of Mary's heart and its character of quasi necessity. The divine fire demands that everything combustible be burned.

Christ's priestly action thus acquires through Mary's *fiat* a kind of new efficacity, or more accurately, a new extension. Mary offers a virgin soil to her Priest; she offers an intelligence and a will wherein God alone has entered and acted. She

---

91. Cf. M. J. Scheeben, *Mariology,* Vol. Two, pp. 223-224: "Mary's cooperation in Christ's sacrifice attains its complete hieratical meaning in this, that her soul or her heart must be regarded as the living altar, built in and from mankind. On and in this altar the offering of Christ, which came from her flesh or her womb, is offered by the fire contained therein as in the true altar in such a manner that she herself appears as equally filled and touched by this fire. . . . In this way, by Mary's mediation Christ as offering appears not only as sacrificed by and from mankind, but also as sacrificed in mankind, in such a way that He lives in mankind and the latter, on its part, is co-sacrificed in a living manner in Him by a loving participation of His suffering. Likewise, in the capacity of sacerdotal offerer, Christ appears not only as offering Himself in Himself, but also, through Mary's mediation, as offering Himself in mankind, and mankind in Himself. In the meantime Mary's passive co-offering is contained in her effective union with Christ's sacrifice, whereby she bears this in her heart. When this expression is fully understood, it portrays Mary's relation to the sacrifice of redemption as richly and profoundly as the term *deifera* marks her personal worthiness and position."

accepts for Jesus to fully exert His priestly action upon her, by becoming a holocaust with Him. Christ's priesthood could only offer in holocaust the summits of the human intelligence and will thanks to Mary's *fiat,* a *fiat* that began at the Annunciation and was completed and consummated at the Cross.

Of course, we must make it quite clear that Christ the Host's priestly action is perfect and needs no other victim to be perfect. However, since His priesthood is in fact a priesthood of love and since He could have in Mary a new victim to offer, it was "quasi-necessary" (a necessity of wisdom, which wants love to be superabundant) for Him to take possession of Mary's intelligence and will to fully and completely achieve His proper work. Love knows no measure other than its own demands of love; nothing can stop it.

Through this, we see clearly how Mary is in a double sense the Priest's Mother: through communicating to Jesus the matter of His sacrifice, His flesh and blood; and through accepting that her own human life, in its very depths, be offered up with Christ's body and blood, like the water of the sacrifice.[92] This heroic act of love of Mary's heart at the Cross

---

92. Cf. St. Bonaventure, *Sent. I*, Dist. 48, Art. 2, Q. 2: "Yet in no manner is it to be doubted, that Her virile spirit and most constant reason also willed that (Her) Only-Begotten be handed over for the salvation of the human race, since as a Mother She was conform with the Father through all (things). And in this wonderful manner there ought to be praised and loved, what was pleasing to Her, that Her own Only-Begotten was offered for the salvation of the human race. And so much even did She suffer with (Him), that, if it could be done, all the torments which (Her) Son bore throughout (His Passion), She Herself would endure much more willingly [*multo libentius*]. Therefore She was truly strong and pious, equally sweet and severe, sparing [*parca*] with

totally surrenders her to Jesus, Priest and Host, and unites her to Him as a host and holocaust of love. It is the most perfect and most complete gift there is, and this gift is offered in the total darkness of faith and the total poverty of hope. Thus it is offered in the most selfless and pure surrender. Mary responds to Christ's total gift with a total gift, one that is completely interior, intimate and divine, because this is how she will really be able to give herself as the Bride, as the new Eve. Only this gift divinely complements, completes and imitates that of the crucified Jesus. It does not copy it in a material or external way, but penetrates the most intimate depths of Jesus' gift under the direct action of the Holy Spirit, the personal Gift. In this way, we can understand its totally divine character in its nature and its very exercise: it is indeed the work of the gift of wisdom. That is why it is completely silent, hidden, buried in Jesus' wounded heart, and it is completely reserved for Him. It is the Bride's gift: *Sponsabo te mihi in sempiternum.* Outwardly, we see nothing. Mary is standing at the foot of the Cross. She is not dying, not covered with blood, not insulted; she is forgotten. He alone holds people's attention. But divinely in her soul she is dying, she is covered with blood, she is covered with all the iniquities. She is living all the poverty of her Son, but solely for Him and for the Father, in love.

Herself, but most generous [*largissima*] to us. Therefore She is to be chiefly loved and venerated after the Most High Trinity and Her Most Blessed Offspring, Our Lord Jesus Christ, from the enarration of the Mystery of whose Divinity all other tongues fail, because *He is the consummation of sermons*." (English Translation by The Fransiscan Archive, available at http://www.franciscanarchive.org/bonaventura/sent.html).

This love that takes possession of Mary's heart, that unites her so profoundly to the Father's will in and through this total gift to her Son, is a fruitful love, capable of engendering us to divine life, of purifying us, of transfiguring us.[93] This jealous love—jealous since it looks so absolutely at the Father's will and will not consider any other, silencing all the natural aspirations of the intelligence and will—possesses a wonderful universal and divine fruitfulness. It is in order to do the Father's will that she accepts this mystery of compassion. The Father's will is a will of superabundant love, one that has universal efficacy. By willing the holocaust of Mary's soul the Father wills to intimately unite Mary to Christ, the new Adam, and enables her to cooperate in His Redemption, in our salvation and our redemption. Thus we understand how Mary becomes, through such perfect, pure and divine love, our Co-Redeemer, the one who, out of superabundant love, intimately cooperates in the mystery of Redemption, in our new birth in Christ Crucified.

Because of their divine efficacy, this faith, this hope and this love mobilize Mary's entire life in order to offer it as a living holocaust in filial, silent and passive obedience. She is dependent on the Lamb of God; and, by fully conforming to Him, she is a true host of love offered up by Christ the

---

93. Cf. Pseudo-Albert, *Mariale*, Q. 42. "At the Cross, Mary is not assumed by the Lord in a priestly function, but she is the Mother of the Savior and His Helper. All orders in the Church are within a function (a ministry). The Blessed Virgin is not assumed by the Lord in a function, but she is assumed in the community of goods, and she is assumed as the Helper, according to the affirmation: 'I will make him a helper fit for him' (Gen. 2:18)."

Priest. All the teaching she received from Christ during His hidden life was leading to this holocaust in which Jesus the Priest presents her to the Father for His glory. Such is the new service that Jesus asks of her. It is no longer a question of dedicating herself to a temporal service but of giving herself even more divinely to a completely interior service, one totally hidden and reserved for God.

The *Stabat* outwardly expresses this attitude of loving and virile submission. Mary is standing before Jesus Crucified, as close as she can be, to be present to all His bodily sufferings, seeing them, contemplating them, loving them. We can understand why Mary's presence was necessary here, for it is a question of being compassionate toward the physical sufferings and exposed sorrows. In order for her to be truly compassionate with respect to such sufferings, her physical presence must supplement her intimate, affective and loving presence.[94]

---

94. It would be interesting to compare the two presences of Mary with Jesus mentioned by St. John in his Gospel: her presence at Cana and her presence at the Cross. The parallel between these two moments is easily understood: at Cana, Jesus inaugurates His messianic ministry and works His first miracle. At Calvary, He completes His work; everything is accomplished. Mary is with Him during both moments. She is in the company of the first apostles [at Cana], or of the beloved disciple alone, the others having at that point deserted, denied or betrayed.

"For then [at the Cross]," St. Augustine says, "it was that He recognized, who, in truth, always did know. He knew His mother in predestination, even before He was born of her; even before, as God, He created her of whom, as man, He was to be created, He knew her as His mother: but at a certain hour in a mystery He did not recognize her; and at a certain hour which had not yet come, again in a mystery, He does recognize her" (*Tractates on the Gospel of John*, VIII, §9, p. 61).

Jesus speaks to her both times; with the same solemnity, He calls her "Woman." At Cana, He asks her for docility in abstention: not to intervene, for the hour has not yet come. At Calvary He asks her for

The Words of Christ

All the words of Christ on the Cross are Messianic.[95]
The words He addresses to His Mother must be Messianic
like the others, although John in fact does not mention this.

---

docility in intimate cooperation: the hour has come.

We understand in this way Mary's role in her divine cooperation in
Christ's apostolic life. Precisely because her motherhood is a motherhood of faith, her role is not merely an earthly one; it goes beyond all
bonds of flesh and blood. Her role is divine. Through her faith, she
cooperates in Christ's apostolic life, she cooperates in His priestly life
and in His life as a Host, since His apostolic life, in its ultimate character, is none other than a priestly and victimal function.

Since this cooperation is divine, it requires a very great poverty. It is
lived first of all in voluntary separation, then in the bloody separation
of Calvary. This cooperation is maternal and virginal. As Mother she
gives herself with her Son, she offers Him to the Father through the
priest as in the mystery of the Presentation. As Virgin, she cooperates
in this offering by letting Christ's priesthood immolate the inmost depths
of her soul; Simeon's prophecy is completely fulfilled. She is therefore
Mother of the Priest and Virgin-Host. At the Cross, in fact, she enables
Jesus to be totally offered by offering Him in a maternal way. She
enables Jesus to be the complete Host by offering herself with Him
and through Him. In this way, she really enables His priesthood to know
a superabundance of love. As Mother and Virgin she arranges and
prepares the sacrifice of Christ Crucified; she cooperates by allowing
His love to overflow. For this very reason, we can say that she accomplishes and completes it. Of course, nothing is lacking in Christ's
sacrifice, but this sacrifice can be accomplished and can come to
completion in a mystery of superabundance of love.

95. Christ Crucified fulfills all prophecy. In Chapter 19 of his gospel,
St. John makes three references to the fulfillment of Scripture: with
respect to the distribution of garments (v. 24, citing Ps. 22:19); with
respect to the cry of thirst (v. 28, cf. Ps. 69:22 and Ps. 22:16); and
with respect to the burial (vv. 36, citing Ps. 34:21; cf. Ex. 12:46).
Scripture is also quoted with respect to the stroke of the lance (v. 37,
citing Zech. 12:10).

Among the prophecies relating to the Messiah's Mother are Isaiah 7:10-16 and Genesis 3:15; the first concerns the virginal birth; the second, the struggle that will exist between the woman and the serpent: "I will put enmity between you and the woman, and between your seed and her seed; he shall bruise your head and you shall bruise his heel." We must not forget that when John refers to the Old Testament, he quotes the Septuagint. The Septuagint specified what remained vague in the Hebrew text concerning "he shall bruise your head." The Septuagint text opted for the individual sense. The victor over the serpent is the woman's descendant: the Messiah.

Thus it is quite obvious that the Cross, which is Jesus' Hour, represents for John the great duel between the Messiah, the Son of God, and Satan, the prince of this world, God's adversary. Since, as Christ Himself says: "The reason the Son of God appeared was to destroy the works of the devil."[96] The final action of the Son of God could only be to crush the head of the serpent. At the moment of His entry into Jeru-salem, Jesus had said: "Now is the judgment of this world, now shall the ruler of this world be cast out" (Jn. 12:31).

Hence for John the Cross is the great battle between the woman's lineage and the devil's lineage—the great battle between those who are born of God and those who are born of the devil, those who are "murderers" and "liars" (cf. Jn. 8:41-44) like him, the scheming Pharisees, the ambitious high priests and all those who let themselves be guided by them out of fear or utilitarian tactics.

96. 1 Jn. 3:8; cf. Jn. 6:70-71; 7:39; 13:2, 21-27; 14:30.

This duel and this combat cannot be separated—in reality they are one—for one who is a "murderer" and a "liar" is one with the devil; and one who is "born of God" possesses God's seed within himself, he is "son of God." "You are all one in Christ Jesus," says St. Paul, and St. John often tells us that mankind has been given the power to share in the condition of the only Son.[97]

It is with Judas and John that these two identifications will be most clear. They are the heads so to speak of these two lineages.

The devil begins by putting the plan to betray His Master into Judas' heart (Jn. 13:2). Then the devil enters into him (Jn. 13:27) when the plan becomes a definite resolution. At this point, the union between the two is such that Judas can be considered a devil. Jesus states this specifically when He says to the twelve: "One of you is a devil" (Jn. 6:70).

John, on the contrary, is the prototype of those who are born of God. He is the beloved disciple, the one who has always enjoyed a unique intimacy with His Master, a special, reserved intimacy. Thus it is not surprising that Jesus on the Cross should designate him as the Woman's son.

It is in this vast perspective of Revelation as a whole that we must consider Christ's divine words to His Mother and to John in order to understand their divine significance. "Woman, behold, your son!" Jesus' final words to His Mother—words that can be considered as His testament of love toward her whom He has loved so much—reveal to us Mary's role in the economy of salvation. She is the new Eve, the enemy *par excel-*

---

97. Cf. 1 Jn., Ch. 3-5.

lence of the serpent, for in her "God's seed" has come to full bloom. In her the divine seed found good soil, soil in which it could bear fruit a hundredfold. Mary is "the woman," as God in His wisdom willed to recreate her after the fall of the first Eve. Mary is the prototype of the Church, the one who is formed for the new Adam and from Him. All that she has, she received from Him; all that she is, is relative to Him.

Since this new Adam redeems mankind and engenders the Church at the Cross, by virtue of this fact Mary becomes the Mother of that Church, Mother of all the members of Christ.[98] Since John is the prototype of the adopted sons, by showing John to Mary, Jesus shows her the whole Church and commands her to be its Mother.[99]

Mary receives these words of Christ with a bride's faith, amidst the darkness of the mystery of the Cross. His words are infinitely sweet to her, although they are also a sharp sword wounding her heart.

These words ask her to look upon John as her son; they ask her to adopt him as Jesus Crucified adopts him. These

---

98. Let us cite this very beautiful commentary by Salmeron: "We contemplate the mother . . . as the second Eve, or the woman given to the second Adam as a helper resembling him, to engender the world anew according to the Spirit, just as we read that the first Eve was given to the first Adam as a helper to engender according to the flesh. By this contemplation we know that we are his sons according to the spirit" (Cf. *Comment. in Evang. Histor. de Passione et morte D.N.J.C.*).

99. Cf. St. Ambrose, *Letter LXIII to the Church of Vercellae:* "Christ testified from the Cross, and divided the offices of piety between the mother and the disciple. The Lord made not only a public but also a private testament, and John signed this testament of His, a witness worthy of so great a Testator" §109, p. 472.

words enable her to penetrate deeply into Jesus' heart; they allow her to understand the divine unity, the new covenant in blood between Jesus and John. They allow her to understand that John receives everything from Jesus, that he is the Father's beloved child and that in him Christ is looking at the whole Church and asking His Mother to love the Church with Him.

Jesus asks Mary for this divine cooperation and does so in a clear, precise, concrete and individual manner. Jesus' words at this tragic moment are truly a testament for Mary, a last will that divinely wounds her maternal heart. Jesus wants her to receive John in her heart as a beloved son, while the deepest human demands of her maternal heart would like to gaze on Jesus alone in these final moments and think only of Him. Does a mother not have the right—a right that no human authority can take away from her—to be fully present to her dying son, well aware that she is the only one who can help him at this final moment, since she is the source of his human life. Mary, who is a mother in poverty and has abdicated all her rights as a mother so as to exercise them only under the motion of the Holy Spirit, must experience this ultimate poverty in her maternal heart, the deepest poverty of all. She must consent to be deprived of this maternal privilege, which would entitle her to be exclusively attentive to the last breath, the last gestures, the last words of her Son.

It is her Son as Priest who gives her this order. In the mystery of the Finding in the Temple, Jesus, as a twelve year old in the bloom of youth, asked her to look upon the Father and to find Him in the Father's presence. Here, Jesus Crucified, who is going to leave her, asks her to look upon John, the beloved disciple, and to find Him in John's heart. In a very pure act of faith, Mary adheres to these words without making any comparison between Jesus and John. To help us understand Mary's heroism at the Cross, St. Augustine, in a very beautiful homily, draws a comparison between Jesus and John, between the Master and the disciple. He compares them as a theologian, and for us. Mary, on the contrary, made no comparison; she took these divine words of her Son into her heart so that these words might be fruitful and enable her heart to become the heart of a beloved Mother for John, and through John, for the whole Church. In a totally divine faith that crucified and crushed her maternal heart, Mary went beyond appearances to adhere to the divine reality, to the mystery of the Mystical Body, to the divine unity of Jesus and John, of the Vine and the Branches, of the Head and the Body, of the Bridegroom and the Bride.

Through her *fiat* at the Annunciation, Christ came to dwell in her; through her faith, she joyfully conceived the Word Incarnate. Here, through her *fiat* in this sorrowful annunciation, the whole Christ takes possession of her heart. She divinely conceives the whole Church in suffering. There is a very mysterious parallel between the two annunciations, one related by Luke, the other by John; one divine and miraculous, in the joyful acceptance of God's lowly servant; the other altogether divine and mysterious, in the great sorrow of Calvary; one made by the angel Gabriel in strict secrecy, the other by Jesus Crucified in front of the entire universe and the holy city, in the midst of discord and struggle.

Mary no longer asks the *quomodo*. She keeps silent, for her heart is broken and her intelligence itself is completely immolated. She fully accepts in the darkness of the Cross. She thus enables us to understand how the Bride adheres to the words of the Bridegroom, who is for her a Bridegroom of blood, a Bridegroom who wounds her in her heart, in what is most loving and holy in her, and who asks her for this ultimate fidelity that consists in keeping His treasure after His death and living by it as He did.

These last words of Christ for her are also a divine nourishment for her Bride's hope marked by poverty. She can use them to rely even more divinely on the Father's merciful omnipotence and be lifted up in a new *sursum corda*. These words truly require an ultimate poverty from her maternal heart and, by virtue of this very fact, this ultimate poverty enables her to enjoy a special mercy from her Father, since each divine poverty required by God is with a view to a gift of His mercy. By accepting to not be exclusively present to her Son during His final moments, Mary receives from the Father this grace of divine fruitfulness, the grace of efficacious cooperation in her Son's work. She is no longer merely God's servant, but also God's helper. Jesus' affirmation: "Behold, your son," makes this quite clear to her. This fruitfulness concerning John concerns the whole Church, since John is the representative of the lineage of those who are born of God.

Mary receives and lives by this mercy from the Father through Jesus' heart. This divine fruitfulness which is communicated to her is Jesus' fruitfulness. That is why this poverty that wounds and bruises her maternal heart also opens it up, expands it and nurses the wound by intimately uniting it to the heart of Christ engendering the Church.

Thus we can understand the new aspirations of her heart. In and through this mercy, she looks at Jesus in John. She penetrates her Son's heart even more intimately, for she can see its continuation, its extension, in John. This prompts her to lift up her heart toward the Father, understanding more clearly how He is the source of all fruitfulness.

Mary lives these last words of Christ in her maternal and virginal charity. Jesus' command establishes a preference in her, a choice, which the Holy Spirit had already required in a passive way when she was asked to accept the mystery of the Cross. Now she must accept it much more distinctly and must personally commit herself to it. By accepting the mystery of Redemption, Mary was really accepting the Father's will whereby Jesus was to die for our salvation; and for this very reason she was complying with this order of Wisdom: to prefer our divine life to Christ's physical presence with her. She herself must now make this choice and prefer John's divine life to Jesus' earthly life with her; she must prefer being John's divine Mother to continuing to exercise her human motherhood toward her only Son.

By living in love this last will of her Son, she must make the divine choice her own, and she must carry it through. We emphasize the fact that it is a divine choice in the sense that Mary does not have to renounce her motherhood with respect to Jesus in order to adopt John. But she must accept being totally deprived on earth of her beloved Son's visible, tangible presence in order to exercise her maternal role with respect to John's soul. She must accept the fact that Jesus is to die under the sorrowful circumstances of the Cross and that she herself is to live intimately the entire mystery of the

Cross in order to give birth to John, the beloved disciple, in Christian grace, and through John, to the whole Church. She must therefore consent, with Jesus Crucified, to be separated from God as it were so that John may be more perfectly a son of God by being the beloved son of her wounded heart and of the heart of Christ.

Actually, while this choice entails certain renunciations of visible and sensible bonds and closeness, it also brings about a deeper divine unity with the Father in the heart of Christ. Through this choice, Mary lives by the Father's secret concerning His Son, concerning her and the Church. Through this choice, the secrets of hearts, those of John and the entire Church, are communicated and revealed to her. Since Christ's words to Mary reveal to us the divine choice of her heart, they reveal to us, for this very reason, the divine quality of Mary's love for her only Son, for John and for the Church. Any choice, implying as it does a preference, always shows us the quality of love. Through this order, Jesus shows us the complete confidence He has in His Mother. He can ask her for anything. He knows that her sole desire is to conform to the Father's will through Him. He can even ask her at the last minute for this ultimate renunciation and ask for it as a direct order, in all simplicity. By accepting this choice, Mary shows us all the divine confidence she has in Him. She knows how much He loves her, and how strong and totally directed toward the Father His love is. She knows how much He wants her to be totally devoted to Him, yet in absolute poverty, so that she may be totally devoted to the Father, clothed entirely in His mercy. There is nothing weak, sentimental or insipid in their divine love; everything is strong and virile.

Mary loves John as she loves Jesus, with all her maternal heart. She loves him for Jesus and with Jesus' heart. She loves him for the Father and with all the Father's mercy. The sign of her love is her acceptance of her Son's death for him. Just as Jesus could say that "no greater love has no man than this, that a man lay down his life for his friends," so Mary can say to John that there is no greater love than this, to give the life of her only Son, of Him who is everything to her.

Mary's love for John exists for each of our souls. What she says to John, she can say to each of our souls as our Mother.

In order for this maternal love for John to be realized, John must choose her as Mother. That is why Jesus, after speaking to His Mother, speaks to John. He orders him to look upon Mary as his Mother. John receives these words in his faith as the beloved disciple; he receives them as the last will and testament of his Master. These divine words immediately form within him the heart of a son with regard to Mary. He tells us that from that moment on, he took her *in sua* ["into his own"]. From that moment on, John looks at Mary in a completely new way. He looks at her as Jesus looks at her; he loves her with Jesus' heart. He wants to be a true son to her, a son who keeps no secrets from his mother and who lives in her intimacy.

Thanks to Mary, John enjoys a new state of intimacy with his Master. He sees Him in Mary's heart as Mary's beloved Son, as an older brother. Jesus and John both have the same Mother. As a Mother, Mary teaches John the secrets of Jesus' heart. In Mary's heart, John discovers Him in a completely new way, as the One who gives us divine life and safeguards it like the good Shepherd who gives His life for His sheep. Is He not the One who gives the fullness of His divine life to His Mother?

What we have said about John remains true for us; for, since Mary's motherhood with respect to our souls is divine, it can be exercised and realized only insofar as we accept it, that is, to the exact extent that we take her as our Mother, to the extent that the words Christ addressed to John take on their full significance for us, to the extent that we receive these words as His testament of love for us. The new covenant in blood is in fact sealed in Mary's heart. But it cannot be realized without us. Without our divine adhesion to the words of Christ Crucified, Mary may be someone we respect, revere and love, but there is not this intimacy between Mary and us. We have not taken her "into our own" as a divine Mother who has the right to know all the secrets of our hearts and who must communicate all the secrets of her heart to us and point out to us the hidden paths that will lead us more quickly to Jesus.

In this annunciation, Mary thus plays the part of the new Eve: she who is the serpent's fiercest enemy, more terrible to him than "an army with banners" (Song 6:10); she who is the Mother of Jesus, who crushes the serpent's head; she who is the Mother of John and of all those who are born of God. The enmity between Mary and the serpent is such that the latter manages to put Mary's only Son to death through the betrayal of one of the twelve, the jealousy of the Pharisees and the cowardice of Pilate. It is in this terrible struggle, in which no neutral zones can exist—"neither cold nor hot, I will spew you out of my mouth" (Rev. 3:16.)—that Christ presents Himself as a "sign spoken against": one is either with Him or against Him. There is no other way. Mary is there, standing. She no longer flees to Egypt as she did at the time of the joyful mysteries, but she accepts this horrible hand-to-hand combat. Through a divine stratagem, she is going to save her people and the whole Church. Letting the devil seize the human life of her only Son, the latter crushes his head and thereby frees all the children of Eve from his tyrannical domination. Just as Judith's stratagem once saved her people when she cut off Holofernes' head with a sword,[100] so Mary at the Cross saves her people by the sword of God—the divine Word Incarnate—by cutting off the head of the real Holofernes.

Thus the flight into Egypt was really a strategic flight and not an admission of defeat or a lack of courage. The hour of battle had not yet come; it was necessary to gather strength, to flee temptation. At Calvary, the Hour has come: "the prince of this world must be driven away." Through her faith, hope and love, Mary can remain standing and unshaken by Satan's apparent victory. She can give courage and strength to her "Benjamin" and maternally teach him to fight to the end for truth, even if he is alone. Think of the "admirable" mother of the Book of Maccabees witnessing the martyrdom of her seven children and encouraging the seventh to prove himself worthy of his brothers and of herself. This admirable mother is indeed the figure of Mary who, at the Cross, participates in the mystery of the whole Christ and encourages John, the "Benjamin," to prove himself worthy of Jesus and of herself.

---

100. Cf. Jdt. Chs. 12 and 13.

Following John's example, we are all "Benjamins"; and for each of us, when the Cross looms ahead of us, and even more so *within* us, she is there to give us strength and courage, to urge us to be faithful to the end. As she spoke to her "Benjamin," she then speaks to us "in the language of our fathers" telling us over and over again:

> My son, have pity on me. I carried you nine months in my womb, and nursed you for three years, and have reared you and brought you up to this point in your life, and have taken care of you. I beseech you, my child, to look at the heaven and the earth and see everything that is in them, and recognize that God did not make them out of things that existed. Thus also mankind comes into being. Do not fear this butcher, but prove worthy of your brothers. Accept death, so that in God's mercy I may get you back again with your brothers (2 Macc. 7:27-29).

The Piercing with the Lance

To all the wounds and abuses is added the wound of the side and heart, which John witnessed and to which he testifies with such force and solemnity:

> So the soldiers came and broke the legs of the first, and of the other who had been crucified with him; but when they came to Jesus and saw that he was already dead, they did not

break his legs. But one of the soldiers pierced his side with a spear, and at once there came out blood and water. He who saw it has borne witness—his testimony is true, and he knows that he tells the truth—that you also may believe.[101]

Mary is present. She too is a witness of this piercing of the lance, which opened the side and the heart of Jesus' corpse and which caused Him to shed His last drops of blood and water.

Christ did not suffer from this final wound since He was already dead, but Mary did. Hence this final wound was meant for her; it was reserved for her. While this blow could not be mortal for Jesus, it was for her maternal heart: "A sword will pierce through your own soul," Simeon had said. The prophecy is thus fulfilled, and with such violence!

While this wound could no longer sadden and humiliate Jesus nor make Him poorer or more of a beggar, more thirsty for love, it could still sadden and humiliate His

---

101.Jn. 19:32-35. Cf.: "And I will pour out on the house of David and the inhabitants of Jerusalem a spirit of compassion and supplication, so that, when they look on him whom they have pierced, they shall mourn for him, as one mourns for an only child, and weep bitterly over him, as one weeps over a first-born" (Zech. 12:10). "On that day there shall be a fountain opened for the house of David and the inhabitants of Jerusalem to cleanse them from sin and uncleanness" (Zech. 13:1). In St. John's Gospel, we find this affirmation: "As the scripture has said, 'Out of his heart shall flow rivers of living water.' Now this he said about the Spirit, which those who believed in him were to receive; for as yet the Spirit had not been given, because Jesus was not yet glorified" (Jn. 7:38-39).

Mother's heart. Mary saw how little people respected her Son's corpse; she saw the cynical license with which the soldier slashed His side and pierced His heart. Mary then understood how much He had wanted to become poor, a beggar thirsting for the love of men in order to draw them all to Himself. Since He could no longer proclaim His thirst for love or express it with new gestures, it was necessary for His corpse to be able to convey it in its own brutal and absolute way. In His body had to be inscribed the indisputable sign of His infinite yearning for our love: the wound in His side. This wound that touches and pierces the heart is a wound of superabundant love which is added on top of the others. As a wound of the heart and a wound of superabundance, it is indeed a sign wonderfully suited, through God's wisdom, for expressing what no word or gesture could convey. Only death, and death realized in the heart by an open wound, can be the sign of an infinite, absolute love. And the superabundance of this mortal wound gives, as it were, a new emphasis and a unique intensity to the value of this sign.

Mary understands that this wound is first of all for her; she understands that she must receive it in her heart, as a "bag of myrrh" (cf. Song 1:13). These last drops of blood and water are reserved, as it were, for her. She must revere them with a very special love. For they are like tears of blood from her heart, burning tears that are purified in blood. In contemplating this wound and these last drops of blood and water, Mary offers them to the Father. She thus accomplishes her Son's priestly work. As the Helper, the Associate of His priestly heart, she must offer to the Father this immolated heart and these last drops of blood and water, since Jesus as

Priest can no longer do it. John witnesses this great mystery and, as a witness, he lives from it. He lives from it because he is Mary's son.

In these revelations presented to us by Scripture, a sequence can be perceived: the Eucharist, resting on the heart of Jesus, the sufferings of the Crucifixion, the gift of Mary as Mother, the death of Jesus, the piercing of the lance. John had rested on the heart of Christ during the Last Supper. The Eucharist had given him this divine audacity as a beloved child. Jesus' gift of His Mother to him gives him a new divine audacity, that of witnessing the wound in the side. It is through Mary that he can penetrate the inmost depths of Jesus' heart and receive the last silent secret of this divine beggar. The piercing of the lance, having produced such an echo in Mary's heart, imprints itself, through the Mother's heart, in the child's heart. Through and with Mary, John offers to the Father this ultimate wound and these ultimate drops of blood and water.

In this offering, John worships "in spirit and truth" within his heart for the first time. It is indeed this offering and this worship that will be as it were the intimate soul of his priesthood, which Mary needed in order to efficaciously achieve and complete Christ's priesthood. Mary needed this so that she herself—with her soul pierced by the lance—might be offered up as a living host to the Father, in an ever more profound unity with the only Host. This living and immolated host, in order to become more and more united in love to Jesus Crucified, had to be as it were assumed by the Eucharistic sacrifice of him who was her son and her priest.

Thus we understand how Mary, through this intimate immolation of her soul, so closely united to Jesus' soul, became the Mother of John's priesthood. The intense desire of Mary's soul to live more and more by the mystery of her Son's sacrifice, a desire which gave her such a sense of the Eucharistic sacrifice, revealed to John all the demands and all the greatness, all the significance and value, of his priesthood.

Mary is really a divine bond of love between Jesus the Priest and John's priesthood. Is she not the living host in whom John's priesthood will know a more profound union of love with Jesus' Priesthood? Of course, she does not confer the priesthood on John. The Apostle received this priesthood directly from Christ at the Last Supper, yet she enables this sacramental priesthood to be exercised more divinely; she enables all its potentialities and all its riches to become more explicit. This divine power of the priesthood actually knows many possible potentialities that can in fact only fully blossom under the direct influence of Mary, Mother of the priesthood. Is this not the fundamental reason why Mary's first spiritual son is a priest, an apostle, an evangelist, and precisely the one who brings to a close the Revelation of the Word of God, the one who was to reveal to us the intimate secrets of Jesus' heart, the fire of His love and the light of His truth?

CHAPTER 14

THE HOLY SEPULCHER:
MARY IS SEPARATED FROM HER SON

THE corpse of Christ, the corpse of God, must be laid in a tomb. It must be committed to the earth after being given the care prescribed by Jewish burial customs. John tells us:

> After this Joseph of Arimathea, who was a disciple of Jesus, but secretly, for fear of the Jews, asked Pilate that he might take away the body of Jesus, and Pilate gave him leave. So he came and took away his body. Nicodemus also, who had at first come to him by night, came bringing a mixture of myrrh and aloes, about a hundred pounds' weight. They took the body of Jesus, and bound it in linen cloths with the spices, as is the burial custom of the Jews. Now in the place where he was crucified there was a garden, and in the garden a new tomb where no one had ever been laid. So because of the Jewish day of Preparation, as

the tomb was close at hand, they laid Jesus there.[102]

The divine body must experience this final humiliation: it must be hidden in the depths of the earth as though abandoned, since the holy women, Mary and John will not be able to remain present near the divine corpse because of the day of rest prescribed by the Sabbath.

Let us try to understand to some extent how Mary lived this last sorrowful mystery, which is also the ultimate preparation, as it were, for the glorious mysteries. Let us try to penetrate the particularly sorrowful character of this mystery for her maternal heart; how it was for her like the dregs of the cup she had to drain to the last drop.

Scripture clearly indicates that the holy women had to leave the Lord's tomb because of the Sabbath day of rest. Thus we are in the presence of the ultimate separation: Mary had to leave her Son's corpse and return to John's house. It was an ultimate heartbreak for her. Just think of the poignant sorrow that takes hold of a mother's heart when the body of her deceased son is taken away. At that moment, all the previous sufferings, all the anguish suffered during his illness and at the time of his death seem to be renewed with particularly

---

102. Jn. 19:38-42. See Lk. 25:53-56: "Then he [Joseph of Arimathea] took it down and wrapped it in a linen shroud, and laid him in a rock-hewn tomb, where no one had ever yet been laid. It was the day of Preparation, and the sabbath was beginning. The women who had come with him from Galilee followed, and saw the tomb, and how his body was laid; then they returned, and prepared spices and ointments. On the sabbath they rested according to the commandment." See Gen. 23, the first mention of burial in Holy Scripture.

acute intensity. It is the pain of a healing wound that is brutally reopened. This pain is even more dreadful than the first,
for it strikes someone weaker and more delicate. We should
understand that a mother who is truly mother can almost not
accept, in her maternal heart, this ultimate separation. As
long as her child's corpse remains, she still has, as it were, the
illusion of his physical presence; but when the hands of
strangers come and snatch away from her him whom she still
considers her own possession—with a distinct jealousy
because of his very helplessness and death, since she is the
only one capable of defending and taking care of him—she
becomes almost mad with grief. We could cite any number of
examples to illustrate this jealousy that characterizes the love
of a mother fiercely keeping watch like a tigress over the body
of her child.

As the most loving and tender mother, Mary experienced in her human heart this ultimate suffering during the
mystery of the Sepulcher. He whom no strange hand had
touched at the time of His birth now had to be abandoned by
her, as a bloody and disfigured corpse, into the hands of
strangers. She had to part completely with this adorable body
and consent to no longer see it, to no longer contemplate it,
to leave it and return to John's house, while He was resting in
the earth, in the rock, alone in darkness.

This ultimate separation makes her relive the separations of the Finding in the Temple and the apostolic life, and
shows her the huge chasm that exists between this separation, which is beyond all human hope, and the other partial
and relative separations. In her heart, which is now nothing
but "grief," "desolation," tears and a "deep sea of sorrow,"

she must bear this final heartbreak and live it with unique acuity and intensity, since the bonds that united her to Jesus were unique.

Without revolt or resistance, Mary accepts the law of the Sabbath that separates her from the corpse of her Son. This was the last Sabbath imposed by the law of God on His people. This last Sabbath was so that the corpse of the Son of God could rest after His great work, His great task accomplished and completed on the Cross. Yet we have to say that this last Sabbath—the most perfect of all Sabbaths and the one that, in a sense, gives finality to all the others by giving them their ultimate meaning—is a Sabbath especially for Mary's heart, since the corpse of Christ only lives it in a material way and the rest of the divine corpse is for His Mother. It was she—and we in her—who needed it, so that she might experience this final heartbreak. In wanting to respect this Sabbath, Mary surrenders herself even more completely to the Father's will, which wounds her and demands from her this ultimate separation. The entire law as well as all the prophecies of the Old Testament thus come to an end in Mary's wounded heart. Like an anonymous, imperative and divine sword, it comes to give the final blow to this poor, worn-out heart.

It is in faith, hope and love that Mary accepts this last will of the Father. This enables her to not waste any time and to prepare divinely for the new stage: the mysteries of glory.

In her faith she accepts being totally separated from Him, physically and humanly, in order to live divinely with Him and share divinely in Jesus' new state. The physical and human separation had to be complete. Mary is not to return home but to John's house. She is not to live on the past, on the memories of the time when He was still with her. She is not to create for herself, in an imaginative, sensible and affective way, a world of memories in which Jesus would be as though present to her. The Holy Spirit does not want her to live where Christ is no longer present; on the contrary, He wants her to follow the Lamb wherever He goes. In her faith, she must be one with Jesus where He is and as He is. She must live divinely united to His inanimate heart, she must not leave the wound of His heart, which is the proper place of her divine life. For despite the fact that during these three days this wound is the wound of a corpse, it remains the wound of the heart of a God who died for her. In her faith, she must therefore remain united to the wound of this heart and experience with it the icy state of a corpse and the opacity of the earth's darkness.

Mary's faith experienced at that point a darkness that in a sense completed the darkness of the Cross and the Agony. In order to understand something of its proper character, we can use a comparison that is, as it were, providentially suggested by the very circumstances of these various mysteries: the difference between the very obscure darkness of the Cross and the opaque darkness of the Sepulcher. The darkness of night, however obscure, always implies a few landmarks for our eyes; certain contrasts always eventually appear, providing our sight with a bit of satisfaction. The opacity of the earth's darkness is characteristically so uniform that no contrast is discernible. This is the most terrible and oppressive type of darkness for our sight since it is the pure and simple negation of light.

This metaphor can help us perceive all the differences between the Sepulcher and the Cross from the perspective of the darkness of faith in Mary. There is a profound darkness at the Cross, yet Jesus' words are still there, as well as His gestures and His visible presence. During these three days far from the tomb, there is, as it were, an entirely new density in obscurity, for there are no more words or gestures, there is no longer any visible presence. Nothing is left but the closed tomb and the darkness of the earth hiding the corpse abandoned by men. Yet at the same time, Mary's faith progresses in certainty. The intense obscurity of the Sepulcher already heralds the radiant light of the Resurrection for her heart, which so firmly adheres to the divine promises. In her faith she never doubts that Jesus is "the Light of the world," that He is "the Resurrection."

Through the mystery of the Sepulcher, Mary's hope experiences, as it were, an ultimate poverty: does she not have to live, in the inmost depths of her maternal heart, the ultimate and supreme poverty of the heart of Jesus who, in the freezing darkness of the tomb, remains abandoned by men, by His friends? They already considered him as no longer belonging to this universe, as having no further role to play among men, as someone useless and futile (recall the attitude of the disciples of Emmaus). Mary puts all her divine hope in this cold, abandoned heart as the proper instrument of divine mercy with respect to her soul and her life as daughter of the Father and Mother of men. Thus she must divinely rely on this hidden heart, invisible to human eyes, and in and through it, await the Father's mercy, which is keeping silent and seems to have permanently withdrawn, but in which she never loses hope. For the promise of the Resurrection remains alive for her and for her divine hope. Indeed, never has this promise been so intensely lived; never has it been so imminent.

The very intensity of this poor and steadfast longing for the imminent Resurrection must have made this silent waiting of the Sepulcher seem infinitely long for Mary's heart. During this wait, Mary divinely exercises her patience since, humanly speaking, she can no longer do anything. All she can do is yearn inwardly for the deliverance of Jesus' body, for its Resurrection. All she can do is ask the Father for it in the hopeful prayer of a poor woman who has nothing left, who has just been deprived of her last treasure, who humanly speaking no longer has any *raison d'être* on earth and who lives as one rejected and useless.

While the mystery of the Sepulcher is lived by Mary in a faith that is both so dark and so unswerving, in such a poor and steadfast hope, it is also lived in a renewed intensity of love. Mary's heart lives in unison with Jesus' heart and soul. It espouses the lifeless state of Jesus' body, the state of this cold, bloodless body committed to the earth. The charity of Mary's heart, totally given to her Son's heart, divinely blossoms during these three days in a very hidden, very silent way. It is a new stage dictated by the very state of Jesus, of the mystery of His burial.

We shall reiterate the fact that the charity of Mary's heart *blossoms in a divine way;* for, while this stage brings about a blossoming of love in God's eyes, from a human perspective, it requires a sort of lifeless passivity. During these days, Mary's human heart remains like a pierced heart that no longer has life of its own. From a human standpoint, her life no longer has any meaning. Having no further purpose or function to fulfill on earth, her heart is totally disoriented, so to speak. It could only groan in silence, in a completely hidden way, out of the sight of men. Thus we realize in what sense we are to understand this divine blossoming of her heart, and the very particular modality of her contemplation during these three days. We can say that this contemplation is realized in such a deep rest and such docility to the Father's gracious will that she really lives by the mystery of the rest of the corpse of Jesus. Is this not the contemplation of one who lives for the Church the mystery of the Catacombs in its most radical and absolute aspect? The mystery of the Sepulcher is indeed the prototype of the mystery of the Catacombs.

While Mary's heart, in this mystery of the Sepulcher, lives in unison with Jesus' lifeless heart, it also lives in unison with His soul. In her contemplation, Mary lives the mystery of the separation of Jesus' soul from His body. She lives the violent state of this separation, a state all the more violent given the fact that Jesus, precisely because of His mystery as Son of the Father, was not supposed to die. God is Love, a mystery of Unity, is He not? This substantial separation of death, considered in itself, is repulsive to this mystery of Love that is source of unity. God is not the God of death; it is sin that generated death. Mary must live this violent state of the separation of Jesus' soul from His body. She must also live the mystery of the descent of Jesus' soul into the underworld, the realm of the dead.

A clarification is needed here: Jesus descended "to the dead," as we say in the Apostle's Creed. Today, some private revelations say that he descended into Hell. But private revelations are not the norm of our faith. The norm of our faith is the Creed and the Gospel lived in the hearts of the saints and approved by the Church. There is a distinction between "Hell" and "the dead." Hell is the place of damnation. There where there is no love, as Saint Thérèse of Lisieux says. It is the place without love, the place of pride. It is the place of pure anarchy because, when nothing is left but pride, there is no agreement. There is no communion in Hell, no *koinônia*. If today's anarchists could go down for a short time to this place, they would see what anarchy pushed to the extreme is! The devils are "pure" intellectuals who, in their pride, affirmed the primacy of the intelligence over love, thus the primacy of aggression because everyone wants to be first. But there can only be one who is first; that is why Hell is the place of constant fighting and constant anarchy—because of pride.

Jesus could not have descended into Hell, because they would not have received Him, and He respects the freedom of every creature. God the Father, God source of grace, God source of gratuitous love, is rejected in Hell. Only the Omnipotence of God as Creator penetrates into Hell— otherwise the devils would have been annihilated. God, in His wisdom, does not even annihilate Lucifer, the Prince of Demons. God does not annihilate anyone, for to annihilate a spiritual creature is contrary to His wisdom. God does not annihilate His creatures: neither spiritual creatures nor the physical world.

Hell is therefore the place where God's Fatherhood does not enter, the place from which it is banned.

"The dead" is something different: it is the place of waiting, Sheol, the Kingdom of Shadows of the Greeks of Antiquity. It is the place of the separated souls. In this place, there is charity, in a very particular kind of community, which is waiting for the Beatific Vision and which lives in an ultimate eschatological hope in faith and charity.

Jesus' separated soul, united substantially to the Word, descends to the dead in order to liberate these souls (which are separated from their bodies) who are waiting. We can understand the haste of Jesus' priestly mercy: immediately after His death, He descends to the dead to bring an ultimate joy and hope to the righteous men and women who are waiting. He brings them the joy of knowing that the time of waiting is now over and that finally they are going to see God. In this mystery of the descent of Jesus' soul to the underworld, Mary lives, for those whom Christ has given her, this ultimate trial which announces His return, His glorious Resurrection.

Mary patiently waits in love, silently accepting this ultimate trial. We have here the buried, very hidden docility of one who, humanly speaking, is worn-out and, feeling as though bruised and beaten, no longer has the strength to undertake anything new. Docile to Love, she surrenders, waiting for whatever God wants. The liturgy uses the Lamentations of the Prophet Jeremiah to express the sorrowful state of Mary's heart in this mystery of compassion, which comes to an end on this first paschal vigil: *Torcular calcavit Dominus virgini filiae Juda.* "The Lord has trodden as in a wine press the virgin daughter of Judah. For these things I weep; my eyes flow with tears; for a comforter is far from me, one to revive my courage" (Lam. 1:15-16).

In this profound docility, Mary remains awake in ardent love. Her heart does not sleep. While psychologically speaking everything should be plunging her into the deepest state of inertia in order to evade the cruelest despair and try to forget the most absurd of failures, the Spirit of God, who before "there was light" "was moving over the face of the waters" (Gen. 1:2), covers the Woman's sorrowful heart with His love. He "overshadows" her who never ceases to say *fiat* to the Father's loving will. The Holy Spirit enables her to love with an even more ardent flame of love, since it is more restrained, more buried, more deeply hidden. He keeps her heart awake in this love. Is she not more than ever the wise virgin who waits patiently throughout the night for the return of the Bridegroom?

During this mysterious waiting period, during this night that is prolonged to envelop the last "Sabbath" of Israel, Mary's heart, under the motion of the Spirit, remains burning with love, a hidden, buried love jealously reserved for God. Her heart, like burning coal, incandescent but covered with ashes, seems extinguished in appearance but in reality it is ready to flare up and set everything ablaze.

We could make a comparison between the joyful Advent that prepares for the birth at Christmas and this sorrowful advent that prepares for Christ's glorious birth. We would then understand that the passivity, the silence, the poverty and the hidden life can be divinely lived in very different ways and with numerous and irreducible demands. They are both still essentially the mystery of Christian love, hope and faith, but with different modalities. The joyful passivity allowed for certain initiatives of mercy, fraternal charity and certain liturgical activities. The sorrowful passivity of the Sepulcher allows for nothing else; it absorbs everything. It places one in a state of desolation. *Posuit me desolatam, tota die moerore confectam*—"He has left me stunned, faint all the day long" (Lam. 1:13). Everything is as though trampled underfoot, destroyed, reduced to dust. It is a state of divine ruin and overwhelming solitude, in which divine patience plays a major role.

The fundamental reason for this difference lies in the fact that in reality joyful passivity implies presence: Jesus is present during Advent. Sorrowful passivity implies absolute, irreparable separation: Jesus is dead; He is no longer there.

We should take note of all the parallels and differences that exist between the mystery of the Finding in the Temple and the mystery of the Sepulcher so as to understand more clearly what is entirely proper to this stage so mysterious and important, since it prepares for the mysteries of glory. Both concern a mystery of violent separation, but how different they are! One is joyful, the other sorrowful. One prepares for an even purer, greater joy; it is a trial that purifies and leads to greater unity of life. The other prepares for glory and no longer simply joy; it is no longer merely a trial. It is a reality lived in all its realism and absoluteness.

With the mystery of separation before the Finding, Mary must do everything possible to find Jesus. With the mystery of separation of the Sepulcher, Mary must remain exclusively and deeply buried, with divine patience, in her life of faith, hope and love. She must remain passive in sorrow; ardently waiting and yearning, of course, but with patience, totally submitting her will to the will of God.

When the Lord seems in fact to have left us, when He abruptly hides Himself, we must understand that in some instances He wants us to make haste to find Him again. In other instances, He wants us to surrender ourselves completely. We have to discern whether, in fact, we are presented with a mystery analogous to that of the Finding: whether the Lord has left us in order to teach and converse with some theologian, or whether we are in the presence of a mystery analogous to that of the Sepulcher. This is not always easy to discern, and yet it is essential to do so, for our attitude in each case must be completely different. It seems that the major criterion lies in the fact that the separation of the Finding happened without Mary knowing about it, whereas the separation of the Sepulcher happened with her full knowledge. Mary gave her *fiat,* her total acceptance. This was her cooperation in the mystery of the Cross, whereas at the Finding, Jesus was divinely educating His Mother. That is why when the Lord leaves us without our consent, we must look for Him, like the bride in the Song of Songs. When He has asked for our *fiat* and has made us understand that He had to die in us, and be buried in us, let us then remain with Mary in this Sabbath rest, this rest of the Lord, when no occupations are allowed, except those necessary for life. Let us be there solely for Him.

This great rest, lived in sorrow, is a preparation for the mysteries of glory.

PART 5

THE MYSTERIES OF GLORY: BLOSSOMING OF MARY'S CHARITY

CHAPTER 15

THE RESURRECTION
AND THE FREEDOM OF FAITH

SCRIPTURE gives us far fewer details about the sorrowful mysteries of Mary than about the joyful mysteries, and it is even more discreet concerning the glorious mysteries. Mary's presence is only mentioned at Pentecost.

This silence does not mean that Mary was unrelated, as it were, to the mystery of the Resurrection and the Ascension, nor does it mean that these mysteries remained extraneous to her and did not affect her life. Should there be any doubt about this, the practice of the Church in giving us the Rosary would be there to affirm it. This silence therefore contains some other significance, which we must endeavor to understand.

As we have already said, God teaches us not only through words, but also through silences. A human teacher cannot do this. He can only teach by using words, thereby reaching his disciple's intelligence and conveying to it the knowledge he himself has acquired. The purpose of his teaching is to communicate the truth.

The purpose of divine governance, which implies education and teaching, is to communicate a divine and personal truth, which is love. That is why all revelation received here on earth through faith is ordered to the beatific vision, the great Revelation, through growth in love. This growth is the most immediate end, so to speak. Love can in fact be nourished by certain silences that sometimes say much more than words. Thus there is nothing surprising about the fact that some of God's silences, as well as His Words, provide divine nourishment for our faith. We might even say that, whereas the word is primary from the perspective of a society or community (for theology as speculative wisdom and wisdom of the Church can only originate in the Word of God), from a personal point of view, God's Word is ordered to these divine silences, in our intimacy with God. Faith is ordered to divine love, and this love requires silence. Mary is at the Lord's feet, and she keeps silent. Mary keeps God's Word in her heart, whether she understands it or not; but she also and above all keeps God's silences.

It is therefore not surprising that these final mysteries of the growth of love in Mary's heart should be so silent. God keeps Mary more and more for Himself. The more she progresses in divine love, the more He hides her in His divine face, in a purely contemplative life. Thus He places her as it were beyond historical facts and contingencies. When the contemplative life is lived in a totally divine way, it is a life that evades history. It is lived in God. Now the glorious mysteries are essentially mysteries of the contemplative life, for glory is peculiar to heaven. It is only through the contemplative life, which is led imperfectly here below, that we can penetrate into these glorious mysteries and into their specific characteristics. Is contemplative life not a kind of prelude to the life of heaven, the life of glory? It is no wonder then that, in Mary's glorious mysteries, the Holy Spirit, through His silence, wanted us to enter a little further into the silence of Mary's heart. He used the most suitable means for this purpose: the means the most eloquent and brilliant, yet at the same time the poorest, most hidden and most mysterious.

Let us strive to enter into this divine silence of Mary's heart in the mystery of the Resurrection. In order to do so, let us compare Mary's attitude with that of Mary Magdalene, and then Mary's attitude with that of John.

Scripture actually speaks at length about Mary Magdalene, about her mind-set while waiting for the end of the Sabbath, about her zeal to go back to the tomb.

St. Luke, speaking about the women "who had come with him from Galilee," tells us that "on the first day of the week, at early dawn, they went to the tomb, taking the spices which they had prepared" (Lk. 23:55; 24:1). St. John specifies that one of these women is indeed Mary Magdalene: "On the first day of the week Mary Magdalene came to the tomb early, while it was still dark" (Jn. 20:1).

Because of her great love for Jesus, Mary Magdalene is busily taking care of everything needed in order to honor the burial of the One she loves. In so doing, she devotes herself to beautiful and noble things that in themselves are excellent. What is more noble than preparing scented oils with which to honor the body of Christ? We know of Mary's gesture for Jesus at Bethany six days before the Passover: "Mary took a pound of costly ointment of pure nard and anointed the feet of Jesus and wiped his feet with her hair; and the house was filled with the fragrance of the ointment" (Jn. 12:3). In response to Judas' indignation, who pleads the cause of the poor, Jesus comes at once to Mary's defense and not only approves of her gesture but praises it: "Let her alone, let her keep it for the day of my burial. The poor you always have with you, but you do not always have me" (Jn. 12:7-8).

Her fervor and generosity urge her to go as quickly as possible to the tomb. So as soon as the Sabbath is over and she is free, we see her rush to the tomb. On the way, she wonders how she will be able to remove the huge stone blocking the entrance. When she arrives at the tomb, she sees that the stone has been rolled away and that the tomb is empty. In St. John's Gospel, we see how frightened she is by this discovery. Her first thought is that the tomb has been robbed. She runs immediately "to Simon Peter and the other disciple, the one whom Jesus loved, and said to them, 'They have taken the Lord out of the tomb, and we do not know where they have laid him' " (Jn. 20:2).

She returns to the tomb with Peter and John. Whereas the two disciples return home after observing the fact of the disappearance, Mary Magdalene remains weeping outside the tomb. She is in a state of utter disarray. All her plans have failed. He whom she was seeking above all else has disappeared, and she no longer knows where to look for Him. Faced with this terrible void, she is completely helpless. This cruel absence is really a desperate situation for her.

"As she wept she stooped to look into the tomb; and she saw two angels in white, sitting where the body of Jesus had lain, one at the head and one at the feet. They said to her,

'Woman, why are you weeping?' She said to them, 'Because they have taken away my Lord, and I do not know where they have laid him' " (Jn. 20:11-13). Her sorrow is too strong; she cannot pay attention to this apparition, extraordinary as it may be. She is not looking for angels, God's messengers, but for her Lord, and that is why "saying this, she turned round" (Jn. 20:14). After the apparition of the angels, Jesus Himself is present, although He hides under the appearance of a gardener who asks her questions. The Scriptural text tells us:

> She turned round and saw Jesus standing, but she did not know that it was Jesus. Jesus said to her, "Woman, why are you weeping? Whom do you seek?" Supposing him to be the gardener, she said to him, "Sir, if you have carried him away, tell me where you have laid him, and I will take him away." Jesus said to her, "Mary." She turned and said to him in Hebrew, "Rabboni!" (which means Teacher). Jesus said to her, "Do not hold me, for I have not yet ascended to the Father; but go to my brethren and say to them, I am ascending to my Father and your Father, to my God and your God (Jn. 20:14-17).

It is by calling her by name—"Mary"—that Jesus reveals Himself to her. Yet even at that moment, Jesus draws away and does not want to be touched.

If we try to understand the meaning of this first apparition of Jesus to Mary Magdalene, it is easy to see that Jesus appears to her in order to revive and purify her life of faith, hope and love, reminding her of the demands of contemplative life. It appears that, because of the sorrow she was experiencing in an overly human way, Mary Magdalene only agreed reluctantly to leave the tomb and Jesus' body. She obeys the precept to rest on the Sabbath, because she cannot do otherwise, but it seems that she does so reluctantly, so impatient she is to return to the place to which her heart calls her and to render to the body of her Jesus its due honors. The Scriptural text points out this impatience when it says that she came to the tomb "early, while it was still dark."

Scripture also shows us the subject matter of her thoughts during this forced immobility. She makes plans; she thinks about what she will be able to do for Him; she is completely preoccupied about how she will be able to proceed. Actually, by not fully accepting God's will for her (manifested by the precept of the law), Mary Magdalene left the divine rest of her contemplative life in order to devote herself to active works, which in themselves are very beautiful and good but which for her are really pointless. She acts this way because of the depth of her sorrow and the violent wound of the separation. By devoting herself to these concerns, she follows the spontaneous inclination of her heart; it is really natural generosity that takes over and stifles in her the specific demands of contemplative life. And so, wanting to be the first to arrive at the tomb to find Jesus' body as quickly as possible, she wastes time. In reality, she looks for Him where He is no longer present; she worries about things which, in reality, have become meaningless.

So we see that God, in His wisdom, who loves Mary Magdalene because she loves much and shows great generosity in love, wants to reward her by granting her the first apparition; but He paternally corrects her at the same time, because He wants her to remain in a true contemplative life and enter into the glorious mystery of the Resurrection of Christ.

First she finds the sepulcher empty. This is a terrible trial, when we think of her feverish waiting, the intense and burning desire that filled her heart. After these two nights and this day of waiting, when she was totally focused on the sepulcher and lived solely in the hope of finding Him again, of being near Him once again, she finds nothing but this incomprehensible void, which lets her imagination visualize the most terrible things: "They have taken away my Lord."

Next, she finds the angels. They could have brought some comfort to her soul, since they are God's messengers and her Teacher's ministers. But her suffering is too immense and prevents her from paying attention to them and making use of them. She wants Him alone. To find Him again is her sole concern. That is why we can say that the presence of these two angels is another trial for her, for their presence is another intermediary which she cannot, and will not, accept. The peaceful question asked by the angels even seems to irritate her. When we are looking intensely for someone we love, we think that everyone has the same concern we have. To meet people who do not seem to think as we do irritates and hurts us. This seems to have indeed been the case with Mary Magdalene, who does not even expect any enlightenment from the angels. She is apparently irritated by this question which is so far removed from her main concern!

Finally, the very presence of Christ is a trial for her. For He is present and she does not recognize Him; she mistakes

Him for the gardener. This is a harsh humiliation that Jesus inflicts upon her, for when we love someone we always claim to be able to recognize him under any disguise. We claim to possess a sort of intuition capable of detecting the cleverest of tactics which would deprive us of our loved one's presence. Mary Magdalene is near Him, and her love is incapable of perceiving that it is He. Her love does not go beyond appearances and cannot penetrate deeper to find the One it wants. Jesus must take the initiative and call her by name: "Mary." He must reawaken in her, her ideal of contemplative life so that she may then understand that He is present.

And even at that moment, Jesus leads her to understand that He expects from her a new love: one ever more pure and divine. She can no longer touch Him, as at Bethany when she was close to Him and anointed His feet with an ointment of pure nard. From now on she must seek Him near His God and Father. It is primarily for the glory of the Father that Jesus rises from the dead, and it is with Him that He remains—*vado ad Patrem*.[103] It is through a totally divine faith that Jesus must be found, and not only in His divinity but even in His humanity—His body—since His glorified body is beyond our universe and becomes an object of contemplation for Mary Magdalene and all His disciples.

By contrast, Mary, the Mother of Jesus who, as we have already seen, lived the trial of the Sepulcher in a divine way, can immediately live by the mystery of the Resurrection. In her life of faith, hope and love, Mary never left the divine presence of Jesus' inanimate heart and lived these days of trial

---

103. "I go to the Father": Jn. 14:12, 28; 16:10, 28.

in unison with this heart in the silence of death; therefore, in her faith, hope and love, she silently lives by this mystery of triumphant and radiant love, right from the first moment when this divine heart is gloriously restored to life through the Father's merciful omnipotence. Mary does not waste time. She does not want to waste any time for she wants to fully conform to the Father's will for her. We waste time only when we turn away from this will and follow our own voluntary inclination. When, at every moment, we fully subordinate our will to God's, we necessarily live already, while still on earth, by eternity and by the mystery of God's love, as God wants us to live it.

Indeed, we must clearly understand that the Resurrection takes place in the tomb, in the recesses of the earth, where Christ's wounded heart and His divine corpse lie. This heart, which has stopped beating since His death on the Cross, starts beating again by the Father's almighty power. It certainly remains the mortally wounded heart, the heart pierced by the lance; but this mortal wound is transformed into a wound of glory which, far from preventing life, gives it more radiance. God uses this wound so that all the love of Jesus' soul may shine forth in unique splendor in His heart of flesh and, through it, in His entire human body. Jesus' wounded and glorified heart is more than an incandescent coal all ablaze and glowing with light; His heart is the very source of fire and light, capable of transmitting fire and light, capable of burning and setting fire to everything it touches. And this is only a comparison: the love of Jesus' soul, availing itself of the Father's omnipotence, realizes a far more wonderful mystery in Jesus' wounded heart and in His whole body disfigured by the Scourging and the Crucifixion. The union between the incandescent coal and the fire that burns it is infinitely weaker than the union between the divine love of Jesus' soul and His glorified heart, His glorious body!

This first beat of Jesus' glorious heart is first and foremost for the Father, for His glory. But it is also for Mary. If the first beat of the heart of the Child Jesus coming from Mary, His Mother, was for the Father and for Mary (no one else shared in it, it was reserved for them), it is normal for the first beat of the glorified Jesus' heart, coming from the Father's omnipotence, also to be reserved for them. Jesus was returning a hundredfold to Mary what He had received from her.

It is in her faith that Mary lives by this mystery, that she lives on this first beat of Jesus' glorified heart. This act of faith is made in darkness in Mary's soul, yet it is based on the glory and brilliant light of Christ's risen heart and body. This darkness is quite different from that of the sepulcher. It is the darkness that veils the splendor of the midday sun, that gives us the absolute certainty of its presence, yet at the same time hides its brightness in itself. This darkness is imbued with light. It is, as it were, diaphanous and translucent, but it is nonetheless all the more terrible and difficult to bear for the intelligence and heart because it appears abnormal. Is it not abnormal to believe in light, in the presence of light? Light in itself is not an object of faith, but of vision. When it is present, it illuminates everything. In her glorious faith in this mystery of glory, light is there, present for Mary. She is certain of it; yet this light is not given as light, but as pure love.

This divine act of faith has no need of any outward sign. Mary does not need any visible and sensible apparition to believe in the mystery of the Resurrection. Inspired by the Holy Spirit, she spontaneously adheres to this mystery of glory. She follows the Lamb in His new state, as she had followed Him on the holy mountain of Calvary. We do not know whether—out of superabundance as at the Annunciation—she was given a sign, whether Jesus appeared to her. Scripture is silent on this point. This silence must teach us that, even if such an apparition did take place, it was entirely for her, totally reserved for her own divine life. For, beginning with the Sepulcher, the Holy Spirit wants her to remain totally hidden in a pure, solitary and contemplative life. When Jesus appears to Mary Magdalene to strengthen her faith, He asks her to inform the Apostles. His apparition must serve an apostolic purpose; it is a charismatic apparition. For Mary, if an apparition did occur, it was out of pure contemplative superabundance.

This mystery of the Resurrection, accepted in a totally pure and divine act of faith, unites Mary's soul to Jesus in a far more intense way than at the Annunciation. She is as it were secluded in this mystery, as though she herself had risen from the dead with Him and no longer belonged to this world. There follows a profound separation, so to speak, from everything earthly. Does St. Paul not tell us: "If then you have been raised with Christ, seek the things that are above, where Christ is, seated at the right hand of God. Set your minds on things that are above, not on things that are on earth. For you have died, and your life is hid with Christ in God" (Col. 3:1-3).

Seeking only "things that are above," living only on the Risen Christ, Mary lives in total, absolute silence as if she were no longer part of this world. John had to respect this silence without understanding it, without grasping its full significance. For Mary was already living by the mystery of the Resurrection, while John still remained in the sadness of the separation of the Crucifixion and the Sepulcher. That is why, in response to Mary Magdalene's frantic call upon returning from the tomb, he runs with Peter to ascertain the fact.

According to the Gospel's narrative, we clearly understand that John and Peter were living in anxious expectation. They too had abandoned the firm and peaceful attitude of a purely divine and loving faith. So instead of reassuring Mary Magdalene and calming her down, they follow her example and run; "they both ran." It is a race to the tomb. John, who is younger and more loving, arrives first.

Mary's presence and the intensity of her contemplative life do not seem to have enlightened John. He has not yet fully believed in the mystery of the Resurrection. God wanted Mary to remain, more than ever, in absolute silence.

The mystery of the Resurrection illuminates not only Mary's faith but also her hope. Her hope remains very poor, but this poverty is different from the poverty of the Cross or of Christmas. It is the poverty of those who live in direct contact with an infinitely rich treasure, who know that this treasure is for them but who also know that they must wait to possess it perfectly. They know that they are not allowed to take hold of it now, but that they can use it according to the will and pleasure of the one who fully possesses it.

It is the poverty of a servant who no longer understands why he remains there in the same situation as before, for the task which was required of him has been accomplished, fully accomplished. He must wait, although it seems a complete waste of time, without worrying, but with absolute trust in his master, who acts with wisdom.

In this divine poverty, Mary's hope in the mystery of the Resurrection experiences a wonderful *sursum corda,* since her heart has been so thoroughly purified and is firmly anchored in the glorious wound of Jesus' heart. This hope dynamically comes to bloom in a mad desire to be with the Father and solely with Him, through and with Christ, since now Christ can realize this calling. The winter of separations is over. While being totally "in His Father's house," Jesus can be at the same time entirely devoted to Mary. Nothing stops this desire and this dynamism in Mary's soul; on the contrary, everything contributes toward making it more pure and fervent. The mystery of the Resurrection is a testimony for her of the Father's infinite mercy toward Jesus and thus also toward His Mother, toward her who followed Him to the end. In her divine hope, Mary calls down this mercy upon herself. She begs for it, showing how much she no longer has any *raison d'être* here below, how uprooted she is from this earth, how much she can only live close to the Father. But this call remains the call of one immersed in poverty, who abandons herself to God the Father's gracious will.

The illumination of faith and hope implies an analogous illumination of charity. Thanks to this mystery of the Resurrection, Mary lives even more intimately with Jesus. This mystery engages her even more intensely, in what was her entire life, but which is lived with new fullness. Mary's life is more than ever a "unitive" life, a life full of love, completely pacified in love, completely transfigured by love.

Jesus is given to her much more even than at Christmas or the Annunciation, for in the meantime not only was there the extraordinary gift of the Cross—which remains—but now there is the new gift of His glorified heart. Jesus rises from the dead for Mary, that He may be totally given to her, body and soul. Through the Resurrection, Jesus' body becomes the model for all other resurrections, including the future resurrection of Mary's body. Everything in Christ is now a model for Mary, whereas during His earthly life—particularly in the childhood mysteries—He could be only a model for Mary's divine life. This causes a great joy and peace in Mary's heart, since there is a more divine and intimate presence of Jesus in this mystery than in the joyful and sorrowful mysteries—a more complete yet fully divine presence, which, as such, escapes all sensible experience and can be reached only through and in faith.

The divine presence of Jesus Glorified orients Mary's whole life toward the Father. We can say that this is what characterizes this final stage of her contemplative life: truly being a contemplative who, in and through Jesus' heart, divinely reaches the Father and rests *in sinu Patris* (Jn. 1:18). What characterizes the glorified Christ is precisely to be *in sinu Patris,* totally glorified by the Father and for Him. He is the glory of the Father. This is why, through this mystery, Mary also lives with the Father.

This life of faith, hope and love really seems to absorb Mary's entire life, since, beginning with this stage, she can only reach Jesus through the exercise of these virtues. The only thing that attracts her is to live with Him, and, through Him, to live with the Father.

We can well understand how the gift of wisdom actually purifies the exercise of charity in Mary's heart and how it also enables her to live in this unity and peace in this new, silent and secret intimacy. The gift of wisdom enables her to draw from this mysterious silence of God at its fundamental and original source and to grasp all its power and divine fruitfulness, in connaturality with the Trinitarian mystery, in and through Jesus' heart. At that first moment of the Resurrection of Jesus' heart, there must have been a divine, ecstatic experience of the gift of wisdom in Mary's spirit, wherein, with and through the glorified Jesus, she said in silence: "Father, here I am," wherein her soul rose up to face the Father, as His beloved little daughter, who realized through Christ's wounded and glorified heart how much the Father loved her in this divine covenant, the covenant of the blood and water that flowed from the wound of the heart.

Such was the divine peace that Mary's soul tasted on that holy and glorious night, while Mary Magdalene was anxiously waiting for dawn so that she could rush to the empty tomb, while John and the other disciples must have been sleeping, tired as they were after all these terrible, overwhelming and contradictory days. As at the Agony, Mary alone was keeping vigil, no longer to console and comfort but to let herself be divinely carried away and attracted by the wonderful power of her Son's glorified heart.

Let us note in closing that if the risen Christ appeared to Mary out of superabundance, in addition to this divine presence of faith, hope and love, she was then able to enjoy a charismatic presence which took complete possession of her sensibilities and imagination. Accordingly, it was Mary's entire life—divine and human—which was as it were captured by Jesus. This divine, mystical and charismatic presence took hold of everything.

CHAPTER 16

THE ASCENSION
AND THE POVERTY OF HOPE

WE can only understand the way in which Mary received the mystery of the Ascension by comparing her silence with the attitude of the Apostles. From the Resurrection to the Ascension, we know that the Apostles had the grace of receiving certain visits from Jesus Glorified. Jesus came to confirm them in their faith, their hope and their love. He also came to finish forming them by His words and His life.

Being always slow to understand, the Apostles ask Christ a question as He is about to leave them, a question that will actually be their last: "Lord, will you at this time restore the kingdom to Israel?" (Acts 1:6). This is their major concern and their deep desire. The mystery of the Cross did not enlighten them. In their view, Christ's Resurrection should imply a messianism, a kind of earthly reign of Christ over the universe.

Our Lord replies: "It is not for you to know times or seasons which the Father has fixed by his own authority. But you shall receive power when the Holy Spirit has come upon you; and you shall be my witnesses in Jerusalem and in all Judea and Samaria and to the end of the earth" (Acts 1:7-8). These were the last official words Christ addressed to His disciples.

We cannot know when Christ's absolute reign over the universe will come to pass, for this is the Father's secret. We cannot know when the return of Christ as Judge and King of the universe will take place. No one knows the hour of the Last Judgment except the Father. Our Lord thus leads His disciples to understand that they are really asking the wrong question, one for which they cannot receive an answer. Their question reveals a desire for usurpation with regard to the Father's plan.

They should, on the contrary, be concerned with the imminent descent of the Holy Spirit, who is going to transform their lives, transform their timidity into strength and enable them to be Jesus' witnesses throughout the entire world. Thus, before leaving them, Our Lord turns them once more toward the Holy Spirit, as though to help them understand that the Holy Spirit is the one who will give them divine understanding of His words and who will help them remain faithful to the end. It is not a question of dreaming about a messianism *hic et nunc* [here and now]: rather, they must hope for the divine, hidden, inner reign of the Holy Spirit—that is to say a reign of love, in what is most proper and demanding to love.

After these words that prophesy to His disciples' destiny and mission and explain to them their role as witnesses thanks to the love of the Holy Spirit, Jesus disappears. "And when he had said this, as they were looking on, he was lifted up, and a cloud took him out of their sight" (Acts 1:9).

The Apostles were obviously not expecting such an abrupt departure. At the very moment when once more they were longing for Christ's temporal and divine reign over His people, He definitively rejects it by visibly and physically abandoning His position as King of the human community. "My kingdom is not of this world." Stupefied, the Apostles keep looking upwards, in the direction where He had disappeared. "And while they were gazing into heaven as he went, behold, two men stood by them in white robes, and said, 'Men of Galilee, why do you stand looking into heaven? This Jesus, who was taken up from you into heaven, will come in the same way as you saw him go into heaven' " (Acts 1:10-11). The angels have to explain to them what has just happened and direct them back to their duty and the demands of God's will for them.

Given the Apostles' state of mind, we can easily understand that the mystery of the Ascension seemed to them an unexpected and incomprehensible mystery of separation. It is a new separation very different from that of the Crucifixion and the Sepulcher; in a way, it is the ultimate separation. For they were longing intensely for Him to remain visibly present among them. As with any separation which is a bit violent, this one inevitably causes a certain sadness in the Apostles' hearts. Their deepest desire apparently cannot be fulfilled. Yet this sadness is as it were surpassed and overcome by a very firm hope in the coming of the Holy Spirit and the future return of Jesus. This separation, however great, is not total and absolute. He promised that He would not leave them "orphans," that He would send the Paraclete. The separation remains temporary: He will come again.

Mary, on the other hand, lives in a direct way by the mystery of the Ascension. Unlike the Apostles, she had not desired this messianic reign because, at the Cross, she had understood how much Christ's reign was a divine reign, a reign in love. Of course, the Resurrection had increased her trust and hope in Jesus. But she was living above all by the mystery of the Resurrection. She was living by the apparitions she may have received only as a grace of superabundance; she did not stop there. Her love for Jesus was too pure, her faith too divine, to humanize all the consequences of the Resurrection. She was too poor to want to hold on to this visible and sensible presence. That is why Mary can live by this mystery of the Ascension without sadness, in a totally divine and glorious joy.

Although this mystery of the Ascension does indeed imply a separation, it is not first and foremost a new separation for Mary, analogous to the separation of the Finding in the Temple or to that of the Sepulcher. For her, this mystery is actually a new gift, a new, loving intimacy, a new presence of Jesus, for this separation is normal and necessary. The glorified Christ is no longer part of this corruptible universe. Hence He must leave it, visibly and socially, for another place: heaven, His kingdom. Mary, who lives only for Him, cannot be saddened by this glorious Ascension—quite the contrary. The mystery of the Ascension is the final exaltation of Christ's glorious humanity. Since this glorious humanity no longer belongs to our universe, it can no longer be contained by the universe as one of its parts. This glorious humanity transcends this universe and in a certain way contains and measures it, in the sense that Christ's glorious body is a perfect body and lives according to an eminent mode. It is the most perfect body, which thus measures all other bodies. This glorious body is for itself its own place—heaven—and it is indeed the place proper to all other bodies which will be glorified. Is His body not the "Father's house" in which there are many dwellings? Is it not the "Head" which constantly exerts its intimate and direct influence upon all its members?

Mary lives by this mystery in her faith. She adheres to this sort of transcendence of the glorious humanity of her Son, "seated at the right hand of the Father," near the Father as our Advocate, ceaselessly interceding for us as High Priest. We know quite well that the consequence of any new transcendence is to allow for a new immanence. A being can be immanent to the extent that it is transcendent; we can live by its immanence to the extent that we live by its transcendence. The mystery of the Ascension enables Mary to live in an even deeper intimacy with Jesus and to understand how much His presence of Glory is more precious and intimate to her than His presence at the Annunciation or during Advent. During Advent, Mary carried Jesus within her and gave Him life; yet His infant heart, while surely remaining quite close and dependent on hers, was still juxtaposed as exterior to hers. There were indeed two hearts beating in unison, but two hearts juxtaposed and external to one another. In the mystery of the Ascension, Jesus' glorified heart is given to her with all its divine transcendence and glory; and, for that very reason, it is given to her with new intimacy.

In her faith, Mary lives by this mystery of transcendence and immanence. This glorified heart becomes the proper milieu of her divine life, the vital milieu in which her divine life will blossom in a totally divine way, in the sense that she will know a wonderful intimacy with Jesus' heart, receiving everything from it and being as though divinely enfolded in its influence and love. We might say that, through the mystery of the Ascension, Christ's heart is given to His Mother as the "gate" of the divine sheepfold, as the "way" leading to the place, as the "pure sign and instrument" of the Father's love for His only Son and for her. Christ's heart is given to her as the very life of her life, as the inmost and most intimate depths of her own heart, as that gushing spring from which "rivers of living water" (Jn. 7:38) flow, as the beloved heart in which the Father is well pleased, for His sake and for hers.

This mystery of the Ascension also brings about a new extension to the Most Holy Virgin's faith; for, not only must she consider the transcendence and immanence of Christ's heart with respect to herself, she must also consider this transcendence and immanence with respect to John and the entire Church. From now on, in faith she must consider John as her priest, her *alter Christus*, another Christ for her, as the one who holds Christ's intimate authority. She must consider Peter as the head of this nascent Church, as the one who has received from Christ the authority to govern it and maintain its unity. Despite appearances, she must believe in this immanence of Christ in the Church, in the members of Christ; she must believe in Christ's efficacious power, which is communicated according to His will, with diversity and unity. We know quite well that a more divine act of faith is needed to believe in God's authority residing in His deficient, deformed, de-crepit instruments that are apparently so distant from the "Father's bosom" and Jesus' heart. Certain difficulties arising from our critical mind must be overcome in order to go beyond appearances and adhere to the reality of the Mystical Body and, in it, to the priestly and governing authority of Christ, the Good Shepherd.

The mystery of the Ascension enables Mary's hope to consider heaven even more explicitly and intensely as her proper place, her own house, since it is her Son's proper place. Is she not now completely connaturalized to this holy place? In this mystery, her hope acquires a mode of wonderful simplicity, since the desire for heaven coincides with the desire of her maternal heart to be with her Son. It is in the same divine aspiration that she yearns to live by the Father and by her Son. To be entirely in the Father's house is to be entirely with her Son as well, to be reunited with Him and live by Him.

This divine simplicity that gives her desire greater intensity—since all its efficacy and potentialities are channeled in the same direction—also demands a very great poverty. This mystery of the Ascension leaves Mary definitively alone with John until the end of her earthly life. John's presence is certainly a very sweet and loving presence for her, but it is also a very impoverishing one. For it is through John and his priesthood that she must sacramentally receive Jesus' body. She must rely on John's priestly prayer to rely more efficaciously on Jesus' prayer. Must she not be sacramentally offered up and immolated in the mystery of the Eucharist in order to

continue living the offering and immolation that she made at
the Cross?

The service of John's priesthood, like the priesthood of
her Son for her, demands from Mary's heart a very great
divine poverty; for she must accept the fact that through
John's ministry, Jesus is able, and desires, to do greater things
than those He did in a direct manner. We must accept the
fact that Divine Wisdom uses multiple and varied instruments to communicate itself more divinely, in a more merciful superabundance, for this very multiplicity requires from
us an attitude of greater poverty and deeper surrender.

Mary, who had experienced Christ's direct influence,
Christ's direct guidance, must accept from now on for Christ
to lead and direct her through His minister, His priest. This
requires very great faith and poverty from Mary's heart. She
must consent to die to the privileged situation she experienced at Nazareth and even afterwards until the Ascension, in
order to enter deliberately into the common way of the
Church. In order to be Mother of the Church, she must consent to be the latter's *pars principalis* [principal member] and
therefore consent to live in unison with its members.

In the mystery of the Purification, we admired Mary's
humility, which consisted in disregarding her privileges in
order to follow the common law and the precepts of the Old
Testament. We have here a far deeper abdication and humility; she must completely disregard the incomparable grace of
having received Jesus' teaching directly and immediately, a
unique privilege and the sign of a preferential love. She must
consent to follow the common law of the Church's members:
to be led and taught by Christ's sacramental priesthood in

John. Such a total interior poverty enables her hope to be free and utterly simple and to know an efficacity in her desires and aspirations that is entirely new.

Finally, let us seek to understand how this mystery of the Ascension transforms the life of love of Mary's heart; for, the more God demands in the way of purifications of faith and hope, the more freely and abundantly He wants to communicate His love.

By living this mystery, the divine love of Mary's heart experiences a completely new simplicity, since she is now living in unity. Indeed, thanks to this mystery, Mary can embrace, in one single act of love, the whole mystery of love in God—*in sinu Patris*—and this same mystery of love in the glorified Christ. She can embrace this mystery as being fully given to her in Jesus' heart. Her love can rest in this complete unity, which is both Trinitarian and Christian. Her love can then be exercised in a very simple way; for, in the most intimate depths of Jesus' heart, she finds the Father's love, and this love of the Father gives her Jesus' heart as an indubitable "sign" of His love and infinite mercy.

Thanks to the gift of wisdom, this love blossoms into a very simple, divine contemplation in unison with the Trinitarian life in Jesus' heart, a contemplation which enables Mary to live in personal contact with the three divine Persons in their personal and secret mystery. She lives in the Word and through the Spirit; she lives by the Father's ineffable fruitfulness, by all that is unique in His mystery as unbegotten Person and primary source of all love. She lives in the Word this mystery of unity and transformation into Jesus' heart. She lives by the light of the Word, which is communicated and given to her in faith and wisdom. She lives by it directly as the Father's little child, begotten by Him in His light, just as the Word Himself is begotten by the Father in His light. She lives in the Word by this unique gaze of the Father who is her life. Through the Holy Spirit, she lives by this mutual love that unites the Father and the Son, that unites the Father and her soul, for she is loved by the Father in and through the Holy Spirit.

Through the gift of wisdom, her Trinitarian contemplation in Jesus' heart takes possession of her whole being and extends to the entire Church, whose Mother she is according to the Father's will. She carries the entire Church in her prayer, in her faith, her hope, her love. She begets the Church to divine life through a superabundance of love and contemplative life—she especially begets John, who is for her like the firstborn, the archetype of her children. Not only must she use John, but she must do much more: she must spiritually and divinely beget him, bear him, feed him; for he is really her child, the one given to her by Christ. John is part of her contemplative life in the sense that he is the first beneficiary of the divine superabundance of her contemplation. He is the first to share in her life, to receive all its fullness.

Using John as a priest and begetting him as a son are two aspects that are conflicting and mutually exclusive from the perspective of our human psychology; yet from the divine point of view, they complement and intensify one another. The more John is Mary's son, the more he can exercise his priestly power upon her; the more Mary is John's Mother, the more docile and receptive she can be to his authority as a priest, since any increase in love necessarily implies a blossoming of all that is divine in us.

This mystery of the Ascension, which places Mary "at the right hand of the Father" (for she follows the Lamb wherever He goes), also instills in Mary's soul an intense desire to receive the Holy Spirit. Jesus said: "It is to your advantage that I go away, for if I do not go away, the [Paraclete] will not come to you" (Jn. 16:7). Mary is thirsty; she longs intensely to receive the One who has been promised and who is to come. That is why the Ascension is also the starting point for her of a new period of expectation, of a new advent that is completely silent and divine, very poor and very fervent. It is in prayer and prayer alone that Mary is waiting, begging the Father through Jesus to send the One who is to be the divine Comforter of her soul and of the Church.

CHAPTER 17

PENTECOST AND THE
FRUITFULNESS OF LOVE

WHILE awaiting the coming of the Holy Spirit "all these with one accord devoted themselves to prayer, together with the women and Mary the mother of Jesus, and with his brethren" (Acts 1:14). They are all together in the same "Upper Room," the Cenacle; they are all prompted by the same love and pray constantly. Mary is there in their midst.

This advent, which prepares for the full communication of the Holy Spirit and His charismatic gifts, is quite similar to the first Advent which prepared for the birth of Jesus, yet at the same time it is completely different. It is very similar because both involve prayer, recollection, silence, faith in the promise, an ardent desire for its fulfillment, and love for this divine gift. While carrying Jesus hidden within her, Mary remained completely immersed in the silence of her prayer and contemplation. By living inwardly united to Jesus' glorified heart, Mary remains even more deeply recollected in the silence of prayer.

This period of waiting for the gift of the Holy Spirit is very different from the first Advent in the external circumstances of time and place. The first Advent lasted for nine months, the natural length of time for the formation of Jesus' body in Mary; the other advent lasts for only a few days, the time determined by divine Wisdom, according to His good pleasure. One occurs in Nazareth, the other in Jerusalem. During the first Advent, Mary was the only one to live by the promise fulfilled in her; here she lives by Christ's promise along with the Apostles and the holy women. It is really a communal period of waiting. It is the Church that waits. The first was personal: it was Mary's. That is why one was to happen in the ordinary circumstances of human life, without any apparent change, so that everything might remain more hidden. The other, on the contrary, requires a proper place apart from the usual confines of human life and its ordinary concerns, a special setting in which everything is directed toward a specific goal: preparing for the descent of the Holy Spirit. Indeed, we can say that this period of waiting in the Upper Room is the first manifestation of the nascent Church, of this still embryonic Church which is about to be born by receiving the Holy Spirit. We have here a very interesting and noteworthy fact, for this first communal gesture of the Church requires a certain rupture, as it were, with other human, political and family communities. Whereas Mary's first Advent, far from breaking human communal bonds, intensifies them while at the same time making them poorer. This difference reveals to us both the autonomy proper to the Christian community—it is a specific community irreducible to other communities, having its own nature and proper laws—and the rooting of this community in the human family community.

In view of the action of God's wisdom in both cases, could we not say that God wants His Church to be both politically autonomous and rooted in a family community? These two aspects are complementary and inseparable. Otherwise, one might humanize the Church too much by rooting it in a political community—the Church is free *vis-à-vis* all forms of political regime—or, on the contrary, one might idealize it too much by separating it completely from the family community. The Church is not indifferent to any kind of family establishment; the Church possesses its own family doctrine.

But there is an even deeper and more fundamental difference regarding the proper end or the specific intention of these two advents. One concerns the Word Incarnate's birth in time; the other concerns the communication of the Holy Spirit in time, a communal and personal communication. We may think that the Holy Spirit had already been communicated to some in a very personal and intimate way, but in reality He had not yet been collectively communicated, in an ecclesial manner, to the Church as such, and hence in a manner both charismatic and personal.

Because of the difference in time, these two divine recollections in Mary's soul will be very different in nature. One belongs to her joyful mysteries and implies the mystery of the Visitation and the journey from Nazareth to Bethlehem; the other belongs to her glorious mysteries and implies no other mystery. Everything must be reserved exclusively for this period of waiting. It is the only thing that matters and that must captivate Mary's activity, the activity of the Apostles, of the holy women, and of the entire community. This note of exclusivity, of intensity, and activity during these days of waiting is well reported in Scripture. It is a very characteristic.

This first communal retreat of the Church gathered around Mary, entirely oriented toward receiving the Holy Spirit, the Paraclete, is highly significant. It must enable us to comprehend what is quite characteristic of the Christian community as such; for we can say that it is its ultimate disposition, so to speak, which very often reveals to us the proper nature of the substantial form. It is in this particular atmosphere that we must understand the mystery of Pentecost, the visible birth of the Church as Church.

> When the day of Pentecost had come, they were all together in one place. And suddenly a sound came from heaven like the rush of a mighty wind, and it filled all the house where they were sitting. And there appeared to them tongues as of fire, distributed and resting on each one of them. And they were all filled with the Holy Spirit and began to speak in other tongues, as the Spirit gave them utterance (Acts 2:1-4).

Note the "signs" used by God's wisdom to show us the Holy Spirit's action in the souls of Mary and the Apostles. Since they concern a true temporal and visible mission of the Holy Spirit, the value of these signs lies in the realm of pure signification and manifestation, to help us penetrate the mystery. First there is this extraordinary sound, "a sound like the rush of a mighty wind." We know that in the Old Testament, the work of the Holy Spirit is often suggested by the image of a "breath" to express both the flexibility and the wonderful dynamism of divine love.

There is nothing more subtle than wind, which manages to penetrate everywhere, which even seems to penetrate all inanimate bodies, as though giving them a life of their own. It gives them life and moves them. To the idea of subtlety, of flexibility, is added the idea of strength and violence. We have all heard about the incredible violence of certain tornadoes and hurricanes which seem to uproot everything in their path. When it reaches such fury, the wind seems to possess a kind of voice of its own.[104]

Scripture here points out the extraordinary sound that occurred and the fury of the wind. It is easy to understand that all these properties of wind wonderfully evoke those of divine love, which is both the most tender and sweet, and yet strongest thing there is; something that slips in, in such a way that it does not seem to come from the outside and which can then bring back to life or give life to what is lifeless. Divine love is at the same time stronger than death and stronger than Sheol. Nothing can resist Love, for It is the very source of strength and efficacy. Without love there would be neither strength nor efficacy.

We should observe however that this "sound," an auditory sign coming from this "mighty wind," is mentioned here in the Scriptural text simply as a general atmosphere that fills

---

104. That is why Scripture, calling the various realities of the universe to witness so that they might praise their Creator, affirms: "Stormy wind fulfilling his command!" (Ps. 148:8).

the entire Upper Room, the whole house in which they are staying. The specific sign is visual: "tongues as of fire" come down upon each member of the community. Even more precisely, fire is used in Scripture to signify God's love. Think of the apparition to Moses:

> And the angel of the Lord appeared to him in a flame of fire out of the midst of a bush; and he looked, and lo, the bush was burning, yet it was not consumed. And Moses said, "I will turn aside and see this great sight, why the bush is not burnt." When the Lord saw that he turned aside to see, God called to him out of the bush, "Moses, Moses!" and he said, "Here am I." Then he said, "Do not come near; put off your shoes from your feet, for the place on which you are standing is holy ground (Ex. 3:2-5).

This fire that burns without being consumed is indeed the image of divine love, which burns everything without destroying, but rather while giving life. Fire possesses that wonderful subtlety whereby it seems to be able to penetrate bodies, to transform them from the inside, without depriving them of their proper nature but by giving them instead an entirely new manner of being, as it were. Think for instance of incandescent coal and glass.

Fire also possesses that sort of tremendous fruitfulness whereby it constantly spreads and assimilates everything it reaches, even what is most opposed to it, like water. And this diffusion occurs with an amazing and proverbial rapidity.

Fire possesses the property of purifying, of separating amalgamated bodies, and of restoring their original purity through its specific action. And this capacity to purify is so strong and so powerful that fire communicates it to the bodies that it has made incandescent, that it has assimilated. Isaiah notes a vision of a seraphim flying toward him "having in his hand a burning coal which he had taken with tongs from the altar." He touches the prophet's mouth with it, saying: "Behold, this has touched your lips; your guilt is taken away, and your sin forgiven" (Is. 6:6-7).

Because of this ability to purify and to separate what is pure from what is impure, fire will be called to witness as having the power to judge what is authentic from what is false. Think of Elijah's holocaust, from the fire of heaven that burns the victims, the altar—to testify that only this sacrifice is legitimate and accepted by God (1 Kings 18:38).

Such are the many qualities possessed by divine love in a far more specific way than fire, which is only an image of divine love. Divine love possesses an incredible fruitfulness, since it is the very source of all fecundity. All fruitfulness necessarily proceeds from this first love; since love, according to its profound nature, not only attracts everything to itself but is "self-diffusive": *bonum diffusivum sui*.[105] It communicates itself as much as possible, and by nature would never cease to do so. If limits are present in this diffusion, the explanation lies not in love as such, but formally in another aspect of being.

---

105. See St. Thomas Aquinas, *Summa Theologica* I, Q. 5, Art. 4, obj. 2 and 2; I-II, Q. 1, Art. 4, obj. 1; Q. 2, Art. 3, obj. 2, etc. *De Veritate*, Q. 21, Art. 1, obj. 4 and ad. 4.

While love unites and is a unitive force, it is also, from a different perspective, a separating and dividing force. While love unites beings that are alike or that can complement one another, it also separates and rejects whatever might harm this unity. This is how love purifies. And the most demanding, the most profound, the most terrible purifications proceed from love, for "love is jealous" with that holy jealousy that will not tolerate any sharing and wants everything.

And it is equally true that it is not only divine love in itself which has the capacity to purify but also all that this love has transformed into itself.

We can also understand how love has the capacity to judge, precisely because of its capacity to unite and separate. For this capacity to unite and separate necessarily implies a power of discernment and thus of judgment.

Because of this perfect correspondence between the qualities of fire and those of love, we can easily understand the suitability of this symbolism of the tongues of fire as a manifestation of the gifts of the Holy Spirit. We can also grasp the suitability of the double symbolism: the "sound" as though coming from a mighty wind and the "tongues of fire." In order to fully give itself, love requires love. We know quite well that love, in its extremity, is a mutual love of friendship. For to love truly, to be able to give ourselves completely to someone, we must give ourselves to a friend, to someone who loves us.

We cannot give ourselves completely to someone who is a stranger, to someone who is indifferent to us. For we can only impart what is most our own, our intimate and personal secrets, to a heart that is already ours, that is not "other" with regard to us. Christ says that we must not cast pearls before swine. The pearl is in fact the most personal fruit of our hearts, this *verbum cordis* [word of the heart] which conveys our love and our life. The swine, in this case, are all those who are not friends capable of receiving our secret with a love equal to the love in which this secret was conceived and continues to be kept. This double symbolism reminds us both that the Holy Spirit is the proper fruit of the first mutual Love—that of the Father and the Son—and that He can only be fully bestowed if our virginal heart already loves Him and welcomes Him with love.

This enables us to understand the very great difference that exists between receiving Light and receiving Love; it helps us understand that one must necessarily precede the other. One must have good will to receive light; one must not place any obstacles in the way, and especially not the obstacle of pride. Those who are humble receive light. And light can communicate itself. The Word, the Light, became flesh and dwelt among us. All the poor have been evangelized and have received the light; the proud have been rejected.

In order to fully receive Love, it is necessary for Light to have already dispelled the darkness and made our hearts loving and pure. To receive Love, humility is not sufficient: we must already love. Otherwise, Love cannot communicate Itself; It cannot give us what is most Itself. The Word was made flesh and came to live among us. To all who received Him, He gave the power to become children of God. And He promised to send the Holy Spirit to them.

There is a divine order between the two missions, an order of divine wisdom. This is why Advent, which is ordered toward receiving the Word Incarnate precedes the advent ordered toward receiving the Holy Spirit.

After the Holy Spirit's mission there can be no other. For the Holy Spirit is the *nexus,* the "bond" of the Father and the Son, and the One that unites us to the Father in the Son. Unity ends and is completed in Him. The Holy Spirit's mission is to lead us to the Father, *apud Patrem,* in the Son, by making us live by God's Word. The return to the Father's house, *in sinu Patris* (cf. Jn. 1:18),. is accomplished through the Holy Spirit, in the Only Son.

Appearing as tongues of fire, the Holy Spirit took possession of the hearts of the Apostles, the holy women, and Mary. To better understand His divine work in Mary, we must first understand His work in the Apostles, as recorded in Scripture. Then, by comparison, we shall try to enter into the new silence, the Holy Spirit's proper work, in Mary's heart.

The Holy Spirit gives the Apostles a divine language with a divine efficacy capable of generating faith and converting and transforming hearts, capable also of making itself understood by each person in his particular and familiar language. The Scriptural text is quite clear:

> Now there were dwelling in Jerusalem Jews, devout men from every nation under heaven. And at this sound the multitude came together, and they were bewildered, because each one heard them speaking in his own language. And they were amazed and wondered, saying "Are not all these who are speaking Galileans? And how is it that we hear, each of us in his own

native language? Parthians and Medes and
Elamites and residents of Mesopotamia, Judea
and Cappadocia, Pontus and Asia, Phrygia
and Pamphylia, Egypt and the parts of Libya
belonging to Cyrene, and visitors from home,
both Jews and proselytes, Cretans and Arabi-
ans, we hear them telling in our own tongues
the mighty works of God" (Acts 2:5-11).

The outpouring of the Holy Spirit in the form of
tongues of fire thus communicates a charism to the Apostles:
the gift of tongues. This is well attested to and shows us how
this outpouring of the Holy Spirit, in its specific effect, first
affects the Church in its communal aspect.

But there is more to it than that: the Holy Spirit also
communicates to the Apostles, particularly to Peter, the
charism of *sermo sapientiae* [preaching of wisdom]. We need
only examine his discourse to be convinced of this (Acts 2:14-
36). Moreover, this discourse has an immediate divine efficacy: it transforms the hearts of those who are listening.

Now when they heard this they were cut to
the heart, and said to Peter and the rest of
the apostles, "Brethren, what shall we do?"
And Peter said to them, "Repent, and be
baptized every one of you in the name of
Jesus Christ for the forgiveness of your sins;
and you shall receive the gift of the Holy
Spirit." . . . And fear came upon every soul
(Acts 2:37-38; 43).

It is not only the Apostles' language that is changed but also their lives. Fearful and cowardly as they were—think of Peter—they become strong, bearing witness to the divinity of Christ. They are no longer ashamed of their title as disciples of Christ; this title is on the contrary their sole glory. What Our Lord had foretold to them before His Ascension is thus fully accomplished.

The grace of Pentecost transforms not only their attitude toward Jesus, but also their attitude toward each other. A vibrant and very deep bond of fraternal friendship develops among them:

> And all who believed were together and had all things in common; and they sold their possessions and goods and distributed them to all, as any had need. And day by day, attending the temple together and breaking bread in their homes, they partook of food with glad and generous hearts, praising God and having favor with all the people (Acts 2:44-47).

It is easy to recognize the specific effects of the gift of piety and its proper demands. This Christian community has something very distinct that specifies it, and is not just any kind of community. Hence it is indeed a grace of complete and total transformation that is given to them in love, a grace that they can even communicate to others. It is really a "grace of fire" which inflames their hearts, and from their hearts it spreads to all those who listen to them and approach them.

In Mary, the Holy Spirit communicates Himself with unique fullness, for Mary's heart is more pure, more poor and more thirsty for love than the Apostles' hearts. This greater perfection of communication instills in Mary an even more divine and absolute silence. In the Apostles' hearts, the Holy Spirit creates a divine, efficacious language that can bring about conversions. In Mary's heart it creates new chasms of silence. He transforms the Apostles into visible witnesses of Christ by means of their words and their lives. He has Mary live a solitary and hidden life as Mother of these witnesses. Just as the Apostles' words must be as though entirely enveloped in Mary's divine silence, so must their testimony be as though rooted in Mary's solitary, hidden life, a life which is more and more solitary and buried, so to speak. This is why, for Mary's soul, the mystery of Pentecost is indeed the starting point of the final stage of her earthly life, the most divine, hidden and secret stage during which she is to live by that which is most ineffable and mysterious in the effusion of Love.

This mystery implies no charismatic gift in her divine life, but rather a new and ultimate demand for her contemplative life, totally hidden and reserved for God and for her children, for John in the first place and through him for all the Apostles and the whole Church. This is perfectly normal, since this mystery is the communication of divine love in its most specific, intimate and personal aspect. When love fully communicates itself, it communicates itself according to its own demands and according to the suitability of the person to whom it communicates itself. That is why, here below, since love communicates itself in and through the mysteries of faith and hope, it communicates itself in silence, in a secret and hidden way. Mary receives it in silence, in a completely silent *fiat,* in a very intimate and hidden way. The community of the Apostles is there to hide her. Outwardly, she is one of the holy women who pray with the Apostles; she is as though lost in their midst because the Spirit wants to give Himself in this totally hidden way. It is Mary's humility, her poverty, the abdication of all her privileges, of all her distinctions, that enable her to receive Him in a completely hidden and secret way. If we want to penetrate somewhat this ultimate demand of silence in Mary's divine life, we must try to specify what the mystery of Pentecost adds in particular to her life of faith, hope and love, since this silence is the fruit *par excellence* of the divine exercise of her faith, her hope and her love.

Through this mystery, her faith reaches its ultimate challenge, both in terms of extension and intensity. All the mysteries of Jesus' life have successively been the object of her faith. After the Ascension there is nothing left, from the viewpoint of extension, but the very diffusion of the Holy Spirit foretold by Christ.

With respect to intensity, we are also presented with an ultimate demand implying an ultimate difficulty. Indeed, through this mystery, it is the very mystery of Love and its diffusion that becomes the object of faith. One must believe in Love. To believe in Love is the supreme trial of faith. For while it is normal to believe in somebody's word and more normal still to believe in God's Word—since faith orients us toward the vision and the full knowledge of the truth—it is "abnormal," so to speak, to believe in Love. Psychologicaly speaking, love is an object of experience and not of faith, whereas words can be an object of faith. No one can ask someone to believe in his love without any direct and immediate experience of it. The realism of love is repelled by that which is indirect and somewhat abstract to faith. Only God can ask His creature to believe in His love, and this is the supreme trial of faith. Since His authority is supreme and the communication of His love is eminently free and depends solely upon His gracious will, He can demand this act of faith, so that the creature may more deeply acknowledge the supreme rights of God in the order of love, so that the creature may thereby be able to pay Him supreme homage and attest to God his supreme dependence. God will then be able to act more freely and accomplish His work of love more superabundantly, since this act of faith demands that the creature recognize the sovereign rights of God. Thus while such an act of faith has no psychological support, it remains supremely reasonable simply because it is God who demands it. It would be supremely unreasonable with respect to any other kind of love.

In this mystery, Mary believes in God's love, which is even more fully communicated to her and is communicated to the Apostles. Of course, Mary has always believed in God's love; but in this mystery, her faith in God's personal Love, in the Holy Spirit, becomes even more explicit and intense. She believes in this "Gift" *par excellence:* the Holy Spirit is fully given to her. Through her faith, she adheres to God's love, poured into her heart by the Holy Spirit who is given to her. *Charitas Dei diffusa est in cordibus nostris per Spiritum Sanctum, qui datus est nobis* (Rom. 5:5). The Spirit does not give only a particular blessing or a gift: He gives Himself. And in the mystery of Pentecost, He does not communicate only charismatic gifts: He gives *Himself.* Even more totally, He makes Mary's heart His home and His temple, the place where He dwells, where He likes to rest.

More than ever and with a new intensity He is the "gentle Guest" of Mary's heart and soul. Our Lord had promised to the one who loves God: "We will come to him and make our home with him" (Jn. 14:23). These words are fulfilled primarily in Mary.

In the mystery of Pentecost, the Holy Spirit, who has dwelt in her ever since the mystery of her Immaculate Conception, truly comes to take root in her and establish His dwelling in her with new jealousy. Under this even stronger influence of the Holy Spirit, in and through Him, she fully lives by this divine life of love in Jesus' heart, with the Father. Is not the Holy Spirit the Father and the Son's mutual Love? This mutual Love is given to Mary so that she may be united even more personally and intimately to her Son and to the Father. The Holy Spirit is to repeat to her in a very interior way everything that Jesus has told her, with a new penetration of love. For Jesus wants His doctrine to take possession of her intelligence in such a way that it may truly be the doctrine that the Son received from the Father, a doctrine so vitally linked to her intelligence that it is like her own thought. "The [Paraclete], the Holy Spirit, whom the Father will send in my name, he will teach you all things, and bring to your remembrance all that I have said to you" (Jn. 14:26). "When the Spirit of truth comes, he will guide you into all the truth," Jesus tells his disciples, "for he will not speak on his own authority, but whatever he hears he will speak, and he will declare to you the things that are to come" (Jn. 16:13).

And the Holy Spirit "glorifies" Jesus in Mary by making her live more and more intimately in faith all His words, as words of life and love. The Holy Spirit enables her to live fully this spirit of adoption whereby she cries: "Father" (Rom. 8:15).

In this new communication of Love, she returns to the Father with a more intense and ardent love. It is the Spirit's life-giving fire that burns her soul with love for the Father. She lives by His loving fatherhood and abandons herself to it with a new upwelling of love so that the Father may take possession of her whole life and mark it with His own hold and influence.

In this way, she truly remains in God and God in her, for she remains in Love. The silent *fiat* whereby she receives the Spirit is made in an act of faith in the Trinitarian mystery communicated by and in the Word Incarnate. This adhesion of faith to Love knows no other limit than that of the love which is given to her; it is measured by the infinite love of God Himself. Thus it is infinite and does not tolerate any internal or external limitation. These are really the ultimate justifications of the human intelligence, which must then abdicate all its rights, so to speak, in order to hide itself in divine love and surrender itself voluntarily as a prisoner to the proper demands of divine love—understanding that in practice it is better to enter the kingdom of God "voluntarily one-eyed or blind" than to have tried to measure or limit God's Word by determining it.

Love, taking full possession of Mary's life, demands as it were a new surrender of her intelligence so as to let divine truth take even greater hold of everything, even unto the most hidden and intimate recesses of her human intelligence. Divine love is entitled to everything. It can demand everything in order to have greater freedom and communicate itself more and more.

It is thanks to the gift of intelligence that faith makes such profound abdications with respect to the exercise of the human intellectual faculty, yet at the same time this gift gives faith a far more penetrating force which enables it to directly adhere to the sole necessary thing—leaving aside whatever is secondary, whatever is not love. Through love, this adhesion of faith goes beyond all formulas, all accidental realities, all that is secondary, in order to concentrate solely on the essential. Such a faith enables Mary to be completely secluded in the mystery of God's love, the most personal and most communicative mystery of love, in and through her Son's glorified heart. Such a pure, divine faith both separates her from all that is not love—this is one of love's proper demands—and puts her in intimate, direct contact from within with all those who receive this love or might receive it. Through her faith, Mary has never been so hidden, secluded, absorbed by the transcendence of the God of Love; and she has never been more a Mother, she has never been closer to all those who are her children and who are entrusted and given to her by the Holy Spirit.

Through this mystery, Mary's faith experiences a wonderful fullness and penetration, coming from Love. In and through her faith, she looks at the invisible as though she were seeing it; in and through her faith, she carries her children, the whole Church—those who are truly faithful and those who find it difficult to be faithful. She believes in the love poured into our hearts.

The ultimate divine demands which we have just considered from the perspective of faith are also found in hope. This hope is directed toward Love. It relies on the Love that is already given and aspires to the Love that is promised. So it is very simple and very divine. It is boundless, since God's love knows no bounds. It can thus be wonderfully daring, and its audacities are inspired by love and are totally directed toward love; they are divine audacities that can only be found in "little ones" and "spouses" whose fidelity has been tested at length by suffering.

But while such hope can rise so high because of the purity of its origin and direction, it also demands total poverty, the poverty required by Love and all Love's caprices. There is no limit to such poverty; inwardly it is without barriers or boundaries. It can ravage Mary's whole soul in total surrender. More and more, God's sole good pleasure is the only thing that matters in Mary's sight.

A hope rooted in such poverty—which explains all the divine audacities of the little and the poor who do not know the true intrinsic value of realities—enables the Father's mercy to use Mary just as He likes. There will be no infiltration of human determinations that humanize and thus diminish and limit divine efficacy.

In this mystery, the love in Mary's heart discovers the very love of God, in His personal and diffusive mystery, as her own divine nourishment. Accordingly, her love possesses incredible purity, intensity and simplicity. For it is the Holy Spirit Himself who enables Mary's heart to love. He enables it to live in unison with the heart of Jesus and the Father. He binds Mary's heart to Jesus' heart and in Him to the Father's love.

Thanks to the gift of wisdom, Mary can respond to this magnificent gift bestowed on her. She can love and give everything. She can freely strive to respond, in purity and spontaneity, to the gift of the Holy Spirit, and in and through Him, to settle in the Father, remain with the Father, *apud Patrem*. Through her, Israel fixes its dwelling definitively in God its Father.

This return occurs in the darkness of faith, in the deep desire of hope, but also and above all in the gift of wisdom, in peace, security and in full divine consciousness.

In this final stage of her life, Mary's contemplative life takes hold of everything else so that it may truly be hidden in God's love, in the Father; so that everything may be as though buried in God's love. At the same time, this contemplative life is extremely fruitful. It divinely blooms into a mystery of spiritual motherhood.

Mary lives with John, with the one given to her by Christ. She divinely adopts him so that all her treasure may be his. Mary keeps no secret from him, as child and priest. They wonderfully share their ideal, their divine life, with all its demands and all its requirements. This intimacy with John is the model, so to speak, of what happens with each of Jesus' beloved disciples, the other "Johns." This life with John is as it were the superabundance of her contemplative life with the Father, and is a kind of milieu that disposes one toward new movements of love.

Everything is simple and divine in this final stage. There is no longer anyone except Him and John, indissolubly united in her love. She remains in the Father through her Son; she remains with John through her Son. The gift of wisdom enables her to live by the Father's secrets and by those of John. It enables her to unify in a divine way these two activities of her charity in the silence of her excessive love. This is why Scripture keeps silent about this final stage of her life, which is as though entirely reserved for God: to understand that when God hides us in Him in this way, He gives all our activities a totally divine, loving, and infinitely fruitful note.

CONCLUSION

THUS we can see that the stages of the growth of charity in Mary—which are the mysteries of joy, sorrow and glory—actually represent three successive stages, each having its original and proper character. In the mysteries of joy, Christ's presence is what predominates. It is Jesus who acts in Mary's soul, educating her in a divine way and asking her for the material service of her physical motherhood. With the mysteries of sorrow, separation from Christ is predominant. Christ is still acting directly in her soul, but now in a sorrowful way. He acts more divinely in her and demands a gift that is even more total. Jesus asks her for a more spiritual service: that of cooperating in His Redemption. With the mysteries of glory comes divine presence in separation. Jesus is divinely present to Mary, but He is no longer part of this universe. He acts more than ever but upon her faith, her hope and her love.

Already within the mysteries of joy, some heartbreaks are felt. They are prophesied and partially fulfilled. Absolutely pure joy lasts only a short while and it always implies a demand for poverty.

In the mysteries of sorrow, there is a certain joy that remains: divine joy takes hold of Mary's soul since she is accomplishing the will of God, the will of the Father. However, there are many heartbreaks in her human psychology and sensibility.

In the mysteries of glory, joy remains, as well as sadness; yet the sadness is as though overcome by something quite particular: a note of glory, of unity and of peace.

Thus we can comprehend how charity first blossoms in conformity with the most basic demands of our human nature, then it requires separations, withdrawals and ruptures. At this point it struggles against certain demands of nature. Then it is strong enough to bloom by itself, independently of its conformity or nonconformity with our human psychology. It is then as though totally free, above and beyond any human contingencies. Everything can be good and can become divine nourishment if it is willed by God. In the final stage, Mary in fact lives in a totally divine unity with God, in and through Jesus, as though she were indifferent to whatever is not Him, yet entirely surrendered to whatever is from Him.

Moreover, the various stages of the mystery of the growth of charity in Mary show us in a unique manner the dimensions of the Father's mercy toward His little child, the new creature fully redeemed by Jesus, as well as the construction of the temple of the Holy Spirit in Mary's soul.

Indeed, the mystery of the Immaculate Conception shows us the first gesture of the Father's prevenient mercy toward His beloved child, toward Mary. We could compare this act of mercy to the mercy that God showed toward Adam and Eve, our first parents. They had been created in a state of innocence out of sheer gratuitousness. The Creator's act toward them—a radical, fundamental act of mercy—is actually, before sin, inseparable from the communication of sanctifying grace. Moreover, the latter is also a completely gratuitous act of mercy, since it is not owing to human nature. Adam and Eve's first sin of pride broke this initial harmony willed by God between the demands of human nature and those of grace. The first sin placed an obstacle in the way of this supernatural communication of grace, by opposing man's will to that of his God and Father. This opposition deprived Adam of his preternatural gifts and put his human nature in a fallen state, a state of servitude with respect to human goods.

God then allows all of Adam's descendants to be born in sin, due to the first sin. Since Adam was the head of the human race and responsible for all mankind, it is normal for all his descendants to suffer the consequences of his first sin of pride. Had he not sinned, his descendants would have inherited his privileges: God would have communicated sanctifying grace to them at the same time that He would have created their souls. But since in fact he let himself be seduced by the temptation of pride, his sin stands in the way of God's mercy; not only toward him but also toward his descendants, in such a way that in creating a human soul in the body of Adam's sons, God allows this soul to be immediately contaminated, stained by original sin. This permission of God is with a view to a greater good, a greater mercy: the redemption of Adam's descendants by the blood of Jesus Christ. Of course for us this redemption is not immediately accomplished in its entirety: the consequences of sin remain, even after the gift of grace. Man redeemed by Christ does not return to the Garden of Eden; he has to struggle and endure temporal punishment which is the consequence of original sin. But this redemption is achieved in a perfect way, radically and fully, for Mary: she is conceived without the stain of sin, receiving from the Father a wonderful royal dowry, a unique fullness of grace. The efficacy of Jesus' redemptive blood is total in Mary; nothing in her escapes the hold of the Savior's mercy. By virtue of the merits of Christ Crucified, the Father performs a unique gesture of mercy for Mary. In creating Mary's soul, He sanctifies it by giving it a unique fullness of grace and beauty, which radically separates it from the kingdom of darkness. This gesture is wonderfully prevenient. It intimately envelops Mary's body and soul in the Father's jealous mercy.

In her mystery of the Immaculate Conception, Mary goes ahead of us. She announces to us that one day, in heaven, we will all be immaculate too, enveloped in this same prevenient mercy. Yet she also shows us that already here on earth, to the extent that we are her children, this mystery of the Father's prevenient mercy and of the full efficacy of Jesus' blood is given to us. The Father's jealousy toward Mary is a divine jealousy; it is not exclusive like our passional jealousies. It is a superabundant jealousy arising from an excess of love. Although the Father showers Mary with His mercy, although He reserves her for Himself, He also gives her to us, and He does so with all the more intensity because He has reserved her for Himself. Her Immaculate Heart, formed solely by the Father, is unreservedly given to us. It is the heart of our Mother.

In the light of the mystery of the Immaculate Conception, we can comprehend more clearly why God, in His mercy, allowed this mystery of original sin to occur. He allowed all of Adam's descendants to suffer the consequences of their father's sin of pride, in order to more perfectly show His prevenient mercy toward her whom He chose to be the Mother of His Son and the Mother of the whole Church. The gratuitousness of this prevenient mercy thus appears in unique splendor!

Actually, in the light of God's wisdom, everything must be understood in terms of this initial prevenient mercy toward Mary. It is the mystery of the Immaculate Conception that shows us why God permitted this mystery of original sin. It is the mystery of the Immaculate Conception that shows us how God, in His merciful wisdom, uses the consequences of Adam and Eve's sin of pride to accomplish a more beautiful and divine work. The original unity that existed between nature and grace in Adam and Eve is found again in Mary—and it is even more divine. The fullness of grace, initially given to Mary, is greater than that which was given to Adam and Eve. It is a fullness of Christian grace, which orients Mary toward Christ Crucified. For Mary there was only one conception and one birth: a divine and human, natural and supernatural birth. Thanks to the mystery of Redemption, the Father's mercy can again be radical, both creative and supernatural. For us, there are really two births: one according to flesh and blood, the other according to water and the Spirit; there is a fundamental duality which remains here below between the "old man" and "the son of God." Yet, in heaven, unity will exist in and through Mary. Is she not the "gate of heaven"? God hastens His work; already here below this unity strives toward fulfillment.

Finally, this first gesture of prevenient mercy—which is so significant and so wonderful since it recreates human nature in Mary in a manner which is both harmonious and perfectly ordered to God—is bestowed in a totally hidden way. It is in the womb of Mary's mother that this unique gesture of mercy is carried out. No one knows about it. And the Holy Spirit only officially revealed it to the Church in the nineteenth century of the Christian era, by manifesting it to us as the great heavenly sign of the Father's prevenient mercy toward us. Indeed, when God reveals a mystery, it is so that we may live by it. All Revelation is relative to our faith and is not merely a speculative, abstract knowledge; it is a divine knowledge which intends to make us connatural to the mystery that is revealed and enable us to live by it. When the Father reveals to us the "follies" of His merciful wisdom, it is for us to admire them, to contemplate them in a divine way, i.e., to live by them. It is the "bread" of children. As Satan's attacks become more and more violent, as the power of the "beast rising out of the sea" (Rev. 13:1 ff) becomes more and more manifest, we Christians of today must, more than ever, enter deeply into the mystery of the Father's prevenient and jealous mercy so that our faith, hope and love may be more resolute. The secret of His mercy has thus been reserved for us, so to speak. The extent to which God allows the beast to have great power is the extent to which He intensifies His mercies.

The mystery of virginal consecration in abandonment shows us the second dimension of the Father's mercy toward

Mary. Prevenient mercy is ordered to another mercy which consists in educating our souls by teaching them how to present themselves voluntarily to God. Mary presents herself to God her Father by virginally consecrating herself, body and soul, in a very simple and complete abandonment. Abandonment is the most divine form of desire, for it alone does not diminish it. Such is Mary's first act of cooperation with respect to the Father's prevenient mercy. She responds to this completely gratuitous mercy by surrendering herself, i.e., by opening herself to all the potentials of this initial mercy without trying to limit them to her own understanding. True divine knowledge of oneself, of one's nothingness, is at the root of all the blossoming in one's divine life. It leads us to acknowledge that we can do nothing on our own, nothing without this prevenient mercy which envelops us, carries us and enables us to live. One can only build a high edifice by founding it on the rock of the Father's mercy. Thus consecration in abandonment is really the first stone of the temple of the Holy Spirit.

This consecration in abandonment is completed in and through the act of fraternal charity toward Joseph. By confiding her secret to him—and Joseph making it his own—Mary divinely binds herself to him. Both will lead a communal life totally reserved for God, in mutual divine abandonment, eager to accomplish His sole will.

The mystery of the Annunciation shows us the third dimension of the Father's mercy toward Mary. If the Father's mercy wants our cooperation with His merciful action, it is to establish a very intimate, personal covenant with us, in mutual gift. The Father's mercy toward us really arises out of

His excessive and superabundant love. Thus His mercy leads us to live by His love, to receive the fullness of His love, i.e., to receive the personal gift of His Son. At the Annunciation, the Father shows Mary His merciful love by giving her His Son: "God so loved the world that he gave his only Son" (Jn. 3:16). In giving His Son, He gives Himself. However, one can only give onself to someone if the latter gives himself. Every personal gift requires a personal gift. The personal gift of the Son requires the personal gift of Mary. In His mercy, the Father wants Mary to give herself in the simplest and most profound way. He wants her to give herself as a mother gives herself to a son. In the Father's mercy and through her *fiat,* Mary truly gives herself as Mother to the Father's beloved Son. The Father wants her to cooperate in a very efficacious manner in His personal gift by becoming the Mother of His beloved Son and becoming His Mother in the most perfect and complete way possible.

To cooperate in the Father's personal gift by giving herself personally requires perfect love, with pure receptivity to the Father's gift and with unreserved generosity, in unison with this gift. Through her living faith, which is very pure and limpid, Mary receives the gift of the Word Himself in the inmost depths of her spirit. Her *fiat* expresses the divine openness and welcoming of her soul which allows itself to be transformed and transfigured by the Father's "Light." Her soul opens totally to the gift of the Son, so that the Son may take everything. To welcome the gift of the Son is to divinely step aside before this gift, so that this gift may be the Life of her life, the Love of her love. This is indeed the true meaning of evangelical littleness.

The latter is required because of the personal gift of the Son. One can only receive this gift by disappearing into love. "He must increase, but I must decrease" (Jn. 3:30). In her pure faith as the Father's tiny child, Mary receives the Father's secret; this secret becomes her own. Buried in this secret of love, she is completely secluded in the Trinity and draws life from It's silence.

Through her pure and realistic faith, Mary's whole life is involved in this gift. The receptivity of her soul, which is so pure, enables her to be generous without focusing her attention on herself. Through her fiat, she cooperates efficaciously in the Father's gift by becoming the Mother according to flesh and blood of the Son of the Most High. The Father's beloved little child, who receives His "secret," is at the same time His "faithful and meek" servant. Mary yields all the strength and energy of her human nature to the gracious will of the Father's omnipotence, so that she may perfectly accomplish the task asked of her. A faithful servant who gives herself without any reservation, a meek servant who humbly gives herself without imposing her own personal opinion, Mary is also a poor servant who abdicates all her rights with respect to the work the Father asks her to accomplish. Mary is poor in her maternity. She accepts having no rights over her Son; she uses in a divine way all the bonds the Father has brought about between His Son and her, yet without making the least claim on any of them. She uses them according to the Father's gracious will, in the manner willed by Him.

While the maternal generosity of Mary's soul is total, it is nevertheless infinitely poor and thus forms a perfect alliance with the littleness of her faith. Not only do the Father's "servant" and "child" live together in Mary's soul due to this poverty, but they also mutually perfect each other: the poor servant hides the child; and the child, through her divine secret, fortifies the servant. The latter enables the Son of God to become incarnate by assuming the flesh and blood of His creature, and in this way she cooperates with respect to God's physical presence and the establishment of His kingdom. The child receives her God and, through Him, lives His life as the Father's beloved Son. This wonderful alliance between God's "servant" and God's "child" in Mary's soul establishes her as the beloved Mother of the Father's Son.

The mystery of the Visitation shows us the fourth dimension of the Father's mercy toward His beloved servant. Not only does the Father have mercy on Mary, but He also wants her to participate in His life as a merciful Father. So He wants her to be, like Him, a source of mercy. In this mystery of the Visitation, the Father does not order her to perform this gesture of temporal mercy toward her elderly cousin; and the latter, for her part, asked for nothing; she kept silent. But God's messenger, Gabriel, merely mentioned Elizabeth's situation. Does mercy not need to flow out of superabundance and gratuitousness in order to be exercised in a completely divine manner? It must also be exercised with meekness and humility. Mary humbly puts herself at her cousin's service. She greets her first. Jesus uses this gesture of temporal mercy to perform a work of spiritual mercy toward John the Baptist. Through Mary, He sanctifies John the Baptist, and, through John the Baptist, Elizabeth.

This mystery of gratuitous and superabundant mercy, so gentle and efficacious, culminates with Elizabeth's greeting and Mary's *Magnificat.* Mercy, coming from God, must rise up again toward God in praise, thanksgiving and glory. Elizabeth glorifies Mary; Mary glorifies her Lord and Savior. Mary immediately offers to God the first praise she receives from her cousin proclaiming her dignity as Mother of God. She keeps nothing for herself. She is poor in her divine motherhood; everything is for the Father and His Son. In her own eyes, she is nothing: what is "great" is what God has accomplished in her. Such is the divine magnanimity of her soul which has no fear of acknowledging that God "has done great things" for her; yet her soul is not touched by any vainglory. Accordingly, she renders Him high praise with all her strength.

The mystery of Christmas shows us the fifth dimension of the Father's mercy toward Mary. The Father wants Mary to rest in the joy of His beloved Son's presence. The Father's mercy is completed in the communication of His joy. The Father's joy is really to live, in full light, by His beloved Son's presence. The Father is totally given to His Son; the Son is totally given to the Father. This mutual, substantial and personal gift results in a unique presence of interpenetration. For there is unity of nature in the duality of the Persons. The Father's joy is a joy that is consubstantial to His person and to that of His Son. In His mercy, He wants this joy to overflow in Mary through the mystery of Christmas, since in this mystery Mary enjoys the presence of His Son, the Father's only Son. All the providential circumstances of Jesus' birth are ordained to intensifying this divine joy of Mary's heart so that her whole being may joyfully exult in her Son. But this joy is lived in poverty, for although the joy of Christmas is indeed a completion, and although the birth of Jesus does bring the waiting of Advent to a close, it is also a new point of departure. It is the beginning of Jesus' earthly life. The joy of Christmas expands Mary's soul while strengthening it. It is indeed a very divine act of the Father's mercy to strengthen Mary's soul by enabling it to become intimately associated with Jesus' whole life and most particularly with His sorrowful mysteries.

These first five mysteries of Mary's life are divinely ordered to the very pure joy of Christmas. But with the mystery of the Purification, sorrow appears. Now sorrow in itself is neither constructive nor intelligible. It is not luminous; quite the contrary: it breaks everything and very often prevents us from comprehending the order of divine wisdom that lies hidden behind it. That is why these first five mysteries show us the dawn of the new law in a unique and striking way, as in full light. In the prevenient mercy of pure gratuitousness flowing from the wounded heart of Jesus, the Holy Spirit constructs in and with Mary the temple of the Most Holy Trinity. The first stone of this temple is the virginal consecration in abandonment and the fraternal trust which divinely binds her to Joseph. The second is the *fiat* given in response to the divine Word, the *fiat* of the "little one" who is born to a divine life of filiation by receiving the gift of the Son, the Father's personal Secret. By keeping this Secret, the soul is silently hidden in the Father's mystery; it is secluded in this mystery. In silence it says, *"Abba, Father,"* with the only Son, Jesus. Without seeing its Father, it looks at Him "face to face" as if it were already entering the beatific vision. It is the *fiat* of the faithful, meek, useless servant, of the one who wants only to serve God and accomplish His will. These two *fiats* are inseparable, for the Father's adopted daughter remains a creature who must serve Him, since grace does not destroy nature. The third stone is the temporal and spiritual mercy of the Visitation divinely exercised with strength and gentleness. This divine mercy rebounds in praise and thanksgiving for all God's acts of mercy. The fourth is divine joy: living fully by God's loving presence for its own sake.

The first three "stones" of this temple can quite clearly be split in two, so to speak. So we would have six stones instead of three, and seven with the joy of Christmas. These seven stones show us the primary order of divine wisdom in Mary. Now Mary is as it were the wonderful prototype of the Holy Spirit's work in our souls. So we can consider these seven stones as revealing to us the architectural order of the life of grace in our souls. If we reflect upon the character of these seven stones divinely sculpted by the Holy Spirit in Mary's soul with her own cooperation, we can see in them a kind of living reflection of the three divine Persons. Abandonment to the Father and to Joseph is a kind of divine echo of the Father's omnipotence; the silent *fiat* of the little child and of the servant is like the echo of Him who is the "substantial *Fiat*" of the Father, the Beloved Son; the mercy springing forth in glory is like the echo of the Holy Spirit. As for joy, since it is that which completes and brings to an end, restoring everything to unity, it is the divine echo of the very unity of the three Persons. The Holy Spirit sculpts this living image of the Trinity in Mary. He cannot but reproduce in her the intimate face of the Trinitarian God so that she may be the beloved Mother of Him who "reflects the glory of God and bears the very stamp of his nature" (Heb. 1:3).

With the mystery of the Purification, we can see how the Father, in His mercy, introduces sorrow into the joyful soul of His beloved servant. It is still an act of mercy, one that is altogether characteristic of the Father and of which He alone can be the Author: associating a mere creature with the proper work of His incarnate Son, with His work as Savior. When mercy is exercised in a manner connatural to our human hearts, it tries in every possible way to get rid of all misery and suffering; for it wants to help the destitute by removing everything that hurts them, thus restoring to them the full flourishing of their lives. By raising the widow of Nain's only son, Jesus performs an act of mercy: He wipes away this poor mother's tears. By restoring sight to the blind and speech to the dumb, He again performs an act of mercy. We can easily understand such gestures of mercy. But the Father can exercise His divine mercy in a totally different way: He can ask us to accept to live the mystery of Jesus' Agony and Crucifixion, to accept to carry His Cross with Him, so that we may cooperate in the work of Redemption and thereby intimately know His Son's heart and be able to live by His life as Savior. We cannot truly be somebody's friend unless we live by his secret and cooperate in his personal work. Such is the characteristic demand of the Father's mercy toward us: He wants us to be entirely His sons, completely one with His beloved Son, with whom He is well pleased. More than any other creature, Mary received this jealous mercy of the Father and divinely lived by it.

The mystery of the Purification is the announcement of the "sword" which is to pierce Mary's soul. All the prophecies of the Old Testament are brought to a close in this prophecy of Simeon, intimately associating the Mother's destiny to that of her Child. This is a prophetic annunciation which will be fulfilled later, whereas the angel Gabriel's joyful annunciation is fulfilled immediately through Mary's *fiat*. This prophetic annunciation immediately concerns only Mary's intimate life. In her outward life nothing has changed. For her living faith, however, this prophecy is real. Indeed, the Father wants her to live it first in a completely hidden way so that this sorrowful foreboding may further increase her love and maternal devotion for Jesus, and intensify above all her divine silence. The secret revealed by Simeon is added to the secret communicated by the angel. Although the Father gives His Son to Mary very gently, He also gives Him to her in a violent way, with all the violence of the sword. Jesus is given to Mary as the Word of God that wounds her maternal heart, that pierces her soul. Mary's virginal and maternal heart, mortally wounded, can offer itself as an intimate, invisible and hidden holocaust. Hence her heart is in unison with the heart of Jesus who has just been officially offered to the Father. The holocaust of the two little doves is symbolic; the two very pure hearts of Jesus and Mary are in fact the sole victim accepted by the Father.

This prophetic announcement is first partially fulfilled in the mystery of obedience with the flight into Egypt. Because of Herod's rage, Joseph and Mary must leave with the Child to take refuge in a foreign country and accept the slaughter of other "innocents," those closest to Jesus in age and place. Mary carries very deeply in her heart the sorrow of these mothers mourning their children, since this sorrow is brought about by Jesus. He who should have brought only "a great joy to all the people," as the angels proclaimed on Christmas night, causes this terrible slaughter through Herod's jealous ambition. Jesus is a sign that is "spoken against."

This prophetic announcement is partially fulfilled a second time in the mystery of the first separation from Jesus that Mary experiences. Without telling her, Jesus stays behind in the temple at Jerusalem, with the teachers of the Law, while Mary and Joseph return home. This is the first great divine sadness that wounds Mary's soul. She experiences this first separation under very difficult circumstances, which make it more intense. The separation lasts three days, three days of searching and anguish. When they find Jesus among the teachers, the sword of the divine Word deeply wounds Mary's heart, rendered so vulnerable by this agonizing wait and intense sadness. It is Jesus, her Jesus, who for the first time is surprised at her behavior: "How is it that you sought me?" And He reveals to her the intimate demands of His heart: "Did you not know that I must be in my Father's house?" (Lk. 2:49).

The third partial fulfillment of Simeon's prophecy occurs at Cana. Jesus' response to the merciful request of Mary pleading for the good people at the wedding feast seems to be a refusal. He leads her to understand that during her Son's apostolic life she must be as though visibly and outwardly separated from Him. He no longer needs her temporal services. But when His "Hour" has come, she will again have to be present.

These three partial fulfillments of Simeon's prophecy are three more trials whereby the Father, in His mercy, progressively forms Mary's heart and soul. He "connaturalizes" her to sorrow, to struggles that are violent and crucifying, and to the sadness of the final separation.

Simeon's prophecy is perfectly fulfilled in Jesus' great sorrowful mysteries during His Agony, His Crucifixion and His Burial. The sword mortally pierces Mary's soul at this point. Mary lives the mystery of Jesus' Agony in solitude and silence. She lives in her soul Jesus' mortal sadness: the sadness of divine abandonment, of the Father's rejection. Like Him, she accepts being anathema in the Father's sight, for the sake of the poor people who are not really concerned about all this or who fall asleep from weariness.

Mary lives the mystery of the Crucifixion before the whole world, in the presence of Jesus' enemies and executioners. She carries in her soul all the scars of Jesus' scourged body, the deeper wounds of the Crucifixion and the mortal wound of the heart. It is in Mary's soul that the piercing of the lance produces its ultimate effect, since Jesus' heart no longer suffers. In her soul, Mary suffers in His place. Her soul is pierced out of love for Jesus; she too drains the cup to the dregs.

Mary lives the mystery of the Sepulcher "buried" in John's home. This is the final separation. Mary accepts having her Son's dead body snatched from her arms. She accepts having strangers' hands take hold of this divine body, touch this blood, these wounds, this wounded heart. Out of respect for the law of the Sabbath and before the Pharisees and the high priests who have just destroyed the true Temple of God,

she consents to leave the tomb, letting it be guarded by soldiers on official duty. These chasms of sadness and suffering
divinely wound Mary's soul by violently and cruelly depriving her of any human support. Through these mortal sorrows
and sufferings her heart is divinely purified. Her divine love
becomes more deeply rooted and intensifies in a new way. It
uses these sorrows and sufferings as divine nourishment given
by the Father in His mercy.

Nevertheless, under the motion of the Holy Spirit and
in the Father's mercy, Mary continues to live her mystery of
total abandonment, her mystery of *fiat* in silence and poverty,
her mystery of mercy and praise, her mystery of joy. These
mysteries, at first lived in full bloom, take even more radical
possession of her soul in sadness and suffering. They are as
though buried in God, hidden from the sight of men.

Thanks to the trial at Cana and the mystery of the
Agony, Mary lives the mystery of the *fiat* of the Annunciation
in a completely new way. Indeed, in the mystery of the Agony
she receives the "Gift" of the Father under circumstances that
for her maternal heart are extremely contradictory. She must
then receive the "Gift" of the Father in a *fiat* of a living and
totally pure faith that goes beyond apparent contradictions.
Through her *fiat,* she must receive Him who is overwhelmed
by sadness and abandoned by His Father, by allowing her
soul to be overwhelmed by the same mortal sadness and by
experiencing the same abandonment. Receiving Christ in
agony means letting her soul suffer divinely under the weight
of sorrow and consenting to have her heart crushed in unison
with Jesus' heart in agony. Divinely receiving Christ in agony
as the Father's gift of excessive love means receiving the

Father's personal "Secret." Christ in agony confides His secret to Mary: totally surrendering to His Father's loving will: "not my will, but thine." The Father's will takes possession of Mary's heart to unite it, in the silence and solitude of the Agony, to her Son's infinitely sad and solitary heart. In this silent *fiat* of the Agony, Mary efficaciously cooperates in the "gift of the Father," in the gift of Him who is in agony. She cooperates in this no longer as a "servant" but as the "helper" of Him who is in agony. It is an intimate cooperation in faith, hope and love. Living the mystery of Jesus in agony in her faith, hope and love, Mary allows the sacrifice of the Cross to attain its full dimension. She allows Christ's holocaust to end in a bloodless holocaust, that of the summits and depths of her soul. Accordingly, she consents to die in her maternal heart; she accepts having her work as a servant destroyed, annihilated under her eyes; she accepts having all her work appear as a complete failure.

In the Agony, the attitude of the Father's child and that of the servant—or more accurately, of the "helper"—are identical, for the only service required by the Father is the service of faith and loving hope through the apparent failure of all the work previously accomplished. She must consent not only to disappear as a servant, but to see the complete, radical and violent destruction of all her work as a servant, of all her efficacious cooperation in the Father's governance. It is truly totally divine faith in love, totally silent patience in mercy, that the Holy Spirit demands from Mary.

Thanks to the trial of the flight into Egypt and the mystery of the Crucifixion, Mary lives the mysteries of mercy and of the *Magnificat* in a new way. The Father asks her to draw life from the crucified Christ's infinite mercy, the mercy of Him who, as Lamb of God, takes upon Himself all the iniquities of the world. At the Cross, Jesus forgives men their sins; He forgives by consenting to be responsible for them before the Father. Mary must live in unison with this redeeming mercy. At the Cross, Jesus gives Himself entirely to the beloved disciple and He wants His mother to give him everything as well. He wants her to be John's beloved Mother as she is His own beloved Mother. Mary makes this superabundant mercy of Christ Crucified her own. At the Cross, she becomes for us a Mother of mercy, the one who engenders us to divine life, with and in Jesus Crucified. Such is the new mercy in Jesus' blood. Mary is the Mother of the whole Christ.

The *Magnificat* of the Crucifixion is the new praise, the new worship "in spirit and in truth." It is a praise that finds its source in this totally divine mercy which demands the sacrifice, the holocaust, of what we love most according to our human hearts and according to the grace of God; and it is a praise that asks us to cooperate in this sacrifice by being ourselves immolated. This completely silent praise possesses a new depth. It is very much like the silence of the *fiat* of the soul that receives the Father's secret. It is a praise full of love in a fiery immolation which consumes even words. When our intelligence, the cause of our speech, is part of the holocaust, our praise becomes silent out of love. This is the *Magnificat* of the Cross.

Thanks to the trial of the Finding in the Temple and to the mystery of the Sepulcher, Mary lives by the mystery of abandonment in a new way. Despite the outward circumstances which, humanly speaking, should immediately bring about anguish and bitterness, disappointment and despair, the Father asks Mary to remain totally surrendered in her soul to His merciful power and joyful in her divine love. Surrender is heroic and divinely lived only when all that is dearest to us, humanly and divinely speaking, is brutally taken away from us, as though we were never to recover it, as though the help of the Father made visible in His "Gift," in His "Messenger" had suddenly let us down, and as though we were reduced to nothing and totally deprived of everything. This then requires heroic abandonment to His mercy "without repentance," to His "faithful" mercy, even though everything around us and even in us, according to our human consciousness, seems to tell us the opposite. It requires the surrender of the "little one" who accepts the desert with its parching thirst and infinite solitude, without any attempt to understand, without any attempt to save himself by his own means. It requires the surrender of one who gives himself up by burying himself, through his loving faith and poor hope, in the depths of the merciful omnipotence of the Father, who alone can make everything new, recreate everything, restore everything to life. This heroic abandonment of the "little one," who wants to know nothing more than the depths of the Father's merciful omnipotence and wants to hide himself in it like a "little one" in his mother's womb, implies an infinite desire without any limit other than the very mercy of the Father. Mary also exercises this heroic abandonment to the Father toward the one that Jesus gave her as a son and priest: John. In absolute trust, she exercises a new fraternal and maternal charity toward John, whom she has chosen. This Mother trusts her son because he is loved by Jesus.

Thus we can see in a practical way how all the "stones" divinely sculpted in Mary's soul are found according to a new mode in these sorrowful mysteries. Here these "stones" are, as it were, much more buried in the soul. For this very reason, their distinctive and original characters are seen less clearly. In a certain way, one might say that all the "stones" are present in each of these mysteries of trial and sorrow. However, it is no less true that some of these "stones" are more explicitly in act in each of these mysteries. For the Agony is a more secret and intimate mystery than the Crucifixion; and the Burial is the mystery of solitude which brings to fulfillment and consummates Jesus' earthly life. Finally, the sorrowful mysteries, that of the prophetic announcement as well as those of the fulfillment, do not give us any new principle of organization regarding the Christian life. They do not manifest to us an architectural character of the temple of God, but convey to us, as it were, a new spirit, a new light, in which the whole divine edifice is as though recreated, purified, simplified, clarified, more divinely rooted in the Father's mercy.

That is why, in the light of the sorrowful mysteries, we can say that the seven "stones" are reduced to three: the silent *fiat* of the sorrowful gift; the mercy that snatches and immolates what one loves most; the heroic abandonment in the face of apparent failure. As for joy, it is completely hidden in its source: the will to love the Father's will above all else. The aspect of passivity, of submission, of obedience, is much more evident in these sorrowful mysteries; this thereby implies a growing importance of exterior elements and certain violent interventions. The whole mystery of struggle then becomes primordial as does for that very reason the mystery of patience, the loving attitude of a soul that suffers in order to love more. It is no longer only the living image of the Trinity, the reproduction of the face of God that the Holy Spirit sculpts in Mary's soul. It is the living image of the Savior, of Christ Crucified, of the Son who, in order to save us, consented to be "the Lamb of God" who bears all the iniquities of the world,[106] and to become the One whose "appearance was so marred, beyond human semblance" (Is. 52:14).

The three glorious mysteries show us in an ultimate manner the Father's mercy toward Mary. Like love, mercy is always in a hurry, it wants to take short cuts. The Father wants Mary to live the life of heaven, already on this earth, in anticipation. The glorious mysteries are indeed the preamble to heaven. Merciful love, triumphant over death and over all the consequences of sin, pride and Satan's hatred, a love that shines forth in the mysteries of Christ's Resurrection and Ascension, comes to take Mary's heart. In the glorious mysteries, the Father's mercy gives her a divine life which is exercised in full freedom, the freedom of God's children, those who experience this holy indifference toward whatever is not immediately God's will for them.

Mary lives the mystery of Jesus' Resurrection in a living and absolutely pure faith. It is her Son, Jesus Crucified, who rises from the dead for the glory of the Father and for her own glory. The risen Jesus is given to her by the Father in a new way, which is even more intimate and complete than at the Annunciation and the Cross. The sacrament of the

---

106. Jn. 1:29; cf. Is. 53:4-7.

Eucharist is given to her as a divine sign to manifest and realize this new gift, a gift in a substantial unity of life, realizing in her this mystical presence, so profound and intimate, of the dead and risen Christ. The risen Jesus is given to His Mother to realize with her a unity of life that reproduces His union with the Father. The Father asked Mary for this cooperation in Christ's sorrows with a view to this unity of love. Such is the new secret of love that the Father communicates to Mary, a secret so divine, so extraordinary, that the Father willed that it be expressed through the Eucharistic bread: words alone no longer suffice. This substantial unity of life requires a stronger and more realistic sign, a sign that is at the same time a reality, a *res*—the *res par excellence* that can still be a sign: the divine body. The sacrament of Christ's body commits the Father's omnipotence to the immediate service of the most humble yet also the most efficacious gift, the one that is most used: food, the bread which is the body of Jesus.

The *fiat* to the gift of the risen Christ, exercised in and through the Eucharist, enables us to comprehend the new quality of Mary's silence in these glorious mysteries. It is the silence of unity, proceeding from the complete gift of the Risen One, expressed and realized by the gift of the Eucharist, in which the source of life is hidden under the appearances of bread—ground grains of wheat. Mary's heart is also ground; yet the Source of life, of light, of love, is present in her, living in her soul in a manner more intimate than her soul is intimate to herself.

This silent *fiat* is also that of the useless servant who no longer has any human, conscious and visible reasons to remain on earth; the *fiat* of the useless servant who dedicates herself to whatever God wills, no longer judging the importance, the significance, the usefulness, of the work that is required, but considering only the Father's will. After being a servant and mother for Jesus, Mary accepts being John's servant and mother, without comparing the difference that exists between these two states; she simply loves to be more hidden and lowly by serving the disciple.

Through the mystery of the Ascension, Mary lives in a very poor and very free abandonment. She consents to remain on earth as long as the Father wills, with an increasingly burning desire for heaven. Through the mystery of the Ascension, the Father's mercy draws closer and closer. With unique intensity, Mary lives this affirmation of St. Paul: *Si consurrexistis cum Christa: quae sursum sunt quaerite, ubi Christus est in dextera Dei sedens: quae sursum sunt sapite, non quae super terram*—"If then you have been raised with Christ, seek the things that are above, where Christ is, seated at the right hand of God. Set your minds on things that are above, not on things that are on earth" (Col. 3:1-2). Mary's heart is entirely with the Father since her treasure, Jesus, is there. The sacrament of the Eucharist is really her viaticum: both the pilgrim's sacrament, giving her the strength to continue her journey in the wilderness; and the sacrament of glory, directing her whole spirit and soul toward the glorified Christ and toward heaven. She also lives by this abandonment in poverty with respect to John: her son and priest.

Through the mystery of Pentecost, Mary lives by the mercy of the Father and Jesus who send her the Holy Spirit, the Comforter. The Holy Spirit is given to her in the form of a flame of fire to burn her soul in a divine way. The Father uses the separation from Jesus, which Mary fully accepted, to communicate the fire of love to her in superabundance. "It is to your advantage that I go away" (Jn. 16:7). So that she may live the mystery of divine motherhood with respect to the nascent Church, the fire of the Spirit burns her maternal heart and makes it a great furnace of love from which her maternal mercy flows for all Jesus' Apostles and for the whole Church. Like Jesus the Host she is given to each member of Christ. It is her maternal heart that is given to each of her children; her heart is their true place, their supernatural milieu.

In a pure praise of love, Mary glorifies God for all His merciful fruitfulness. Her praise is silent, like that of the Host.

It is the reflection of the glorified Christ that the Holy Spirit sculpts in Mary's soul. She is the living mirror of His glory, after being the mirror of His disgrace.

Finally, there is this ultimate mercy of final perseverance, which is given by the Father to Mary in the final act of her earthly life, this act of ecstatic love in faith and hope. Everything culminates in this luminous mercy of the beatific vision. The Father brings Mary into His glory; she lives by His Life, contemplates in His Light, loves with His Love. The beatific vision, which realizes the substantial unity of life and love in the Word, radiates over the whole of Mary's human nature to beatify her.

All the "stones" sculpted by the Holy Spirit in Mary's soul, all the sorrowful mysteries, all the glorious mysteries, all these mysteries are held together by the mystery of obedience.

Obedience is what divinely unites, in love, such diverse activities and demands. This is, moreover, the major role of obedience: to bring about unity of love in diversity of operations. Obedience can bring about this unity without suppressing the specific diversity of human activities, for it has no proper matter. It is essentially the virtue of exercise, of execution. It puts into execution a dependence upon the one who has authority and whom one obeys. In all her activities, Mary obeys God in a perfect way. This obedience is yet another fruit of the mercy of the Father who wants to associate her very intimately with His paternal governance. It shows us the proper authority of paternal mercy, but is in fact carried out according to the various ways in which the Father exerts His merciful authority.

In the mystery of her virginal consecration, Mary seems to obey directly the prompting of the Holy Spirit who invites her to consecrate herself totally to God and to choose Joseph as her spouse. In the mystery of the *fiat* of the Annunciation, Mary obeys the angelic, contemplative messenger of the Father. In the mystery of the Visitation, she is docile to the inspiration of the Holy Spirit that is revealed to her by the sign the angel gratuitously gave her: Elizabeth, the sterile woman, is expecting a child. It is under the inspiration of the Holy Spirit that she praises Mary: Mary responds to this divine praise with her *Magnificat* which also springs from an inner divine inspiration. As for the joy of Christmas, Mary receives this in a divine way. She lets herself be completely overcome by this great divine joy that comes to her from the Father; it is again another mystery of inner docility to the prompting of the Holy Spirit.

Thus these mysteries of joy are really bound together by a mystery of obedience—obedience with respect to the internal forum in the precise meaning of the term. This obedience is above all joyful and gentle, for the Holy Spirit dwells in Mary's soul. He moves her from within in a very intimate and loving manner.

The mystery of the Purification, which is a kind of divine prelude to the sorrowful mysteries, implies obedience to the law, a law which seems inappropriate for Mary. Obedience to the law of purification thus requires great humility on her part. Mary does not consider her personal privileges; she considers only her dependence with respect to the law, hence with respect to the common good of her people.

Obedience to this law enables Mary to meet Simeon and to hear his prophecy. Through an old man chosen by God and representing the whole people of Israel and all mankind, the Holy Spirit announces to her that a sword will pierce her soul. Mary receives in obedience this prophecy that wounds her soul.

After the adoration of the Magi, it is Joseph who directly receives the angels' message, for he holds the authority as head of the household. Mary must obey him in all that concerns the common good of the family. This obedience to Joseph is carried out in a sorrowful context and in itself implies a sacrifice; they must leave their country without having time to prepare. The order must be carried out by night.

In the mystery of the Finding, Mary obeys providential circumstances. Having lost trace of her Son Jesus, she must do everything possible to find Him. These three days of anxious searching are indeed ordained by providential circumstances which are unforeseeable and beyond her control. When she finds Jesus, her Son teaches her for the first time as one sent by the Father, which requires from her a very intimate obedience, but that nevertheless wounds her heart.

At Cana, again because of unforeseeable and providential circumstances beyond her control, Mary makes this first official request to her Son: "They have no wine." For the second time, Jesus teaches His Mother as a priest and demands from her an obedience concerning the internal forum that wounds her heart.

In the mysteries of the Compassion—the Agony and the Crucifixion—Mary obeys the prompting of the Holy Spirit and Christ's words. She obeys the law of the Sabbath during the ultimate separation of the Sepulcher.

It is easy to note that the sorrowful mysteries are as it were directly dependent upon certain acts of obedience concerning the external forum, whether it be obedience to the law, to Joseph's authority or to providential circumstances. These acts of obedience concerning the external forum are, as it were, ordered to other acts of obedience concerning the internal forum as regards priestly authority, the authority of the Old Testament in prophetic form and the authority of Christ. Finally it is an act of obedience concerning the external forum that completes and perfects these sorrowful mysteries.

It is normal for obedience concerning the external forum to cause suffering, for it is always somewhat violent. The law is a universal precept which, for any given individual considered in his own existential individuality, always seems inappropriate and often seems unjust. Moreover, since it is applied as something exterior, the law always seems to do violence to the individual considered as a certain personal whole. One might make similar observations about authority concerning the external forum, giving individual and particular precepts. Again, these precepts are orders coming from the exterior, for no matter how prudent the superior may be, he never knows perfectly all the vital needs of the one whom he commands. His order may always appear unsuited to the one who receives it. As for the authority of the priest, this is ordered toward sacrifice; his priestly words are a sword. So, we should not be surprised to find that if we remove obedience in the external forum, we separate human life from the mystery of the Cross. On the other hand, the mystery of the Cross takes possession of human life to the extent that we submit our lives to this obedience.

As for the glorious mysteries, all three put Mary under the direct motion of the Holy Spirit. The mystery of obedience begins with docility to the Holy Spirit, and it ends with this same docility, which alone is eternal. The Holy Spirit really has the authority to direct and rectify our divine life. Yet here below, joyful docility to the Holy Spirit must lead us to obedience to God's angelic messengers, to the signs given by God, to providential circumstances, and to all those who are mandated by God to lead us to the Father's house, even if such obedience hurts and crucifies us. Here below, obedience to the Holy Spirit is true only to the extent that it blossoms into forms of obedience which may be inferior, but which are totally characteristic of our earthly way of following Christ and of living His mysteries. This mystery of obedience thus appears not only as a necessary condition for the true growth of charity but also as an essential part of this mystery, clarifying our condition as "sons of God": "He who has my commandments and keeps them, he it is who loves me; and he who loves me will be loved by my Father" (Jn. 14:21).

The mystery of the growth of charity in Mary, which shows us in a unique way the construction of the temple of God in the human soul, ultimately amounts to the construction of these divine "stones," the joint work of the Father's mercy and Mary. This construction is first undertaken in joyful desire, which is the particular modality of the first mysteries up to Christmas, then in sorrowful patience, finally in loving freedom. The unity of this divine construction is achieved in a spirit of obedience that is ever more demanding and that enables Mary's soul to flourish in joy, which frees her in the fire of the Holy Spirit.

Moreover, the mystery of the growth of charity also appears as being first a great advent, a joyful expectation; then a great ascent toward Jerusalem, with trials, struggles, battles and with above all what seems a total failure; finally as a sort of glorious waiting for the return, when heaven is already present, although in utterly barren poverty. This shows us, as it were, the four great components of our Christian life on earth: it is a radiant and joyful expectation; a trial in struggle and battle; a total human failure; a death; finally, it is heaven already begun, the waiting for Christ's return. We recognize in these the great tendencies of every Christian life. If we isolate and separate them, we fall into certain forms of false mysticism that reduce Christian life to being nothing more than a perfect humanism, or a trial in struggle for conquests, or a failure in death, or an exclusive waiting for Christ in His glory. If we want to remain in the truth, we must always maintain these various aspects and their divine equilibrium, and consider her who is given to us so that we may understand them, as St. Bernard so wonderfully affirms:

> Mary . . . is interpreted to mean "Star of the Sea." This admirably befits the Virgin Mother. There is indeed a wonderful appropriateness in this comparison of her with a star, because as a star sends out its rays without harm to itself, so did the Virgin bring forth her Child without injury to her integrity. And as the ray does not diminish the brightness of the star, so neither did the Child born of her tarnish the beauty of Mary's virginity. She is therefore that glorious star, which, as the prophet said, arose out of Jacob, whose ray enlightens the whole earth, whose splendor shines out for all to see in heaven and reaches even unto hell[107]. . . . She, I say, is that shining and brilliant star, so much needed, set in place above life's great and spacious sea, glittering with merits, all aglow with examples for our imitation. Oh, whosoever thou art that perceiveth thyself during this mortal existence to be rather drifting in

---

107. To be understood as "abode of the dead."

treacherous waters, at the mercy of the winds and the waves, than walking on firm ground, turn not away thine eyes from the splendor of this guiding star, unless thou wish to be submerged by the storm! When the storms to temptation burst upon thee, when thou seest thyself driven upon the rocks of tribulation, look at the star, call upon Mary. When buffeted by the billows of pride, or ambition, or hatred, or jealousy, look at the star, call upon Mary. Should anger, or avarice, or fleshly desire violently assail the frail vessel of thy soul, look at the star, call upon Mary. If troubled on account of the heinousness of thy sins, distressed at the filthy state of thy conscience, and terrified at the thought of the awful judgment to come, thou art beginning to sink into the bottomless gulf of sadness and to be swallowed in the abyss of despair, then think of Mary. In dangers, in doubts, in difficulties, think of Mary, call upon Mary. Let not her name leave thy lips, never suffer it to leave thy heart. And that thou mayest more surely obtain the assistance of her prayer, see that thou dost walk in her footsteps. With her for guide, thou shalt never go astray; whilst invoking her, thou shalt never lose heart; so long as she is in thy mind, thou shalt not be deceived; whilst she holds thy hand, thou canst not fall; under her protection, thou hast

nothing to fear; if she walks before thee, thou
shalt not grow weary; if she shows thee favor,
thou shalt reach the goal.[108]

The path of the righteous is like the light of
dawn, which shines brighter and brighter
until full day (Prov. 4:18).

---

108. St. Bernard. *Hom. II, supra "Missus est,"* 17, P.L. 18, 70, 71 (cited in
     Doctor Mellifluus, §31). In this encyclical from May 24, 1953, Pope
     Pius XII exclaims that there is no praise more beautiful of the Virgin
     Mother of God than this one.

ABOUT THE AUTHOR

FATHER Marie-Dominique Philippe, O.P., was born in 1912 at Cysoing, in Northern France and entered the Order of Preachers in 1930. He studied theology and philosophy at the Dominican house of studies of Le Saulchoir and at Paris, and was ordained a priest in 1936. He taught philosophy at the Pontifical University of Fribourg, Switzerland, from 1945 to 1982. From 1982 until two months before his death on August 26, 2006, he continued teaching philosophy and theology at the houses of studies of the Congregation of Saint John in France. His published works include studies of Aristotle, Saint Thomas Aquinas, and Mystical Theology.